The bullet smoked by within two inches of my head, and I can still feel the memory of that frightening moment today. A very lucky split second before the VC sniper squeezed the trigger, I had turned my head toward the shooter, and instead of hitting me square in the side of the head, the bullet cracked by my ear. I had been motioning with my arms to change my platoon's formation.

At first, I thought the soldier behind me had fired a round by accident, but seconds later, all hell broke loose. . . .

Books published by The Random House Publishing Group are available at quantity discounts on bulk purchases for premium, educational, fund-raising, and special sales use. For details, please call 1-800-733-3000.

MEKONG
FIRST
LIGHT

JOSEPH W. CALLAWAY JR.

PRESIDIO
PRESS

BALLANTINE BOOKS • NEW YORK

A Presidio Press Book
Published by The Random House Publishing Group
Copyright © 2004 by Joseph W. Callaway Jr.

Published in the United States by Presidio Press, an imprint of The Random House Publishing Group, a division of Random House, Inc., New York, and simultaneously in Canada by Random House of Canada Limited, Toronto.

Presidio Press and colophon are trademarks of Random House, Inc.

www.presidiopress.com

ISBN 0-89141-816-4

All photos courtesy of the author

Manufactured in the United States of America

First Edition: April 2004

OPM   9 8 7 6 5 4

In memory of Captain Dan Monahan,
one of the finest men I have ever known.
He gave me the confidence and leadership
skills that helped me survive Vietnam.

Letter to Dan Monahan's Daughter

June 24, 1984

Dear Maureen,

The past eighteen years, I am sure, seem long to you, but to me April 1967 was only yesterday. Your father and I were good friends. We knew each other only a few months but were bound inextricably together with the common purpose of doing our job and preserving life under the most dangerous and hostile conditions. We depended on each other. I was his point platoon leader, a young lieutenant. I was always the first guy in and the last guy out on every operation. We trusted each other's judgment.

We tried to bring some sanity to an environment of incredible violence. This life-and-death drama brought out the worst in many men—selfishness, hate, racism, fear, brutality, etc. I watched some men literally crumble before my eyes. Your dad provided a ray of hope in this harsh Vietnam world. He was concerned about human life. He was a good soldier, but more important he was a great man. He was concerned about others. He loved his fellow man. His bravery was commitment, and his courage was consistency. He was more a hero for his great compassion and character than for giving his life. His loss is our tragedy. He tried to build better people, and I shall always remember him.

In the days between your birth on April 6 and his death on April 14, he was very happy. Dan was very proud of his new daughter. He talked about you often. He always had that great Irish wit and subtle humor, and he was never better than during this period. I came to see you when you were a baby, but decided I could only bring sad memories to your mother and grandparents. For these many years, I have made no contact with your family but have always remembered. I knew you would be graduating from high school this year. The diamond pendant with the three connecting gold circles, which I have sent, not only is recognition of your achievement but is symbolic of your father's love for you, your mother, and your grandparents. I will always be a friend, and please stop by if you ever travel west.

Last fall, I went to Washington to visit the Vietnam Memorial. I found the names of many friends, including Daniel Francis Monahan. I was proud to have known your dad. He was a good friend.

Love,
Joe

CONTENTS

ACKNOWLEDGMENTS

This Vietnam history is written for the American soldiers who served in the war and their families and friends, and to my sons, Tucker, Casan, and Quinn, for their grandchildren. You three young men brought joy into my life. I am proud of you, and I love you.

I want to thank Millie Lindsay for her tireless editing effort, Ron Murphy for his historical research, and Gary Linderer, who never gave up on getting this book published.

PROLOGUE

Over a period of almost two years in Vietnam, I served as an infantry platoon leader in the 9th Infantry Division; an infantry tactical combat adviser for the Queen's Cobra, the first Thai army regiment deployed to Vietnam; and an officer in the 5th Special Forces Group. Vietnam was an unbelievable adventure requiring incredible will to execute the responsibilities and to survive. I completed my final year in the army in the 10th Special Forces Group. In these high-profile, intense assignments, I learned a considerable amount about war, life, and myself.

My story is about personal development and growth—the courage, responsibility, and character that evolved during my participation in the war. The unimaginable terror is still buried within the recesses of my mind. Vietnam has had a strong positive and negative impact on my postwar life. I have never been able to escape its influence—even to this day, more than thirty-five years later.

My story is also about truth. War is never glorious, only brutal, no matter how noble we try to make it. Vietnam was a particularly savage and destructive guerrilla war. It seemed to destroy most everything and everybody. Even today, these many years later, many of us do not understand how or why America became involved, how the war was fought, what really happened on the battlefields, and why America has yet fully to recover emotionally. To find truth and meaningful value in the Vietnam War is not an easy task. This story is an honest description of my experiences. It is my truth—a truth that I needed to clarify for myself to continue a productive life.

About twenty-five hundred years ago, some five hundred years before the birth of the Christian religion, the Greek philosopher Plato wrote, "In the world of knowledge the idea of good appears last of all, and is seen only with an effort; and, when seen, is also inferred to be the universal author of all things beautiful and right . . . and the immediate source of reason and truth in the intellectual; and that is the power upon which he who would act rationally . . . must have his eye fixed."*

Many young men, particularly after adolescence, engage in high-risk behavior in order to try to satisfy their sense of self-worth. They correlate risk directly with courage, and courage directly with self-esteem. Much of the male human species, without regard to race, manifests this inherent "rite of passage" competitive drive through macho actions that run the gamut from athletics, mountain climbing, and parachuting to fast cars, motorcycles, sexual activity, and bar fights. We often correlate risk with hierarchical status; combat warriorship, where the risks are the greatest, is the ultimate in competition status and macho-driven self-esteem.

Satisfying the need for self-esteem evolves into less risky behavior as we age, but it still surfaces. We do not outgrow this compelling, instinctive drive; instead it changes from taking physical risks to seeking power. Older men usually view their youthful high-risk activities, in retrospect, as idiocy.

It is the competitive drive and fearless, risk-taking behavior of youth that are integrated with the foundation of war. All wars are funded with the blood of youth and built upon

*Plato, The Republic, Book 7.

their willingness to fight and suppress their fear of death in their macho actions.

The concept of warriorship entails a symbiotic relationship between young and old men that passes down from generation to generation. The philosophy and economic interests of old men start wars, but they need young men to fight them, and young men are more than willing to cooperate. Most young men believe they are invincible, and the military throughout world history has manipulated this admirable but naive human characteristic. The military also stresses the concepts of heroism and nationalistic patriotism to bolster its position.

Older soldiers are seldom put in combat frontline positions because they usually have accumulated some responsibilities that depend on their continued existence, and they understand better the frailty of life and the arbitrary nature of fate. Younger men are much more willing to challenge fate because they believe they can prevail and will not die. They are less inclined to hesitate and can often function without regard for logic or reason. Emotion is a strong power in their lives, and heroism and patriotism are emotion-driven concepts. Young men also rationalize their actions as altruistic. What they do is for the good of the community. It is a behavioral trait evolved from our tribalistic heritage.

Our youth supposedly go off to war to help the elders protect our land and way of life, but most often it is really an attempt on the part of the elders to force their doctrines and codes of living on other societies. Our elders rationalize their decisions because their own sense of failure, which focuses on the fear of losing control, is so great that war becomes the best option.

Young men feel this societal stress, have not matured enough to fear individual death, and willingly go off to battle. Yet they never truly understand a war's purpose and certainly do not understand the human cost. Youth go off to make their sacrifice. We lament their loss, applaud their courage, resolve that war is a poor option. We experience peacetime for a while, then enter the war cycle yet again.

THE EARLY YEARS

My father was a young artillery lieutenant in the 81st Infantry Division (Wild Cats) stationed at Fort Rucker, Alabama, and my mother was a beautiful young lady from the adjacent town, Enterprise. They were married on November 13, 1942. I was a war baby from a war marriage, and my father would soon be shipping out to the South Pacific islands.

On October 3, 1943, as I sucked in my first breath of Alabama air, World War II was raging in Europe and Asia. Events were also beginning to take place in Southeast Asia that would ultimately lead to America's role in the Vietnam War and my eventual participation. Ho Chi Minh and his troops, the Viet Minh (the future North Vietnamese Army), fought with the Allies, repatriated downed Allied fliers to south China, and gave information to the Allies on Japanese troop movements. Their actions attracted the attention of the American Office of Strategic Services (OSS), a precursor to the Central Intelligence Agency (CIA). The OSS sent an American advisory team, code-named Deer Mission, to Vietnam, and the team, led by Archimedes Patti, gave selected troops of the Viet Minh army their first instructions in automatic weapons, demolitions, mortars, field tactics, and the like.

My father served overseas in Anguar, Pelilue, the Philippines, and the initial landings on Honshu, Amori, Japan, and fortunately survived the war. When World War II ended, the world split into two distinct philosophical and organizational blocks—the democratic capitalistic countries led by the United States, and the communist dictatorships led by the Soviet Union. Russia, our ally during World War II, became our enemy. These opposing ideological forces engaged in a cold war struggle for global supremacy that lasted more than forty years, until America's industrial might finally collapsed the Soviet Union's economy and empire in the late 1980s.

Both nations created highly developed nuclear military capabilities, causing the industrial nations to live under the shadow of a potential nuclear holocaust and bringing the world to the brink of nuclear annihilation on at least one known occasion, the Cuban missile crisis in 1962.

During this political, economic, and military cold war, geographic hot wars occurred in third world countries such as Korea, Laos, Cuba, Vietnam, and Afghanistan as the two military giants, often using surrogates, faced off and battled across the globe for world domination. For America and its combat soldiers, the most important hot wars were the Korean War, in the early 1950s, in which my father, Capt. Joseph W. Callaway, Sr., participated, and of course my 1960s war, which was Vietnam.

After World War II, my dad had stayed in the Alabama and Mississippi National Guard. As the Korean War expanded, his unit, the 31st Infantry Division, or so-called Dixie Division, was activated in 1950. He was separated from the division because he had already completed the Artillery Officers Advance Course. Ultimately, after being bounced around with his family from Fort Sill, Oklahoma, to Fort Jackson, South Carolina, to Fort Benjamin Harrison, Indiana, he was sent to Korea, where he spent almost a year. It was a difficult period for me, and I spent considerable time with my granddaddy and his black employees. My mother, little sister, and I lived across the street from my maternal grandparents in Enterprise, and we all waited patiently, praying for my dad's safe return. In Korea, my father was a senior military adviser KMAG (Korean Military Adviser Group) officer to a Republic of Korean Army (ROKA) medium artillery battalion. His artillery firebase was overrun by the Chinese shortly after he left.

Finally, in 1952 my dad returned safely from Korea. While he was away I kept thinking about my friend Joe Tursic, whom I played with every day for months when my family was stationed at Fort Jackson, and how his family one day received a telegram notifying them of his father's death in Korea. We lived across from them in old World War II barracks that had been converted into family housing. The Tursic family's crying, sadness, and remorse was almost more than I could bear. And although I was happy my dad was home, it was tough to adjust to him, because I had gone almost a year with little supervision and discipline.

In the early 1950s, Vietnam had already experienced nearly twenty years of almost continual warfare. The nationalistic struggle began in the 1930s against the French colonialists, who controlled Vietnam; it gained momentum in World War II with the Vietnamese's tenacious resistance against the Japanese, who starved the Vietnamese by commandeering their rice supply to feed Japanese troops in the South Pacific.

When Japan surrendered to the Allies, the French, who had surrendered to the Japanese without a fight, returned to Vietnam to reclaim their colonial empire. The Vietnamese nationalists, led by Ho Chi Minh, aligned with the communists, the only option available to them, because the United States supported its European ally, France, and French colonialism in Vietnam. In 1946, Ho Chi Minh's forces revolted against the French, and after years of warfare delivered them a stunning defeat at Dien Bien Phu in early 1954. The French government called for a Geneva conference to arrange a peace settlement.

President Harry Truman's administration had financially supported the French during the war because Ho Chi Minh's Vietnam was communist, and President Dwight Eisenhower had continued this policy. The decision in Geneva to divide Vietnam into two parts eventually led to civil war in Vietnam. It was America's irrational fear of communism and intervention in the civil war that led to our Vietnam quagmire.

While these international conflicts were exploding around the world, I was just a happy little Alabama boy growing up and learning the art of survival in an agricultural environment. Southeastern Alabama in the late 1940s and early 1950s was rural and isolated. White people, as Alabama Caucasians referred to themselves, were skeptical of Yankees, completely distrusted the federal government but worked hard to manipulate it for personal advantage, and generally considered Alabama to be the center of the world. They were still not exactly sure they had lost the American Civil War.

You could buy a Coke for five cents at the store and a roast for fifty cents. We had no television, and the most notable entertainment and social events were the community radio station (WIRB), the *Enterprise Ledger* newspaper, the local class D minor league baseball team, Protestant churches, the picture show (movies), hunting, fishing, and an occasional trip to the beaches in Panama City, Florida. Local folks often sat together in their homes, talked about their problems and experiences, and told one another stories.

Sometimes at night we would sit around the radio and listen to programs. My granddaddy always listened to the New York Yankees baseball games when they were broadcasted. All the farm families came to town every Saturday to shop and socialize, and everybody knew everyone's business. My family continued to live on North Rawls Street in a house across the street from my grandparents after my dad returned from Korea, and I roamed around town freely without any concern from dawn to dusk. I was Jo Jo Callaway and did just about anything I wanted.

My buddies and I, by the age of five, were traveling all over town on our bikes. At around age eight or nine, our little group of juvenile adventurers was so bold we would climb into the rafters of the local cotton and peanut oil mills, break into warehouses, and crawl over mountains of cotton bales and oceans of unhulled peanuts to hunt and catch pigeons. We would even sneak into the attic of the Coffee County Court House while court was in session to catch pigeons as they came in under the roof eaves. We stuffed the birds in a croaker (burlap) sack as we caught them. Sometimes we would use a flashlight to engage in these pigeon hunting activities at night; the birds were much easier to catch in the dark. We all had pigeon pens. Owning a large, colorful flock was a status symbol among us, and we engaged in constant trading. Most of our daily activities were dangerous; we were almost wild and completely fearless little boys. First grade was a real bore, and I felt very constrained. I had no interest in sitting in a classroom and wanted to be out in the world seeking new adventures.

Southern Alabama was the land of magnolia trees, azaleas, camellias, kudzu, persimmons, blackberry patches, watermelons, field peas, collard greens, fresh boiled peanuts, pecans, cotton, mimosa trees, mockingbirds, snakes, fig trees, Saint Augustine grass, red clay, brutal thunderstorms, and extremely hot, humid weather. Mules were still used for plowing fields because tractors were too expensive and labor (unskilled black Americans from poor families) was so cheap.

The streets of Enterprise were safe because there was very little crime, but the town had a rigid and well-defined social

structure, and there wasn't much economic mobility for anyone, white or black. It was a traditional southern, racially
segregated environment. The African Americans, usually
called "colored people" or occasionally "Negroes," lived in a
number of well-defined pockets around the periphery of
town. These areas were referred to as the "colored sections."
The white population lived in the nicer areas near the town
center, almost the reverse of our urban living patterns today.

The black citizens congregated in the colored section of
the town's business area but also patronized the white commercial section of town, and the white merchants encouraged their business. Cash was green and usually color blind.
However, public drinking fountains and bathrooms were dis-
tinctly marked white and colored. In public buildings, blacks
had to sit in the designated colored section, which, at the local movie theaters, was the balcony. They never ate in the
front section at white restaurants, but always in the back near
the kitchen, where black cooks prepared the food.

The blacks had their own churches and schools. When my
parents were married in the Enterprise First Baptist Church,
the balcony was filled with blacks. No one told them to sit
only in the balcony. It was just the accepted practice in a
white church when blacks visited for a special event such as
a wedding or funeral.

When we rode out to my granddaddy's farm, we often
drove through the colored section in a hollow, called "the
bottom." All the government-subsidized shacks, lined up in a
row about thirty feet apart along each side of the road, were
painted the same (noticeably peeling) brick red color. The
landscaping was red clay and kudzu vines. The houses had,
at the most, two rooms. Some had no windows, or had windows without glass panes; some had city water, few had refrigerators, most had hand-pumped well water, and all had
outhouse facilities out back. Only the Enterprise white people had indoor plumbing.

All the houses were mounted on top of concrete cinder block pier foundations about two to three feet off the ground, depending on the slope of the land toward the bottom of the hollow. Mangy, flea-ridden mongrel dogs usually lived underneath the structures. Occasionally, one would contract hydrophobia (rabies) and had to be shot. A neighbor—Ray Johnson, owner of Johnson's Superette, a convenience store that serviced the bottom at the other end of North Rawls Street—once used his store pistol to kill a mad dog, crazed and foaming at the mouth, that had staggered out of the colored section and up near our house.

Most black families had big black cauldrons out back and kept fires burning under them to heat water. These large pots were also used for personal laundry and bathing. Those belonging to the local washwomen were used for doing white people's laundry as well.

The disparity between the blacks' lives and ours bothered me when I was a child. At around five, I can remember staring out my granddaddy's truck window as we drove on the red clay dirt road down through "the bottom" and worrying about the living conditions of the blacks. I felt that something was terribly wrong. They seemed content, but in reality they were living only a step above slavery and abject poverty.

My white neighbors and relatives never made degrading comments about the black community, so my perception of the black citizens of Enterprise was simply that they were hardworking, polite, happy people who, because of the rigid social structure, did not have the opportunity to do better.

Seldom did anyone use the word "nigger." The word represented the fear of whites who lived on the economic fringe. These whites directed it at those they perceived as lower in the social structure—people they could feel safe humiliating. The expression revealed that nasty human characteristic of seeming to feel better about ourselves by degrading or ridiculing someone else. Only the most uneducated and less advantaged whites, in competition with the blacks for employment, including the better sharecropping jobs, used "nigger." This white socioeconomic group, occasionally referred to as "white trash" or "rednecks," really was at the bottom of the social pecking order. The community's successful whites had little sympathy for rednecks, particularly when they picked on the blacks. There was no Ku Klux Klan here.

Blacks came to town, almost without exception, spotlessly clean in their best clothes. Coming to town was a social event for whites and blacks alike, and dressing well meant the blacks would be treated respectfully by the whites they encountered. I remember the little girls vividly because they often braided their hair into multiple pigtails and some wore snow-white dresses. Whites called the girls "pickaninnies," which is a racially offensive expression, but even the successful whites did not consider the term bigoted. Our house was between "the bottom" and town, so every day I saw blacks as they passed by. A few drove very old cars, some came piled in mule-pulled wagons, some walked, but many used black-owned taxis.

Enterprise was a dry town, meaning there was no legal drinking of alcohol, but side dealings in moonshine were common. Generally, the black taxicab drivers ran the local black moonshine business. The taxis were cheap, because the entrepreneurial drivers made most of their money running "shine." The taxi money just subsidized their gas cost and was a front for the black shine business. The bootlegging taxi drivers were basically left alone by the local authorities. The police seldom did anything in the black community unless someone had a clear-cut, significant grievance. Murder of another black person or—for certain—anything that threatened the white community was considered significant. In Enterprise, as in most of the South, the legal standards and systems favored the whites in any white-black personal conflict.

In the South, there was not much money, and few white people were in a position to improve their own lives let alone anyone else's. This was the residual effect of the collapsed slave-based economy after the Civil War. The South's economy struggled terribly, and the federal government did little to help except dole out crop subsidies and locate military bases in the southern states. Enterprise was fortunate to have Fort Rucker Army Base located adjacent to the town to help its economy. It was soon to become the army's primary helicopter pilot training base for the Vietnam War.

Perhaps the first step toward integration in the South occurred at the military bases. President Harry Truman's executive order forcing integration and ending segregation in the armed services in 1948 opened a door that brought about the beginning of progress in the advancement of civil rights for African Americans. The order stated that all American soldiers would fight together in integrated units regardless of race, creed, or color. I believe integration of the armed forces was much more significant than Jackie Robinson breaking the color barrier playing major league baseball for the Brooklyn Dodgers.

In the 1930s, before DDT and other insecticides, the boll weevil insect had decimated the local cotton crop, which meant that little work existed for blacks, who used to pick the cotton or work in the cotton mills. And industrial equipment and even some farm machinery were replacing many of the local manual labor jobs.

The death of Enterprise's cotton industry forced the farmers to grow peanuts to survive, and they quickly became the primary crop for southern Alabama. This created such an economic windfall for the farmers that right in the center of Enterprise they erected a monument to the boll weevil—a huge enlargement of the insect mounted on a pedestal and surrounded by a fountain. The pedestal is a marble Greek goddess with her hands above her head holding an oversize bronze boll weevil. The Boll Weevil Monument is still there today. I often think there should be another monument to memorialize the person who invented peanut butter.

My granddaddy, Cliff Brunson, who owned a slaughterhouse and meat market, was innately kind and had a good relationship with the black community. The blacks seemed to respect him and often solicited his advice on decisions. I do not remember ever hearing him make a racial slur or discriminatory remark. Many of the blacks he trained in his meat market business left the South to go north, where they used those meat cutting skills working for big meat packaging companies, such as Swift, and made substantially more money. It could be said that my granddaddy ran a little meat cutters' training program. He always hated to lose good employees, but he was happy for them because he knew they could build a better economic life in the North.

The Grubbs brothers, Emmett, Monroe, and Willie, were black employees of my granddaddy's, and I spent a lot of time with them—Monroe in particular. Monroe was one tough, hardworking, honorable man, and my granddaddy trusted him implicitly. Sometimes I would spend an entire day with Monroe when my dad was away in Korea.

On occasion, Monroe would take me on his daily work routine. We would go out to my granddaddy's cattle farm in the country, single out a steer, take him by truck across town to our solid concrete slaughterhouse, then kill and butcher him for my granddaddy's meat market, located in downtown Enterprise.

Monroe would shoot the steer right in the forehead, then disembowel, skin, and quarter him. There was lots of blood, and the smell was foul, especially after Monroe split the steer right down the middle, spilling the intestines onto the concrete floor. I was always amazed by how clean and fresh the meat and slaughterhouse looked and smelled when Monroe was done, after he had hosed the blood and unwanted parts to the outside into a slop trough for the hogs.

Monroe saved my life when I was about nine. We were looking for a cow and her newborn calf in a brush thicket along a creek bed on our farm. I found the cow, which, most likely to protect her calf, went crazy and started charging at me. I ran as fast as I could, trying to reach the nearest climbable tree, but the charging cow closed in quickly. She was not more than twenty feet behind me when Monroe appeared, yelling and frantically waving his heavy butcher's apron in the air to get the angry cow to turn. Monroe would have broken that brindled cow's neck if it was necessary, and, believe me, he was strong enough to do it. He would never have let anything happen to Mr. Cliff's grandson. Monroe was a man of courage, and he left a lasting impression on me. The memory of his quick willingness to risk his own safety to help someone else served me well in the rice paddies and jungles of Vietnam.

Against my mother's wishes, my dad gave me my first BB gun when I was five years old. From the age of five to eleven, I hunted constantly, developing the natural instincts, mindset, and visual acuity of a predator. I went through at least five guns before reaching the age of ten, when my granddaddy gave me a .410-gauge shotgun to supplement my BB gun arsenal. I hunted every day and killed every bird in our neighborhood with my BB guns, and every squirrel, rabbit, and snake on my granddaddy's farm with my shotgun. The neighbor ladies used to get angry with me for killing their mockingbirds, doves, and redbirds (cardinals), and frequently threatened to call the police. One of the Enterprise policemen, Robert Pascal, was my mother's cousin, though, so I did not worry too much about the law.

Hunting was a way of life in the South. Constant hunting

developed within me the unique perception and basic tactical skills I would use in the war. In Vietnam, I read terrain well, picked up the nuances in village activity or unusual Vietnamese behavior patterns in the rice paddies, had an instinct for guerrilla tactical warfare, and anticipated situations well. I calculated early that I had to be highly disciplined, prepared, and able to out-think and out-quick the Viet Cong. I knew how to be a predator, but, most important, I knew how to use the thought process in reverse and avoid being a predator's victim.

After the defeat of the French army at Dien Bien Phu the Geneva Conference was held in July 1954. The Viet Minh, headed by Ho Chi Minh, wanted complete control over Vietnam. In a concession to the French, who were withdrawing their military, and at the urging of his allies, Ho Chi Minh agreed to a temporary partition of his country at the seventeenth parallel. Self-determination elections to reunify the country were to be held in July 1956. The Soviet Union, the People's Republic of China, the United Kingdom, and France signed the accords—a diplomatic concession to defuse the issues and only postpone the inevitable. The United States delegation, headed by Secretary of State John Foster Dulles, did not sign, because at the time the American government was paranoid about communism and knew that Ho Chi Minh would win the 1956 election with a huge majority. Ho Chi Minh and his communist allies also knew this, which is why they signed the accords.

In a 1955 referendum encouraged by the United States to circumvent the accords, Ngo Dinh Diem was elected president of the Republic of Vietnam, the area south of the seventeenth parallel. Diem refused to recognize the Geneva Accords. Ho Chi Minh was not amused and denounced Diem's actions. The United States supported Diem, who was a weak Catholic puppet in a Buddhist country, an arrogant elitist who never participated in the French Indochina War and was controlled by his heroin addict brother's wife, Madame Nhu, the infamous "dragon lady."

Thus began the second twentieth-century Vietnam War, which was a nationalistic fight for the homeland that started as a civil war sponsored by the reigning international military superpowers. Communist North Vietnam was financially supported by the Soviet Union and China; South Vietnam was supported by the United States. When it became evident that the South was no match for the North, America gradually escalated its commitment and participation in the war, and awoke one day to discover that it was engaged militarily, on a full-time basis, in the Vietnam civil war.

The National Liberation Front (NLF) was the North Vietnam–sponsored political organization in South Vietnam, and the Viet Cong (VC, or Victor Charlie) was their sponsored military organization. Their mission was to bring about revolution in the South to reunite it with North Vietnam. As the United States committed more troops and support, North Vietnam committed more North Vietnamese Army (NVA) troops to the war in the South and received more support from its superpower sponsors.

Our military commanders and politicians underestimated the situation. Our gradual increase in military pressure and resources never brought about resolution, only made our predicament worse. America bumbled into an Asian civil war, even though our political and military leaders had watched the French commit almost 200,000 troops a little more than ten years earlier and be resoundingly defeated. Ho Chi Minh, the father of Vietnam's nationalistic spirit, had said to the French in the late 1940s, "You can kill ten of my men for every one I kill of yours, but even at those odds, you will lose and I will win." Our government officials and military commanders would have done well to heed those words.

America's involvement in the Vietnam War was born from our country's 1950s communist phobia. The atheistic communist doctrine challenged the structure of our political, economic, social, and religious existence, and this created a high level of unrest and fear in America. Politicians and the military whipped the population into a frenzy over the threat that our communist adversaries posed to our national survival.

The American people lived with the fear of imminent nuclear annihilation by the communists. Our paranoia caused significant domestic disruption, because many Americans who did not agree with our government on a variety of issues were immediately suspected of being communists and intensely investigated by federal agencies. Senator Joseph McCarthy and the House Committee on Un-American Activities, in particular, conducted vicious and destructive investigations and attacks on Americans whose activities and political positions they deemed suspicious.

American politicians sold the war to the public with the domino theory, the belief that if South Vietnam fell to communism, the rest of Southeast Asia would systematically be engulfed by communist expansion. Politicians worked the American public's well-developed fear of communist world domination.

In 1954, as the French in their Vietnam War were being defeated in the final battle at Dien Bien Phu and driven from the country by the Viet Minh army, and American civil rights legislation was about to start desegregation of the southern school systems, my family moved from Enterprise to New Canaan, Connecticut. My dad could see the societal storm on the horizon for the South and wanted more economic opportunity. In Enterprise he was the sales manager for a large peanut mill operation and did lots of business with Procter & Gamble, particularly after the company learned to homogenize peanut butter to keep the oil from separating. He also had worked for the J. Walter Thompson ad agency before World War II and was able to get a job with a New York ad agency with the help of an old friend employed by the firm.

New Canaan was a fashionable New York City suburb and a small town of immense wealth and education. It was the last stop on a New Haven Railroad spur line that ran to and from New York City and boasted it was "the next stop to heaven." It was indeed a beautiful place, a town of opulent estates, not just big homes. The IBM Watson's estate was there. Other New Canaanites included Nicholas Katzenbach, President Johnson's attorney general; one of the Bundys (either McGeorge or William), both presidential advisers or high-level cabinet staff; Stanley Resor, secretary of the army under Johnson; Philip Johnson, a renowned architect; and Admiral Nimitz, Jr.

The town also was a community of many legal, artistic, entertainment world, and business superstars—wealthy commuters who worked in New York and lived in New Canaan. This was one of Connecticut's Fairfield County towns, along with Westport, Darien, and Greenwich, where New York's successful power elite lived. My father worked in New York on Madison Avenue for a prestigious, major advertising firm, Dancer, Fitzgerald and Sample. He left home before light every morning and returned after dark. When my children were growing up, each of them saw more of my father than I ever did at the same age.

My first date was with Amy Cousins, a fourteen-year-old curly tressed brunette goddess whose father, Norman Cousins, was the famous editor of the *Saturday Review*. I knew the kids of Vance Packard, a well-known author in the 1950s who wrote *The Hidden Persuaders* and *The Status Seekers,* and I also knew Freda Freed, the daughter of the first famous New York rock 'n' roll disc jockey and self-ordained king of rock 'n' roll, Alan Freed. These people were not my friends; they were just people who lived in the same relative geographic space as I did. My functional world was very distant from theirs.

New Canaan's social structure was very stratified. It had an upper class, the extraordinarily wealthy and powerful American aristocracy; an upper middle class, the wealthy New York commuters; and a middle class, which consisted of the local merchants and the support services population. New Canaan had few interdependent relationships except among members of the local business community, who supported one another to improve their economic interests.

Perhaps the most noticeable delineation in this society existed at the adolescent level between the "preppies" and the "townies." Preppies were students from wealthy families who went away to the most prestigious private secondary high schools, which were conduits to the Ivy League institutions. Townies were the children like me who went to the local high school. All upper class children were preppies. The upper middle class split; and all children of the local support population went to New Canaan High, an excellent public high school. Most of the kids I knew seemed to have a chip on their shoulders, which was initially confusing to me because most seemed to have so much. They seemed defensive and competitive in every aspect of life. I could sense a latent underlying cynical bitterness. Sarcasm and snobbish behavior were the wealthy and educated's humiliation tools and ego crutches. For all its wealth and advantages, this was not, at least for me, a happy place.

I was accustomed to going up to Montgomery, Alabama, to the cattle auction to buy Black Angus and Hereford cows or steers, not mentally engineering some way to make someone look and feel bad. I was from a rural town where a big deal was castrating young male calves into steers in spring or going squirrel or coon hunting. These kids were going to Europe, to Florida, and to Harvard, Princeton, and Yale football games, to Broadway shows and Yankee stadium, and even to California. Some girls were debutantes, not just girls. I had to go to dancing school conducted at the New Canaan Country Club and wear a dark suit, white shirt, tie, and white gloves. I felt awkward in this environment. It was a difficult transition for me and gave me even greater empathy for the Enterprise black people.

In Connecticut I admired New York Giant Willie Mays, the "Say Hey Kid," for his marvelous skill and graceful ability to play the game of baseball. He became my hero. He was not the hero of most young New Canaanites, who idolized white players such as Mickey Mantle, Stan Musial, Duke Snyder, and Ted Williams, and I felt a small sense of individuality and self-esteem for having selected this extraordinarily gifted athlete as my hero. New Canaan kids had difficulty understanding Willie when he talked, but I had no problem. His diction was familiar to me. He was a connection to the southern culture and helped me psychologically to move through the initial societal complexities I faced when we relocated north.

Watching Willie Mays play baseball helped me escape mentally from a world I did not understand. Also, not coincidentally, he was a young black man from Alabama who was now functioning in a social and economic world quite foreign to him, yet on the baseball field, where only his ability counted, he was the greatest. There has never been a better baseball player.

The affluence and wealth in New Canaan did not foster development of the strong bonding relationships that existed in a place such as Enterprise, where there was much need for interdependence. The privileged existence also did not foster the creation of strong family units. It was an enormously competitive town—almost predatory.

These inherent societal weaknesses greatly impacted the community's adults, who were lost in their social worlds and alcoholic and sexually promiscuous behavior. The adults in this environment were products of the times. They were not bad people, but they were obsessed with success and self-importance. They were caught up in an expensive, quick-moving, cutthroat life. They could not see or anticipate the damage they were doing to themselves and their families. Most parents either did not understand or were not willing to invest time in the development of their children. Many of their capable but essentially unsupervised children were often turned over to boarding schools and left to pass through adolescence without much nurturing. The children gravitated to early sexual relationships and alcohol, looking for solutions to the social complications, competitive frustrations, lack of structure, and emotional voids in their lives.

Although many of the teenagers were from what we today call dysfunctional families, they were better educated, more motivated, and more sophisticated than I was. I had not developed in the elementary school years the fundamental educational building blocks needed to construct the foundation on which to build advanced academic thinking. When my dad was recalled into the army for the Korean War, we moved from army post to post, and I transitioned often between Alabama public schools and army post schools. In all I changed schools seven times at the elementary level. In Connecticut I was educationally and culturally far behind my peer group. My only saving grace was that they were about as emotionally challenged as I was.

I could do short spurts of above-average school performance but did not have the inclination to stay focused. Eventually, I gave up and drifted into failure. When everyone else was planning future education, short-term objectives, and long-term goals, I could not even find the motivation to get to school. I just wasted time and pretended I did not care about anything.

For me, going to school was just putting in time. It was a place to congregate, a place to talk sports, a place to see friends. I did not understand the purpose of school. Getting an education was not a consideration. Studying was hard for me, and my reading skills were poor. I tried to please my parents but never felt comfortable or motivated by the work. It was just a grinding, relentless, boring task, and I despised it. Yet I could not face the next step in life because I had no idea what it was or how to do it. To me, whatever I was supposed to do after high school seemed like stepping off the roof of a thousand-foot-tall building. In high school, I was confronted with a paradox. I was afraid to leave, to take the next step, but I did not want to go to school to face my limitations.

In my senior year, I missed seventy-eight school days and was late twenty-one others. All I needed to graduate were two and a half credits, but I just could not make it. The worst night in my life prior to Vietnam was the night my high school class graduated without me. My friend Alex Reid did not graduate either, so we went out drinking. Alex was gregarious and had a great sense of humor, but even he could not make me laugh that night. I was a lost and lonely person with no place to go.

In my late teens, I developed a little business stealing booze from the wealthy New Canaanites' pool house bars and reselling it at below market value prices. I was careful to take only a small percent of their inventory to keep them from noticing, and I dealt only in high-quality brands. This was a top-of-the-line operation that required patience and stealth, because the execution was always at night. I used my job as the Lang's Pharmacy prescription drug delivery boy to recon my targets.

I looked at myself as a young suburban Robin Hood, because I robbed the very rich and sold at discounts to the less rich. Sometimes I sold the booze back to a local liquor store. I did this for only a short period. Fortunately for me, another kid in town who was stealing TVs was caught, and I decided my activities were frivolous, senseless, risk taking. It was not for the money. What I was doing was really an escape to offset my inability to compete and perform in the New Canaan environment. It was no more than displaced personal frustration and discontent.

I did hang out with a group of young men who were interesting and somewhat wild—basically young men trying to grow up. They amused me, and I admired them, but because I had no achievements of my own, I found myself living vicariously through their accomplishments and lives. This little group of cohorts gave some meaning and social structure to my life and helped me through some difficult years—years that could have been even more disastrous without their valuable although somewhat limited friendship.

I could write a novel about these characters, but they might not appreciate it. A modern-day suburban Tom Sawyer/Huck Finn crowd, they were always a lot of fun to be around. They helped take away the pain of my failure. These defiant young bucks, who in their own way challenged the New Canaan social hierarchy and aristocracy, on occasion could be bad boys, but they supported one another in ways that reminded me of the life in Alabama I had lost and missed. These friendships would later become very important to me—so important that they may have saved my life.

After graduating from summer school and finally high school in August 1961, I spent a year in postgraduate private school. Saint Luke's School for Boys, a local prep school for rich kids whose parents did not want to send them away to school, mercifully gave me a chance. But even though I started well, I failed academically once again.

I was a pretty good basketball player for this level of competition, but I ran into trouble after a team trip across the border into New York State. We drove to the game in cars. Most of the players became lost and did not show up for the game, so we had to forfeit. Mike Cowenhoven, the tall, rangy team center, and I, the only players who did not get lost, decided to down a couple of Budweiser six-packs; we could drink legally back then at age eighteen in New York. Unfortunately, back at St. Luke's we encountered our coach, Dick Whitcomb, a stern, husky man with a squeaky little voice, and he kicked me off the team, probably for stupidity as much as for drinking. I had created another tangible way to fail, avoid work and responsibility, and the future.

St. Luke's miraculously found a college that would take me; the next year I went to Monmouth College, a small school located in the western part of central Illinois, Carl Sandburg country, near the Mississippi River. But this became another academic and social disaster, and I was in and out of this school every other semester from fall 1962 to spring 1965.

During my first academic year in the second semester, January 1963, I went to Europe—actually traveled all over Europe by myself for three months. My apparent motivation was chasing a lost high school girlfriend, but I was really running away from the social adjustments and work requirements of college. Martin Luther King had already given his famous "I have a dream" speech in Washington, and I was watching racial events in the South only on TV. President Kennedy was assassinated on November 22, 1963. Life was confusing to an underachieving twenty-year-old who grew up without much education and direction in two diametric environments.

On another college sabbatical in 1964, I was employed at the Pepperidge Farm Bakery in Norwalk, Connecticut, for about four months. Starting work at 4 A.M. and lifting hundred-pound bags of sugar and flour all day was hard, but it helped give me physical and mental strength and discipline. This definitely improved my self-confidence. And on my last academic stress break in spring 1965, I went to California's Newport Beach for a few months' visit with my paternal grandfather, Jesse Thomas Callaway. Here I bemoaned the loss of my most recent true love, Kit Rafferty, a beautiful lady who had just gotten a job with Eastern Airlines as a stewardess and had moved on to a better dating market than spending time with an immature college dropout with no job prospects in sight.

After these hiatuses from school, Monmouth College was not going to protect my military selective service deferment anymore, so I decided in June 1965 to join the army, simply because I had no idea what else to do with my life. I was, without doubt, going to be drafted into the army anyway, because the Vietnam War was starting to heat up and the military was expanding rapidly.

America's struggle against the communist empire in the little backwater, third world country of South Vietnam was not going well in the early 1960s. Our financial and military advisory support was not producing any significant gains. In fact we were systematically losing ground, and South Vietnam was getting weaker each year, so the United States backed a regime coup d'etat in which President Diem and his brother were assassinated. But America also needed a reason to make a more concerted effort and commit more resources, including greater airpower and conventional ground troops, so the administration used the Gulf of Tonkin incident, in which a few small North Vietnamese patrol boats supposedly attacked a mighty American destroyer. On August 7, 1964, following the House of Representatives unanimous yes vote, the Senate voted eighty-eight to two to support the Gulf of Tonkin Resolution and gave President Lyndon Johnson unlimited authority to increase dramatically America's participation in Vietnam.

The events surrounding the naval incidents in the Gulf of Tonkin remain in doubt and were challenged by Senator Wayne Morse (D-Oregon). On August 2, 1964, South Vietnamese naval boats had bombarded two islands off the coast of North Vietnam. The American destroyer USS *Maddox* was in the area and reported an attack by North Vietnamese patrol boats.

One patrol boat was severely damaged by the *Maddox* and two others were chased off by U.S. aircraft from the carrier USS *Ticonderoga*. The United States insisted that the North Vietnamese attack was unprovoked. The main controversy is whether there was a second attack on the *Maddox* on August 4. Evidence suggests that the second attack did not occur, and many historians assert that the Johnson administration fabricated the second attack to gain congressional approval for the resolution. The fact that the very document that became the Gulf of Tonkin Resolution had been prepared in May 1964, some three months before the "unprovoked attacks" took place, certainly supports this point of view.

Senators Ernest Gruening (D-Alaska) and Wayne Morse, men of foresight and courage, were the two senators who voted against the Gulf of Tonkin Resolution. Gruening was opposed to sacrificing a single American boy in this venture. He said we had lost too many already. Senator Morse stated that the Senate was about to make a historic mistake in passing the resolution.

President Johnson and Secretary of Defense Robert McNamara had convinced all 416 U.S. congressmen and 88 of the 90 senators who voted on the resolution to give the president unlimited powers in prosecuting the Vietnam War. Because the Congress of the United States abrogated its power, giving up its constitutional right to be the only branch of the government that can declare war, American public support for military action in Vietnam was no longer required, and President Johnson could conduct the war on his own terms.

After the election in November 1964, President Johnson did not have to face the public again in an election until 1968. These fours years were the most divisive in American history since 1861–65 when President Abraham Lincoln prosecuted the American Civil War. Senator Wayne Morse was right in predicting that future generations would look with dismay and great disappointment upon a Congress that passed the Gulf of Tonkin Resolution.

DESTINY'S PATH

For my entire life prior to Vietnam, I had, in my estimation, screwed up everything. I screwed up school. I screwed up sports. I screwed up my social life. I had very few friends. I had no self-esteem. I did not have confidence in my ability, could not develop the will to achieve, and lived with an attitude that success was not important to me. I did not have the faintest idea how to stick with a task or accomplish a goal.

But somehow I began to click in the army, and in Vietnam I found my mission. When I first arrived in-country, it was like a bad dream to be in that godforsaken place. I often asked myself how I got duped into this. To avoid being drafted and going to Vietnam as an infantry private, I enlisted in the army and signed up for missile school, hoping to train at Fort Bliss in El Paso, Texas, spend lots of time carousing in the cantinas across the border in Juarez, Mexico, and later spend my entire army tour partying in the German *hof braus* and traveling around Europe. If the possibility existed, I also hoped to go to officers candidate school (OCS) but still end up in Europe in some noncombat function. I took an IQ test in the Fort Dix, New Jersey, army induction center and learned, for the first time, that I was very bright. I did not have a college degree but passed all the intelligence entry tests and qualified for OCS.

In the eight-week basic combat training (BCT) program at

Fort Dix, I was the first acting platoon leader of my training unit. I enjoyed working with the young men in basic training and helping them improve in their tasks. I could always explain and show them easier ways to do things and tried to help the physically weakest through the tough physical requirements. Many were frightened by this military experience. Some had never been away from home. I found newly discovered gratification in helping my fellow soldiers and in the subsequent respect I was given. They knew I cared about them, and the men looked up to me. I began to feel good about myself for the first time in a long while.

I almost went AWOL (absent without leave) three-quarters of the way through the program, though. I was relieved as the acting platoon leader by Staff Sergeant Parker, the drill instructor (DI), because I marched the troops into the side of a building by accident. Marching the troops, calling cadence, keeping everyone in step, and giving the correct directional commands were always difficult for me. I had no sense of rhythm and was self-conscious at this stage of my leadership development. I took this demotion hard. I hated the army. I hated the discipline, the degradation, and the regimentation. I hated someone being able to tell me what to do.

I decided to leave Fort Dix. I could not take it anymore. I tried to call Kit Rafferty but was unsuccessful. Right before leaving the post, while standing in a phone booth near the Fort Dix front gate, I broke down and started crying. I suddenly realized there were no viable options left in my life. This was the end of the line on running from responsibility. I had to take a stand.

If I went AWOL, all opportunities in the army would be lost forever, so I elected to return to my basic training unit and go to OCS, even though I knew it was a direct ticket to Vietnam. The company commander had asked me and three other qualified trainees from other platoons to sign up for OCS halfway through basic training, but initially I declined.

The army was desperate for infantry lieutenants for the Vietnam expansion. At this point they gave almost anyone who could pass the intelligence tests the chance to go to OCS, although the army decided what OCS program the person attended. The three combat arms options were infantry, artillery, and engineering. Those OCS candidates with college degrees had some leverage, but guys like me were strictly infantry line doggie meat. Initially in order of preference, my OCS selections were engineering, artillery, and infantry.

After basic training and before OCS, the army sent me to infantry light weapons advanced individual training (AIT) at Fort Dix. This was another eight-week program and a definite clue regarding what was going to happen to me. The training company commander and the DI, platoon sergeant Mallory, a huge, robust black man, knew I was going to OCS. They gave me a couple of squads of the worst performers in the company, and my own area in which to work with them, then said, "Do the best you can." Sergeant Mallory gave me lots of latitude, and this turned out to be an inspiring responsibility.

These problem young men were sincere and willing but slow thinking. Working with them and shaping them into soldiers was challenging, and I gained a real sense of accomplishment as they gained pride from their own progress. I taught them how to be better organized by preparing ahead of time, explained the training more clearly to help them learn, and gave them confidence that effort brings success. I found men with good hearts and new enthusiasm and energy—men who before knew only failure and humiliation.

By the end of training, in some performance areas, my group was doing better than the regular troops. They were especially proud of themselves after the last inspection when they received the highest rating in the company. I almost cried when I saw how happy they were to be recognized for achievement. Positive reinforcement had given them self-respect, improved their morale, and motivated them to work even harder. Success had built success.

Christmas 1965 was around the corner. Everyone had applied for a two-week leave after AIT and expected it would go through, just like the two-week leave we were given right after basic training. Then, we all had received a special three-day pass the weekend before graduation because the company had done so well; everyone was elated and returned from the weekend with great enthusiasm for the final training week. A few days before the end of the AIT training, however, during a company formation the commander announced, "All leave requests are denied. The entire unit is leaving for the 1st Air Cavalry Division in Vietnam on Saturday, except for Private Callaway, and he's going to infantry OCS at Fort Benning, Georgia, in January." I was then very happy I had applied to OCS.

The army had to station the military police (MP) around the barracks every night to prevent desertions. These were not happy troopers. They felt betrayed by the army and did not understand why the army would not at least let them go home for Christmas before sending them to Vietnam. The troops' mood changed quickly from euphoric to cynical and bitter.

I was happy not to be assigned to the 1st Air Cav but was concerned for my rapidly improving group to be going to Vietnam without me. I hoped they were led by people who would understand and help them. When Saturday arrived, I shook their hands and sadly watched them depart on a bus going to McGuire Air Force Base. From the sidewalk I could see them through the bus windows as they drove off on the first leg of a long, lonely trip to Southeast Asia. It was a solemn moment for me as I realized for the first time that the government owned the lives of those in the military. I went home to Connecticut on Christmas leave and enjoyed the holidays in picturesque New England with my family, while my Vietnam-bound buddies were in a violent, frightening life on the other side of the world. I never saw any of them again.

There is no such thing as freedom in the army. Gradually, I learned that the best option in the army was to be good enough to impact decisions regarding your assignments, which gave you some control over your destiny. You needed to distinguish yourself so you were not just a piece of slaughterhouse meat and to learn to engineer your own career.

Infantry OCS is the ultimate leadership program and one of the best ever designed. The program is structured to teach leadership fundamentals. I learned that to be an effective leader, you must have vision and organization skills, an ardent passion for your task, technical knowledge, high energy drive, concern for those you expect to lead, and the ability to inspire confidence in the execution, strategy, and mission objectives. You must be able to communicate these leadership skills and personal characteristics and demonstrate them through your actions. Your troops learn in part from your behavior and your commitment. You must be a patient teacher, and your troops must be willing to work hard in training preparation and learn to work as a team. You must create willing action and the desire to improve.

Infantry OCS is also a difficult, demanding six months. The program is designed to tear you down, then rebuild you the way the army wants you to be. The OCS program humiliates the officer candidate not just to see if the individual can take it, as most candidates believe. The army wants the infantry lieutenant to learn never to abuse the significant power given to him. The army teaches you how it feels to be psychologically degraded. The infantry lieutenant must inspire his subordinates to follow willingly his direction; this can be accomplished only through positive leadership, not dictatorial and humiliating management. On the battlefield, power has little value. I later learned in Vietnam what "Follow Me" really meant.

Infantry OCS was particularly difficult for me, because I was not fond of military discipline and regimentation. But my goal was to get through the grueling program, which was basically structured to make you quit. I also struggled because, for this rigorous and intense level of training, I was very disorganized and had poor time management skills. Every day was a survival challenge for me.

My bunk mate with the Cheshire cat grin, the bright and polished Ernie Parker, who later served with me in the 2d of the 60th Infantry in Vietnam, helped me get through OCS. He knew I hated the harassment but was willing to endure it because I felt driven to complete the program. I needed a significant achievement in my life. Ernie was a compassionate person and a strong individualist; without his support and encouragement, I may not have lasted.

At this time, I still hoped to end up in Europe in some noncombat function. In fact I never thought about killing anyone, or that killing was where all this infantry training would ultimately lead. I just wanted to get through OCS. Graduation day, June 21, 1966, as an army infantry gold-bar second lieutenant, was one of the happiest and proudest days of my life. I had actually finished something and was overjoyed, ecstatic. My parents came. At the age of twenty-two, I had finally made an important graduation and achievement goal. My parents finally saw something I had done for which they could be proud. Becoming an army officer was my first noteworthy accomplishment in life other than the most valuable player award that Coach Tom Wood gave me when I was twelve, in the New Canaan Little League baseball program. Coincidentally, the coach's two sons were to play an important role in future decisions that I would make in life.

I had continued an important family tradition, as did my father, and my paternal grandfather, who was an infantry officer in World War I. Becoming an army officer was the best way to redeem myself in the eyes of my family after my adolescent failures. After graduation I went to Fort Riley, Kansas, the home of the recently activated 9th Infantry Division, to join and train my infantry rifle platoon.

I spent a mere four months at Fort Riley, located on the plains of central Kansas. The 1st Division (the Big Red One) had trained here before it deployed to Vietnam. The 9th Division was mobilized in the vacant space. What we conducted was just fundamental army tactical training. We worked on the basics—weapons and tactical formations and movement. We had only one day of helicopter training. The terrain here did not even remotely resemble Vietnam, but the Kansas summer was hot, so this was a good indoctrination for us.

During this period the 9th Division men got to know one another. I worked my men hard with all I knew about military training and tactics, which was limited. In late October we conducted a brigade field training exercise (FTX); three men were accidentally killed. Most of November we spent packing for Vietnam and taking two-week leaves prior to deployment, so we had only three months to actually train. However, the leadership responsibility of being a platoon leader was helping me mature as a man.

Prior to the army, I made only marginal improvement each year in direction and focus and drifted, trying to find some motivation or a goal in life. In June 1965, when I joined at the age of twenty-one, the army presented a new beginning. It was a chance to start on a new and even playing field again. Although I almost self-destructed a couple of times during training, I made strong, consistent improvement in my focus, determination, and character with each new hurdle.

I simply could not escape the Vietnam War. The more I tried to avoid it, the closer it came to me. The army and Vietnam made me strong. Without them to help me reposition my life, the future could have been a much rougher road. I might not have become confident enough to do much in my life. My years in the military taught me that life and, in particular, achievement is about hard work and believing in oneself.

A LONG WAY FROM KANSAS

In 1967 it seemed I should still be a kid driving around my hometown with my rowdy buddies looking for a party. But there I was—a twenty-three-year-old lieutenant, an infantry platoon leader for the 1st Platoon, Company C, 2d Battalion, 60th Infantry, 9th Infantry Division, United States Army— conducting combat operations in the remote Southeast Asian country of South Vietnam. That year my old life ended and the person I am today began in the same place—a bone-dry, dusty rice paddy with a group of young soldiers I loved and admired because they accepted and executed this grueling, brutal Vietnam task with nothing to gain but the satisfaction of doing their duty for America. They were the most heroic, courageous, and unselfish men I have ever known.

Our combat unit, the 9th Infantry Division, the Old Reliables, established its reputation and proud traditions in World War II by crushing Axis forces in North Africa, Sicily, and Central Europe. The first soldiers to enter Germany in World War II were wearing the red, white, and blue double quarterfoil, the 9th Division's shoulder patch. The emblem was worn by the men who helped defeat Rommel in North Africa and by the liberators of Belgium as well. In World War II the 9th's most notable achievement was taking the Ludendorff Bridge, near the small village of Remagen, before it could be destroyed by the Germans. It was the last bridge left standing to cross the Rhine River, and the 9th became the first infantry unit to battle across the Rhine since the Napoleonic Wars.

Now the 9th was going to war again, but this was an Asian guerrilla war and very different from World War II, in which courage and relentless power dominated the action. In the Vietnam War courage was required, but patience, tenacious discipline, and guile were also valuable. The 2d of the 60th Infantry, with the motto "To the Utmost Extent of Our Power," was about to face a new, brutal test. And we, along with much of America, were also about to learn a painful lesson: The spirit we used to build our great country is not unique to us. Other societies love their countries too, and simple human will can be a far greater power than technological and resource superiority.

Charlie Company, 2d Battalion, 60th Infantry, 9th Division, departed from Fort Riley for Vietnam right before Thanksgiving in 1966. We were part of the 9th Division's 3d Brigade, also known as the Devil's Brigade. As we loaded onto military buses, I had a minor incident with Pvt. Bruce McKee's parents. They held on to their only child, preventing him from getting on the bus. I pulled him from their arms and assured them I would take good care of him—a promise I would come to regret for the rest of my life.

The buses took us across the rolling hill plains of central Kansas to a northern Kansas railhead, where we loaded aboard trains. I looked out my window and watched western America pass by. The iron horse ride through the majestic Rocky Mountains and the gorgeous surrounding scenery was a fitting way to say good-bye to America. This was a great adventure, but it was hard to get excited about the journey. We tried to comprehend the distance of the trip and the significance of what was taking place, but it was a stretch for our young minds.

We laughed and acted as if we were having a grand time

on the train. The jovial troops horsed around and behaved like young boys. We wanted to feel as though we were going on vacation, but in our hearts we knew that was not true. Many of us would not be coming home again, and the lives of the survivors would be changed forever.

For us war was only a romantic event, shaped in our minds by the movie industry and stories we had heard about World War II and the Korean War. I didn't feel as though we were really going to war. In fact, I had never seen a Vietnamese in person, only on TV, and I wasn't sure what any of them had done to make our government so upset. I certainly wasn't angry with them, but I never asked myself why we were doing this or whether it was right or wrong. We were conditioned and trained to do what the army told us.

Our train arrived in Oakland, California, at about 0300 because the army wanted to avoid the war protesters from the University of California at Berkeley. I was the first soldier off the train—most were sound asleep. As I looked down the long, lonely string of dimly lit cars packed with young innocent men, then back up to the train engine, steam jettisoning out its side and dissipating quickly in the cool air, I felt that this was going to be an experience that would forever alter my life. I stood there in the damp night air, waiting for angry, belligerent student protesters carrying antiwar signs to come marching down the tracks. Little did I know that more than thirty-five years in the future, my two oldest sons would have graduated from this great university and that most of my adult life would be spent in Danville, California, in the morning shadows of Mount Diablo not much more than thirty miles from this location.

Our troopship, the USNS *General William Wegel,* was docked at a pier right across the railroad tracks. We loaded about two thousand soldiers, each with one duffel bag, from two trains onto our ship sometime before daylight. It was a quick and orderly process, and later that day we sailed under the Bay Bridge, past San Francisco and Alcatraz, and out across San Francisco Bay. My first view of the Golden Gate Bridge—awesome and striking but surprisingly not "golden"—was essentially from the bottom up. Beyond the Golden Gate was an endless expanse of ocean. Vietnam was a small Southeast Asian country on the other side of the world and more than ten thousand miles from home.

The troops were packed in the *Wegel* like sardines. Bunk beds were stacked up three and four high with only about six inches between our noses and the bunk above us. Once we passed the Golden Gate, the ocean became extremely rough. The ship began to pitch and roll, and most of the soldiers got seasick. The men were sandwiched so tightly together that vomiting became a chain reaction.

There was vomit and its putrid stench everywhere. The entire ship reeked; the latrines filled up and sick soldiers lined the ship's railing. I did not get sick, but I did feel ill for a couple of days. A sailor had told me to keep my stomach full to reduce the slosh effect, so I ate as often and as much as possible, and it seemed to work. The motion sickness continued for about a week until everyone adjusted to the rolling pitch of the sea.

We were assigned scheduled deck time, each day, and our units exercised in their designated space and at their allotted time. Everyone was surprised to learn that we jumped a day ahead at the international date line. At the date line, we conducted the traditional King Neptune ceremony to haze all those crossing for the first time, which was almost everyone on board except the sailors. The soldiers, stripped to their shorts, had to get down on their hands and knees with a bucket on their head and crawl up to the feet of and pay homage to the exalted ruler of the high seas, King Neptune. A senior sailor, dressed in a regal costume and carrying a large artificial pitchfork in his hand, sat on the ship's bow deck on a throne. His surrogates whacked the soldiers' butts and poured soapy cold water on their bodies. This proved to be a wonderful distraction for the troops, and everyone had a good laugh.

Eventually, however, the trip became quite boring, and we sat around all day playing cards, usually hearts. Some of us overate and began gaining weight. The Pacific Ocean is extraordinarily large. The distance we were crossing was vast and completely beyond my comprehension.

After about three weeks of sailing, we stopped in Okinawa, and everyone was allowed to get off the ship for about twelve hours. This southern Japanese island was the U.S. strategic forces base in the western Pacific; its residents were familiar with American soldiers and were well equipped to handle two thousand rambunctious GIs ready to party. We had a midnight curfew, and the ship was scheduled to sail after sunrise the next morning.

The troops went crazy hitting all the sleazy bars and nightclubs on the island. The place was saturated with decadent massage parlors and brothels. Miraculously, all of the soldiers returned, although some had passed out and were carried back by their buddies. This would prove to be good training for their future tasks. The next morning, a mile out from this oriental den of iniquity, a distraught soldier jumped from the stern of the ship and tried to swim back to Okinawa. No one knew why. He presumably drowned.

About thirty days after leaving Oakland and shortly before Christmas, on December 19, 1966, we arrived at Vung Tau, South Vietnam. As we crossed the South China Sea and approached this town, I looked at it against the horizon and wondered what my future would be. Would this be the end of my life? What was I supposed to do here, and would I have the courage to do it? I felt as though we were going through some kind of time warp into another dimension. The army was going to pay me $303 base pay and $65 hazardous duty combat pay each month, or $368 nontaxable income with free room and board, to enter this unknown and dangerous world for a one-year tour of duty.

Charlie Company deployed with five commissioned officers. The company commander (CO) was 1st Lt. Al Bredleau; the executive officer was 2d Lt. Jim Lehne; and Second Lieutenants Callaway, Johnston, and Torres were the three infantry platoon leaders. Bredleau and Lehne had military experience as noncommissioned officers, but we platoon leaders had been in the army only a little more than a year.

I had seventeen months' experience in the military—twelve months in actual training (basic, AIT light weapons, and infantry OCS) and only five months as an officer. One of these five months was spent on board a ship. I had just turned twenty-three, was Batman 16 (my radio call sign, pronounced "one six," not sixteen), had dog tag serial number 05330111, and was responsible to lead forty-two men on an unimaginably dangerous journey into jungle guerrilla warfare against some tough, experienced, and well-trained light infantry combat soldiers who were highly motivated and committed to their task.

The 1st Platoon's noncommissioned officers/sergeants (NCOs) also had limited experience. My platoon sergeant, Sfc. Paul Dilley, had about seventeen years in the army but had managed an NCO club in Germany for the previous ten years. He must have really angered someone to get this Vietnam assignment. Sergeant Dilley was taciturn and passive. He assumed the ultimate low profile and let me run the platoon, which is the way I wanted it and the way he wanted it. Because of this understanding, we had a good working relationship.

The platoon had three reinforced squads; we took the weapons squad, or 4th Squad, and split the men among the three rifle squads. My 1st Squad leader, the scruffy but effective Staff Sergeant Rasch, and the 2d Squad leader, the consistently professional Staff Sergeant Hunt, were also military lifers; each had about ten years' infantry background but no actual combat experience. My 3d Squad leader—the cocky, sometimes cynical but capable Sgt. Ed Chodyniecki as well as the six buck sergeant fire team leaders and all but three other enlisted men (EM), were drafted; each of these young men had less than a year's experience in the army. We were line doggies conditioned by the army. Its training gave us the courage but not the tactics needed to fight this guerrilla war. That we learned on the job.

The platoon had two fire team leaders in each of the three squads. All but one of my six fire team leaders were exceptional. Sergeant Billy Joe Price, a heroic young soldier from Kentucky, was an excellent point man and fire team leader. Southerners made good soldiers because many were farmers and all usually were hunters. Sergeants Ronnie Bentley, Gary Blaylock, and Jimmy Stanfield—also from the South—were solid young men and dependable team leaders. Along with Chodyniecki and Mark McCowan, who became a fire team leader in Vietnam, they were the young nucleus of leaders who made my infantry platoon effective. These draftees had a good attitude and solid relationships, which helped hold the platoon together during the worst of times. The platoon also had an exceptional medic in Spc. Peter Nero, a fearless declared noncombatant and curly headed blond surfer from San Diego. Also very capable were my radiotelephone operators (RTOs), the dependable Gary Boyd and the gutsy, talkative Phil Hilowitz. Charlie Company's 1st Platoon had a fine group of young men. I was a very lucky platoon leader.

The company first sergeant, Edward Johnson, was a powerful force. About thirty-eight years old and about six foot four, he was a hardcore, tough Korean War veteran with a booming voice that projected his determined will and strong principles. Charlie Company's "top" sergeant, he had an informal power and experience that made him the most influential man in the company. Although respectful to the company officers, "Top" was strongly opinionated and almost unrestrained in arguing if he thought the officers were wrong. He was a professional soldier and forthright man.

The 2d Platoon sergeant, George Marshal, a Korean War veteran, was also a friend and worthy consultant. Although he would occasionally drink too much, he knew how to execute field tactics when he was sober, and he was invaluable, particularly in the field. He was a man of courage and compassion with a subtle sense of humor. More than anyone else in the company, he understood the horror of war from his brutal Korean experience.

IN-COUNTRY

When we disembarked at Vung Tau, some senior 9th Division officers who flew to South Vietnam ahead of us were there to greet the ship. They staged a fake landing for the photographers of themselves getting off a navy landing craft and walking through about a foot of ocean water onto the Vietnam beach. In the background, the flags of the Republic of Vietnam, the 9th Infantry Division, and the United States of America unfurled beautifully in the wind. The officers said it was symbolic of the troops landing, but to me it looked silly and phony.

Pretty Vietnamese girls, clad in their native garb, placed leis around the necks of the generals and colonels. The division band, which had flown to Vietnam, played background music for the ceremony. General William Westmoreland, a strikingly handsome man, a strong command presence, and the commander of Military Assistance Command Vietnam (MACV), was in Vung Tau for the welcome ceremony, not only in his official capacity but also for personal reasons. He had served in World War II in the 9th Division as a commander of the 34th Field Artillery Battalion and was also division chief of staff. After the official welcome ended, General Westmoreland and Maj. Gen. George Eckhardt, the 9th Division's commanding general (CG) walked among us extending a personal welcome to the troops as we gathered our duffel bags and loaded onto five-ton convey trucks.

On the ride from Vung Tau to Bearcat, the new 9th Division headquarters, located near Long Thanh, thirty miles east of Saigon, Vietnamese civilians lined the road near the villages we passed. They wanted to sell us drugs, their sisters, their mothers—anything they had that we might want. Even the children begged for money and cigarettes. They were masterful little beggars and would steal anything that wasn't tied down. There was even some "Fuck you GI" and "Yankees go home." This was not the liberation of France. Many Vietnamese expressed anger at our presence and were disgustingly offensive.

Along the way, we passed an Aussie (Australian) patrol in tiger fatigues with slung AR-15 rifles moving at a forced march pace down the road. They were solemn and grim looking. Our troops were laughing and having a good time, but the Aussies were stone-faced and looked straight ahead as we passed. They did not even acknowledge our presence. It was as if they knew the formidable danger in our future and did not want to know us. On my first day in Vietnam, I sensed that this was going to be a very bad experience.

The Republic of Vietnam extended in a crescent shape along the southeastern face of the Indochina peninsula. The country was long and narrow like California but less than half its width. Extending from its forty-five-mile-long border with North Vietnam at the seventeenth parallel southward to the bottom of the Mekong Delta lay fifteen hundred miles of coastline on the South China Sea and the Gulf of Siam.

The northern two-thirds of South Vietnam is dominated by the rugged Annamite Mountains. South of the mountains, the land descends through flat plains covered with savannah grass to the Mekong Delta. The delta, extending generally southeast of Saigon, is a vast alluvial plain fed by the many mouths of the Mekong River, which starts in the mountains of southwest China and flows more than twenty-six hundred miles through many countries before it reaches the delta and the South China Sea.

At the time, the Mekong Delta, crisscrossed by a dense and extensive system of canals, was capable of yielding five million tons of rice yearly. It was the major rice-producing area of Southeast Asia and home to at least six million people scattered throughout the area in little villages and hamlets. Because two-thirds of the country is mountainous, the overwhelming majority of the population lived in the open lowland plains of the rice-rich deltas. These included the Mekong and a series of smaller deltas along the coast.

The Vietnam heat and humidity were close to intolerable. There were two distinct seasons: blazing hot and dry, and sauna humid, hot, and rainy. In the dry season, it was so hot by 1100 that we could see heat ripples shimmering in the air above the dried-up rice paddies (after a few weeks of no rain, the water in most rice paddies evaporated and the surface mud turned to concrete). In the wet season, the rain never seemed to stop, and the humidity was so high that we would sweat just standing in the shade. All the rice paddies filled with water and were almost impossible to slog through for everything except water buffalo. The mud was everywhere and stuck like glue to our jungle boots. I could not understand why the Vietnamese never had mud on their Ho Chi Minhs, sandals made from tires. We seemed to physically rot in the extraordinarily high humidity, rain, and ever-present mud.

The freshwater swamps and streams in the deltas were full of leeches. Before any freshwater-related mission, and particularly before a night patrol, we covered our jungle fatigues and boots with kerosene to deter these awful creatures. They seemed able to elongate and go right through jungle fatigue or boot fabric. They attached themselves to our flesh, scoured out a small, painless wound, then drank our blood as it rose to the surface. (Leeches exude an anticoagulant, which prevents the blood from clotting at the wound.) These parasites were a lot like ticks only long, slimy, and much larger. They dropped free if you touched them with a lit cigarette or a drop of insect repellent. Soldiers were terrified of a leech getting into the end of their penis. A gruesome story circulated about how this happened to a trooper in another battalion; to remove the leech, his penis was sliced open by an army surgeon. The troops speculated what would happen to the poor guy if he got an erection with the stitches still in the penis.

The mosquitoes were not bad in the dry rice paddies but were awful in the jungles. Hordes of them attacked any exposed part of our bodies, including our eyes, nose, ears, and mouth. Even when we were drenched in repellent, the constant buzzing around our heads drove us crazy. Swallowing orange pills every day to protect us from malaria, carried by the female of one mosquito species, became routine.

The environment in Vietnam was totally alien to most newly arrived U.S. soldiers. The country smelled repulsive, as if everything was in some stage of decomposition. The place was an open sewer.

The 9th was assigned to the Mekong Delta and the surrounding rice paddy area in southeastern Vietnam. The land was flat and barely above sea level. Any land not used for rice crops or rubber plantations was covered with dense undergrowth. Some of the bamboo in jungle thickets was as hard as steel and had leaves like razors. We generally encountered coconut tree jungles with tall nipa palms, which covered the areas adjacent to mangrove swamps and had an undergrowth of thick, lush green foliage. Adjacent to the rivers, which dominated the alluvial plain geography, were muddy swamps, choked with reeds and grass or mangrove palm trees even in the dry season.

Navigating through these dense jungles and muddy swamps was a difficult and sometimes hopeless task. Just traversing the countryside could be almost as dangerous as facing the enemy. Many of our operations covered large areas of hostile terrain, uninhabited except for a Viet Cong (VC) base camp.

Charlie Company's initial exploratory combat operations began in III Corps' dense jungles near Bearcat and Long Binh, northeast of Saigon in Bien Hoa Province. Our most dangerous adversary when we were on night patrol here was our own artillery harassment and interdiction (H&I) operations, which were preplotted artillery fire designed to keep the enemy on edge and off balance around our large base camps.

Our initial in-country operations were relatively safe security patrols around Long Binh and Bearcat, but it was here that I came into contact with the silent deadly killer Agent Orange, the dioxin-tainted defoliant used in Vietnam. Dioxin is a known highly carcinogenic substance. I can remember being actually sprayed only once, maybe twice, and I am sure that I covered myself with my poncho for most of the time on that occasion. Sergeant Jimmy Stanfield, a young fire team leader, and I were on a platoon patrol around the Long Binh area when we were first sprayed. A military plane repeatedly flew over the area, and we could feel the mist coming down. As we were walking, Stanfield told me that this was very dangerous stuff. I told him we were too valuable to the army for them to do anything without checking it out carefully first. I said, "This only kills plant life." He insisted that I put on my poncho and keep my helmet on my head.

The terrain around Long Binh was eerie. Agent Orange had killed all the vegetation, leaving the normally lush green jungle foliage a lifeless brown and gray. The feeling of death's presence surrounded us. The sounds of life from the jungle birds, insects, and animals were noticeably absent. Each soldier's step produced a crunching sound from the dried, dead vegetation on the ground. All that existed was the awful recognition that every living part of the jungle was dead.

Stanfield had remarked, "I didn't go to college, and I'm only a farm boy from Tennessee, but I can tell you one thing, sir, if this shit can kill these forty-foot trees, it can kill you." He added that the trees were a lot tougher than we are, that if you struck one of these trees with a sharp ax it would continue to live, but if you struck one of our legs with the same ax, we could die.

The salty, silty, polluted tidal river water in the rice paddy regions was completely undrinkable. In the jungles we often used iodine tablets to kill bacteria in the water from the streams; sometimes we had no choice but to drink this water to stay alive. The slow-talking, tobacco-chewing Stanfield insisted that the stream water near or in areas that had been defoliated was full of poison, and he was probably right. A few weeks later we conducted operations in the Rung Sat Swamp, where massive quantities of Agent Orange had been used. Most of the operational areas where I participated were remote, dense jungles or major rice-growing terrain, so except in III Corps and the Rung Sat, I was not exposed to major doses of Agent Orange; it was primarily used around permanent base camps such as Long Binh or Bearcat. I did develop non-Hodgkin's lymphoma (NHL) cancer in 1993 and have recovered from the illness. The federal government accepted responsibility for me getting this disease.

Before we moved on to the Rung Sat, our battalion conducted an all-night, coordinated patrol with three rifle companies that cut, slashed, and chopped their way through the dense jungle on several different approach azimuths, to encircle the village of Binh Son, located adjacent to a rubber plantation four miles south of Bearcat and thought to be occupied by a large Viet Cong unit. Charlie Company became lost often during the night. We had to really hump to arrive at the village at about 0500, after a grueling night of dulling our machete blades, and were happy to discover no VC waiting for us. I am sure they had heard us coming three miles away.

We had moved through the jungle like a herd of water buffalo, lost lots of equipment along the trail, and arrived exhausted. Even in the night, the heat was overbearing.

This village had a beautiful stream running behind it, and we were filthy from the all-night patrol, so we took turns going into the water for a refreshing swim downstream from the village. The Vietnamese laughed at us as we swam and bathed, and we were confused about what they thought was so funny. Later, after checking the rear of the Vietnamese hootches (homes), we discovered long, shallow troughs running from the hootches to the stream. We soon learned that these troughs carried raw sewage from their bathrooms into the idyllic stream in which we had been bathing. We had washed and relaxed in their sewer system.

A few days later my platoon was on patrol near Bearcat on a sizzling hot day, and we took a short break. I sat down under a solitary shade tree on a dike in the middle of a dry paddy, and in a few minutes realized I was sitting on the trip wire of a booby trap. My eyes followed the nylon fishing line about four feet down the dike to where it attached to a grenade. The pin was not pulled, and the nylon line was on the ground. I put my hand on the trip line to keep it stationary—so my clothing would not accidentally pull the pin—and got up very carefully, keeping my eyes firmly fixed on the grenade pin. Believe me, it was as if nothing else existed in the world but that small grenade pin. I could see it as clearly as if it was a foot long. I was never that careless again. From that time, I sat in the sun with my men. Vietnam was often just luck—good and bad.

Racial conflict, a major problem in 1960s America, also surfaced in Vietnam. Stress, fatigue, and poor living conditions exacerbated racial issues, and this became my first crisis in-country. All troopers in my platoon except three NCOs were under twenty-three. Most were in their teens. Ninety percent were drafted through the government's involuntary selective service system in effect during the war. Approximately 20 percent of my young men were blacks from urban or farm areas. I found that the blacks and the whites from rural farm and suburban areas got along fine; they were respectful and understanding of one another, given the circumstances.

A major problem, however, existed between the urban whites and blacks. There was a latent war going on between these groups, one that started in the stateside urban neighborhoods. As a suburban kid, I did not fully understand the magnitude of this problem. Until I got to Vietnam, racial problems were what I had seen on TV and were generally related to problems in the South. I did not realize at the time that some of our country's most severe and destructive race problems were taking place in all U.S. cities.

Shortly after we arrived in Vietnam, after the Binh Son night march and while we were still going through indoctrination around Bearcat, I relieved one of my fire team leaders. He was extremely authoritarian and belligerent. Although I had worked with him to use constructive leadership and not abuse his power, he just did not have the maturity or skill to lead. I replaced him with Mark McCowan, a popular black nineteen-year-old high school football star who had a wonderful smile, a well-developed sense of humor, and innate leadership skills. Called "the Cincinnati Kid," he was mentally and physically strong. This replacement caused a significant and unexpected rift throughout the company. Not only had I given authority to an untested black over a white soldier, I had relieved a white soldier to do it.

When my decision became known, my friends Sgt. George Marshal, 2d Platoon sergeant, and the company first sergeant, Sgt. "Top" Ed Johnson, came over to talk with me about the situation. Marshal was black and Johnson was white; both were Korean War veterans. Marshal respectfully questioned my judgment. He asked me if I was doing this for some liberal "do-gooder" reason and suggested we wait until McCowan proved himself in combat, as Marshal had done in Korea.

I told Sergeant Marshal that McCowan was a natural leader and the best man for the job, and when we got into combat we needed the best performers in the most responsible positions. I asked him how many of the Charlie Company white kids in leadership positions had proven themselves in combat. I told him that Mark had great potential, that he was the right man for the job despite the negative reaction to his promotion, and that racial issues had nothing to do with my decision.

Mark McCowan was the first young black soldier to be promoted in our company. Weeks later when my platoon was ambushed, Mark proved exceptional. In fact, he and his fire team were instrumental in helping us break out of that ambush when we were pinned down. The issue of his promotion was never mentioned by anyone again, including the white soldiers. They all listened to Mark attentively when he spoke, and I enjoyed telling Sergeant Marshal that Mark had saved my butt.

Mark went on to become a superior squad leader and was quickly promoted to staff sergeant (E-6). I never experienced another racial issue, although it became a problem of enormous proportion throughout Vietnam in other conventional units. Within many platoons, the troops divided along racial lines.

After a month of indoctrination in the moderately hostile areas around Bearcat and Long Binh in III Corps, we moved to the ruthless, withering Rung Sat Special Zone, a northern section of the Mekong Delta, where the enemy hid in tidal swampland sanctuaries. The army created an innovative concept of war for the 9th Division, specifically designed for Vietnam's delta swamp terrain, called "riverine warfare."

A riverine area is a land environment dominated by water

lines of transportation with an extensive network of inter-connecting rivers, streams, canals, swamps, and paddies ex-tending over broad, level terrain, such as the Vietnam deltas. The swift movement of American soldiers and fire-power into these delta-type areas literally brought the battle to the enemy's inaccessible terrain. On these riverine opera-tions, we worked with the small boats of the "brown water" navy, different in function from our "blue water" navy of the high seas.

After leaving the Bearcat area, Charlie Company spent a little more than a week in the Mekong Delta conducting these river raider amphibious operations as a mobile riverine force. We were in the notoriously treacherous, insect-infested Rung Sat Special Zone, south of Vung Tau, a little north of the Mekong River and inland from the South China Sea. We lived on the USS *Benewah,* an air-conditioned naval barracks ship, and were transported each day from the ship into the massive swamp on armored troop carriers (ATCs)—boats that could quickly move platoon-size units into combat areas and could withstand a direct hit from a rocket-propelled grenade (RPG), an armor-penetrating rocket used by the VC and NVA. The *Benewah* also served as an infantry tactical operations center (TOC).

The hostile terrain made this first Rung Sat operation the most physically demanding and psychologically stressful mission I had led up to this time. On the daily amphibious operation into the swampland, we looked for a VC base camp, which we never found. But we did find 110-degree-plus heat, unbelievable humidity, strong tidal currents, mud two to three feet deep, no water resupply, and voracious, al-most warlike red fire ants everywhere in the foliage. Every squad carried rope just to pull men from the mud. It was so humid and hot that we could hardly breathe. It was surprising that no one drowned in the quicksandlike mud. The only positive thing was that because the water was brackish (partly salty), we encountered no leeches.

Every day we trudged through the stinking mud. Our M-16s were soon mud laden, too, and probably would not have fired had we needed to use them. They had to be disassembled and spotlessly cleaned every night. Every day in the late afternoon we returned to our navy support ship, the *Benewah,* caked in mud, and the navy sailors cleaned us off on the top deck with water from high-pressure fire hoses.

In the evening our officers ate a superbly cooked meal in the navy officers' dining room, called the wardroom, complete with china, white linen napkins, and real silverware. It was nicer than home. Our troops also had quite pleasant living conditions. We all slept peacefully at night with air-conditioning in comfortable bunks with clean white sheets without fear of being attacked. What a contrast to the daylight hours!

Lieutenants Mike Johnston and Torres Torres were quite a story. After we had all spent a little more than a week in the torturous Rung Sat, our company commander, Lieutenant Bredleau, gave us the night off in Vung Tau, a beautiful, secure city just north of the Rung Sat and our USNS *Wegel* port of entry on the South China Sea. The Charlie Company platoon leader officers were allowed to stay overnight in the Vung Tau bachelor officers' quarters (BOQ), a pleasant hotel where we slept on single cots in an open bay because all the rooms were filled with officers who were actually stationed in this paradise-like location. That evening we went out on the town, had dinner, then hit many local bars, but I went back to the BOQ early because we were sleep deprived, and this was a good opportunity to catch a few safe extra hours of peaceful sleep.

Lieutenant Johnston, a tobacco farm boy who chewed tobacco, was a graduate of North Carolina State and the Army

Ranger School. Lieutenant Torres was a small, feisty wise guy, Puerto Rican, who thought he knew everything and loved to pontificate. They were the 2d and 3d Platoon leaders, respectively. They later told me that after I left they got drunk, returned to the BOQ to get a fragmentation grenade from their equipment, and threw the grenade on the front porch of a Vung Tau Vietnamese bar, where they felt that the bar girls had ripped them off. The men had spent lots of money drinking with the girls, who then refused to have sex with them without getting additional money.

Johnston threw the grenade, and it blew a four-foot hole in the bar's front wall; fortunately, no one was hurt. Torres just stood there and watched the incident. Johnston and Torres were arrested, relieved from duty, and reprimanded with Article 15s (almost a court-martial). They were never given the responsibility of a combat assignment again and were asked to leave the army when their tour ended. They were confined to quarters (their tents) in Bearcat for the next ten months. They could go only to and from the mess tent and latrine.

First Lieutenant Al Bredleau stayed with the troops in a tent city compound outside of Vung Tau. He was angry with me because I had gone back to the BOQ and left Johnston and Torres alone. Bredleau knew I would not have let them engage in such a stupid act had I been there, and he was correct. When the lieutenants returned to the BOQ that night to get the grenade from their gear, I was sound asleep. The next thing I knew, Johnston and Torres had been arrested, and the military police were in the BOQ at about 0300 to question me and confiscate Johnston's and Torres's rucksacks and weapons. I think the stress of our responsibilities had caused the two lieutenants to react this way, because their behavior was completely irrational and out of character.

This may have been a fortuitous event for Charlie Company, because Lieutenant Johnston had no confidence in Lieutenant Bredleau to lead Charlie Company in combat.

Johnston had even called a meeting with Lieutenant Torres and me, asking us to go with him to see Colonel Mundy, our First Battalion commander, and try to get Bredleau relieved from command for incompetence.

I argued, and rightfully so, that although Bredleau appeared to be unusually gung ho, exceedingly impulsive, and very self-serving, he had done nothing wrong to justify this action, and Colonel Mundy would have no alternative but to support Lieutenant Bredleau, our commanding officer, in the matter, which meant we would be nothing more than dog shit. My position prevailed. Johnston had lots of exterior bravado, but in spite of his ranger status he was very fearful. He took himself out of the game with the bar girl and hand grenade incident.

Second Lieutenant Roland Ray, who replaced the disgraced Johnston as the 2d Platoon leader, was a two-week hotshot in Vietnam. I watched him practice fire and maneuver drills with his platoon in base camp and told him he was too recognizable and visible in directing his troops. What was taught at Fort Benning did not work on Vietnam battlefields. Ray was executing textbook Fort Benning. I also talked to Sergeant Marshal, his platoon sergeant, about Ray's practice drills. Marshal said that he had already warned him. In a firefight, the VC always tried to locate the rifle platoon leader first, waited for the officer to get in the kill zone, then tried to waste him. The platoon leader officer directed the troops but, more important, he was the one who usually called in the artillery and helicopter gunships. It was smart for the VC not to spring an ambush until they had located the American officer.

Lieutenant Ray, a skinny, fidgety know-it-all, said he would do it his way. He intended to make a big name for himself quickly. I told him he was certain to get killed. He said he believed in reincarnation and already had a son to carry on his name. I asked him if he wanted to see his son grow up, and he told me that he wanted his son to be proud of him, and a man had to take risks to be recognized. On February 26, 1967, in his first firefight, west of Rach Kien in the "rat's nest" along Doi Mai Creek, Ray was shot between the eyes. The more unfortunate consequence was that he took one of his soldiers, whom everyone called Little Gonzales, with him.

Little Gonzales and Big Gonzales, two Hispanic soldiers in Lieutenant Ray's platoon, were not related but were friends. One was a little, skinny guy and the other was a large Mexican—the biggest man in Charlie Company. Little Gonzales was shot in the head. In retreat from the battlefield where Lieutenant Ray and Little Gonzales were killed, Big Gonzales carried over his back the body of Little Gonzales, who was then shot again. Gonzales's dead body acted as a shield and saved Big Gonzales from a bullet meant for him. I tried to console the devastated Big Gonzales back in base camp. The huge man cried uncontrollably over his lost friend and talked about how his dead friend's body actually saved his life. Lieutenant Ray got his Silver Star posthumously. I grieved for the casualties' families and poor Big Gonzales.

Lieutenant Bredleau directed the same firefight that killed Lieutenant Ray and Little Gonzales. He was a mustang (prior enlisted man) and the somewhat impetuous, overbearing commanding officer whom Lieutenant Johnston wanted to get relieved. He also possessed the hero disease. Bredleau's decisions contributed to the death of his RTO, Sp4 John Paul "Johnny" Scoggins, a fine, handsome, blond Southern California boy with a big smile and dreams of being a Hollywood actor.

Scoggins was killed within minutes of Ray and Gonzales when Bredleau led some troops in a charge of a wood line where the VC were entrenched in foxholes and fortified positions. All Bredleau had to do was pound the VC with artillery and follow up with gunships, and he could have walked in and mopped up. But in my opinion Lieutenant Bredleau's ego-driven need for personal glory and recognition superseded reason and true concern for his men. He cared for his men but did not have as a priority the proper regard for their lives.

Bredleau was full of military bravado, was always loud-mouthed, and had questionable analytical ability. He tried to compensate for his lack of skills by grandstanding all the time. One night in the field, in a company base camp near Long Binh, he had brought in four prostitutes for the troops, an incident that Johnston wanted to use to get him relieved. Bredleau was too much show and completely impulsive. He occasionally undermined the authority of his lieutenants with the Charlie Company senior sergeants. A couple times he even belittled us in front of the troops. We were the ramrods, the ass kickers, so this was poor leadership behavior for a company commander. Bredleau was not a bad man. He just was not a commanding officer. He pandered to the troops, and his judgment was diminished by his need to be a hero.

Fortunately, Bredleau had one of his arms drilled in the same firefight that killed Ray, Gonzales, and Scoggins. The bone splintered, and he was sent home with his Silver Star before he could get anyone else killed. I was extraordinarily happy when our new CO, Capt. Dan Monahan, took over. He was a graduate of Penn Military Academy, near his home in the Philadelphia area, and was an inspiring man of reason, compassion, and understanding. He was a leader whom men wanted to follow.

A few days later we moved on to the highly productive rice paddies in Long An Province around Tan Tru, a small village south of Saigon, west of the Rung Sat and South China Sea, east of the Plain of Reeds, just northwest of the Mekong Delta. For years this area had been an uncontested supply route for movement of enemy equipment between the primeval Rung Sat and the Plain of Reeds. Enemy guerrillas

historically collected heavy rice taxes from the peasant population here. This Long An Province area, sometimes called
the Southern Front, was completely dominated by the Viet
Cong and had been virtually cut off from South Vietnamese
government control.

Our permanent 2/60th Infantry Battalion base camp headquarters (HQ) soon followed, moving from Bearcat to Tan
Tru. Living conditions in the 2d Battalion camp in Tan Tru
were not bad and relatively safe. Occasionally, there was an
incoming mortar round or distant sniper fire, but it was a reasonably pleasant place to live. We slept on army cots in GP
(general purpose) tents and always had hot prepared food. We
had outhouse toilets on which we could sit, a real convenience,
especially for the line troops, who did not have this luxury on
combat operations. In base camp, we even had showers, al-
beit short ones because we hand-carried our own water.

The army's term for a combat unit that returned to base
camp from the field was a "stand-down"; it was garrison-like
duty in a combat zone. When on a stand-down in the Tan Tru
battalion base camp, the worst and most detested duty for
troops was the latrine shit-burning detail. It involved the disposal of raw human waste by burning it with diesel fuel in
the halved fifty-five-gallon drums used to catch the waste under the latrine seats. During the disposal process, the waste
had to be stirred to disintegrate the solids. It was a revolting
task, and the stench was awful, no matter how hard the
troops, with bandanna-covered faces, tried to hold their
breath and avoid the smell as they worked.

On a combat mission, and some lasted two weeks, we
lived more like animals than men. The troops were always
exhausted after a few days in the field. Generally, we were
resupplied by helicopter every day in the late afternoon after
establishing our night defensive perimeter. If we were not on
night patrol but part of the defensive perimeter, we slept un-
comfortably on the hard ground. There were two or three

men in each foxhole position in the perimeter, and one was always on guard duty. I would usually sleep in fifteen- to thirty-minute increments and no more than two to three hours a night. Discomfort and fear were our major concerns at night. Dawn's first light was a relief.

Everyone felt much safer in the daylight. Fear was such an overriding factor that few really noticed or complained about the poor living conditions. Simply staying alive was the most important concern. We learned and did whatever was necessary to survive.

The highlight of each day in the field was opening the C-ration units we received. My favorite was the B-1 unit, which was franks and beans and canned pears for dessert. I also liked spaghetti and meatballs, but it came with apricots, which I did not like. Some troops actually liked ham and lima beans. Trading items was always fun and the social event of the day. We ate only canned C rations and used tiny balls of intensely flammable C-4 plastique explosive to heat our food. The material explodes only with a blasting cap or an electrical charge, so C-4, the size of a large marble, was very stable. It was an excellent fuel that heated a can of food or boiled a cup of water in seconds.

We always drank lots of water at night and in the morning to hydrate our bodies, because the next day each of us had to make it through the scorching heat to the afternoon resupply on a single canteen of water. Occasionally, in the evening we had a San Miguel beer, from a Philippine brewery that had supplied the 3d Brigade with 80,000 cases, or a Coke if we were lucky.

Sometimes we would get mail in the field, which we all enjoyed and held very private. We read our mail when we were in a safe position and were always quiet during this time. It was our only connection to the normal world and an escape from our everyday reality. I sometimes would watch the troops as they read. From their faces, I could tell how lonely they were and how much they missed their friends and family. It always made me happy when one of them broke into a wide smile while reading his letter. I think my faithful, diligent father wrote almost every day. I always had mail, lined yellow paper every time. The troops would often kid me about how my dad was killing off the tree population.

When we returned to the battalion base camp after a field operation and had a night off, the southern farm boys would get together and start singing lonesome country songs. I will always remember "The Green, Green Grass of Home," which they used to sing over and over. The CO's radioman, Pvt. Charlie Ford, a young soldier from Texas, kept a guitar in base camp and played rather well. When they were singing, it almost sounded as if they were crying. As the night progressed, they seemed to sound even more lonely and sad. Sometimes I enjoyed listening to them, and sometimes I just wanted to get away from it all. They wailed and whined long into the night yet were always ready to go at first light the next morning. Singing those country songs together seemed to revitalize them.

The army, and in particular the Vietnam soldier, brought out the worst in American contemporary communication skills. The use of the English language was not too bad among the army personnel and trainees in basic training, but with each advanced stage of training, as I moved toward Vietnam, the use of expletives seemed to get worse. By the time we reached Vietnam, the use of profanity was pervasive. After we were in-country two months, our communication skills had degenerated to the base level of vulgarity. "Fuck" was used most often and served as a general all-purpose word that covered for any number of adjectives, adverbs, and even an occasional noun. It seemed to simplify the complexities of our language.

The use of profanity numerous times in any given sentence gave us the flexibility to give any significance or meaning that suited our needs. There was a certain appropriate negativity and ambiguity attached to the words. The message was in the tone. "Get your fucking ass in gear." "Dig the fucking foxholes." Even "It's a fucking nice day." Or multiple undetermined meanings were conveyed in the same sentence, such as, "We'll get the fucking gunships and blow their fucking asses off." "The fuckers shot the fucking chopper."

"Shit" and "son of a bitch" were also popular favorites and frequently used. Sentences such as "Let's kick the shit out of the fucking sons of bitches" were simplistic yet got the point across. Every cussword ever contrived was used constantly and in unimaginable combinations. In retrospect, it was funny and disgusting language, but because we were in a base visceral environment, we worked with a limited vocabulary and language everyone could understand. It would be offensive in our world, but it caused little confusion in Vietnam. Nobody ever said, "What do you mean?" (They would say, "What the fuck do you mean?") Vietnam had its own language of functional profanity. It was also an expression of the overwhelming negativity of this experience.

The Vietnamese from the rice-growing regions lived in small hamlets and villages usually located on or near rivers or streams. Their hootches were scattered about on the higher ground above the surrounding rice paddies and swampland. Most of the hootches were roofed and sided with layers of thick, dried palm fronds, which also served as insulation from the heat and waterproofing against the monsoon rains. I do not remember the floors of the hootches being anything other than bare, hard-packed dirt. A wooden floor was a luxury. Certainly, anything resembling average American housing would have been considered a mansion by the standards of the local Vietnamese. Owning a water buffalo for working the rice paddies was akin to an American farmer owning a deluxe John Deere tractor. This was an economically primitive agrarian society where life was barely elevated over base survival. Crop failures were catastrophic.

In the beginning, we tried to be understanding and compassionate, but we could not relate to the Vietnamese or their lifestyle. Vietnam appeared to be a nation of very young children or ancient, withered adults. We called children babysans, the older women mamasans, and the older men papasans. There seemed to be few young adult or middle-aged people in the rural population. Everyone seemed to go from very young to very old. The wrinkled, leather skin appearance, I am sure, was the result of extended field labor in the blazing Vietnamese sun. You can be sure they never used suntan lotion or facial moisturizing creams. Often they sat by merely squatting and seemed relaxed in that position. They all put nuoc mam, a rotten-smelling fish sauce, on their food, which was almost always rice. The old people chewed betel nut, a type of narcotic opiate, which stained their lips, gums, and teeth a reddish brown. They spit out disgusting tobacco-colored saliva wherever they stood. The drug even made them act a little crazy *(beaucoup dinky dou)*. The Vietnamese men often held hands, apparently a common practice in their culture. This act resulted in a strong homophobic reaction among the American troops who witnessed it.

The Vietnamese communicated with our GIs, an affectionate American pseudonym for our soldiers that came from the term "government issue," by classifying things, events, and people as number one or number ten. We were always number one, the best, and the VC were always number ten, the worst, or at least that is what they told us to our face. When the VC were around, I am sure they reversed the classification. The Vietnamese people came across to us as very two-faced. We also grew to dislike their jibbery language, which we found difficult to understand.

When our soldiers suffered casualties in an area of operations suspected of supporting the Viet Cong, they occasionally turned on the local inhabitants and destroyed their villages, burning their hootches and killing their farm animals. This was caused by the complete frustration experienced by our troops, who could not take casualties without being able to retaliate. Our most effective and often used means of communication eventually became violence.

The life of the American soldier in this hostile environment was arduous, and just getting through a single day in the field was a struggle. Every time leaders selected an easy route over rough terrain, they made their platoon vulnerable to a VC ambush. The VC relied on the Americans eventually to stop fighting the terrain and take the easy trail. These were the areas where the VC placed mines and established ambushes. When leaders lost the strength to push their troops through the most hostile terrain, they put their men's lives at extreme risk.

When leaders failed to vary the direction of march every hour, or they established complacent, predictable patterns in how the troops functioned each day, they put their soldiers' lives in jeopardy. The troops hated intelligent tactical movement that required them to challenge the rugged terrain. They generally wanted to take the easy way, even with the greater risk of death.

We all periodically battled severe diarrhea, and occasionally a soldier came down with dysentery. From our dreadful living conditions, these intestinal maladies, along with extreme fatigue caused by the country's steaming tropical climate and brutal terrain, methodically eroded our physical strength, our capability to function, and our will. Consequently, leaders needed to constantly remind the men that their lives depended on intelligent decision making and steel willpower. Potable water, reliable weapons and lots of ammo, mosquito repellent or kerosene, an extra pair of dry socks, a poncho, and plenty of toilet paper were also critical for life in the countryside of Vietnam. Everything else was a luxury.

Vietnam was a place of endless death and murder. Death came so quickly that there was little time to deal with it. We had to do whatever came next. We just stepped over the bodies and kept going. We had to make the next move right, the next decision right. It was like playing chess with human lives; there were no laws, no rules, no standards. There was only you, the individual, struggling to survive and trying to help others along the way.

In high school, I did not have the knowledge base to compete effectively. I had to think twice as hard and fast to keep up, and always had to figure out the game as it was in progress. In Vietnam, I faced the same problem. I had to figure out the battle as it was in progress, because the VC almost always picked the time and place. I had to be a very quick thinker.

I was also isolated in adolescence and learned to live alone within myself. A rifle platoon leader's job in Vietnam was a lonely job. I was the ramrod and had to make difficult decisions alone and quickly. Again, my adolescent environment helped train me for these difficult tasks.

Because I failed in almost everything in adolescence, I was well acquainted with despair and depression. There was no way an intelligent infantry platoon leader could win in Vietnam. We could not hold terrain and could control only the very ground on which we were standing. Victory was an illusion. Traditional military victory was not achievable. Those who could fool themselves with body count or military bravado and glory could actually deceive themselves into a false perception of accomplishment and success.

Vietnam was only pain and suffering. We all had to be able to fight through the feeling of failure and the pain of personal loss. We had to be able to fight through the mental defeatism that frustration, despair, and depression foster. I understood how to deal with depression, and depression in this wartime environment was something we had to do battle with often. To be a strong leader, I had to be able to beat despair and depression and overcome defeatism in every battle. The environment of my failed youth served me well.

KILLING STRATEGIES

Our superior military strength and awesome war-making capabilities caused the Viet Cong to revert to their age-old guerrilla tactics to engage us successfully in combat. The VC had perfected their skills against the French in the 1950s and were excellent guerrilla fighters. They possessed an almost uncanny ability to disappear into the environment. Charlie, our name for the seemingly ubiquitous yet always invisible VC, was a formidable foe. His reluctance to show himself and stand and fight was frustrating to the American soldier. We had tremendous technological advantages with our helicopters, mobile artillery, starlight scopes, automatic M-16 rifles, M-60 machine guns, claymore mines, M-79 grenade launchers, light antitank weapon (LAW) rockets, communication systems, C-4 explosives, and other modern weaponry. But Charlie relied on the element of surprise to reduce our effectiveness and improve his own odds for success.

Generally, Charlie picked the time and place of engagement, which often offset our significant edge in firepower. Firefights were short, quick, and deadly. We spent our days and nights trying to find the VC. They were an elusive enemy, patiently holding back and waiting for us to make a mistake. When we did, and we always did, they would strike. If they did not inflict substantial damage early in the battle, we would shred them, because we would respond with overwhelming force. We seldom went outside our artillery fire fan; if we did, we usually had immediate helicopter gunship support, so at least one of these resources was always available to us. However, when the fighting was over, we soon realized that the only terrain we could hold was the ground within the range of our M-16 rifles.

We held limited physical space around the objectives of our military successes, which left us with no definable accomplishments for our efforts. The mission was in the killing, which made Vietnam significantly different from our country's other wars. In the past, our soldiers gained a sense of achievement and victory for their efforts and sacrifices by driving back the enemy and physically taking and holding ground. In Vietnam our sole measurement of success was the body count. What was considered victory was computed on the tally boards in the tactical operations centers of every major combat command in Vietnam. Every day we pursued the elusive enemy with the only objective being to kill him and count him. If the VC had not been so heavily armed and such good guerrilla fighters, we would have been guilty of sport-hunting humans instead of conducting military operations.

We always tried to ambush the VC at night when they were on the move, and attack their remote, hidden base camps during the daytime when we could find them. We were usually stationary at night, because in the dark the terrain was extremely hostile to us. The night was the ally of the enemy. In a reversal of roles, the VC tried to ambush us during the day when we were on the move and attack us under the cover of darkness when we were in our night defensive positions.

Vietnam was the war of the helicopter, which included transports, gunships, dust-off medevacs, and observation scouts. We were supported by the division's 9th Aviation Battalion, located in Bearcat. The helicopter made us into an airmobile infantry army, capable of covering vast distances in a short period of time. The stinking Vietnam mud had little effect on the helicopters' efficiency. They could hover above the ground to drop off and pick up troops with their skids never touching the earth. But in the dry rice paddies we often had to exit with our eyes closed, because the blade wash kicked up incredible amounts of flying straw, dust, and other wind-whipped debris.

The choppers offered an operational advantage for us, especially in daylight. We moved everywhere on UH-1D transport choppers, called Hueys or slicks, particularly in the Mekong Delta and in the expansive rice paddies to the north. The terrain was ideal for heliborne troop operations. The slick helicopter was a maneuverable, rapid means of transportation, able to drop a reaction force of troops into a battle zone only minutes after the ground unit made enemy contact. We moved by day in our helicopters, whereas the VC moved at night on the tidal rivers and along the complex network of trails.

The choppers functioned high above Vietnam and, to an infantry grunt like me, high above the war—at least my war. We jumped out of the transport slicks into the muddy or rock-hard Vietnamese rice paddies. If we were lucky, no one would be shooting at us. The aircraft then flew away and left us alone on the ground in the sweltering heat, with predatory insects, slithering snakes, and nasty little VC. While we were fighting the elements and enemy to stay alive, our choppers escaped into the clouds, where the air was cool and life was relatively free and unthreatened. Choppers were at their best when they were on their way back to extract us from the bush and were our saviors whenever we needed gunship support or a medevac dust-off.

Gunships, armed with 1,800-round-a-minute miniguns and 2.75-inch explosive rockets, were weapons of destructive terror that brought fear to the hearts of the VC and saved me and my men many times. But they were merely flying machines, detached and indiscriminate, and on occasion they ravaged the countryside.

The medevac dust-off choppers, which ferried the wounded from the battle site to the hospital, meant the difference between life and death for countless soldiers. The tiny observation scout helicopters, bubblelike choppers, were an eagle eye from which artillery was adjusted, air strikes were called, and enemy movements were tracked. They served also as heliborne command posts (CPs) for infantry battalion commanders.

On occasion my platoon was used on helicopter "eagle flights." In an attempt to make enemy contact, we would combat-assault into a landing zone (LZ) and make a sweep through a dense wood line suspected of being a VC stronghold. If we were lucky enough to engage, a combat skirmish would begin. If there was no contact, we were picked up by chopper on the other side of the wood line and flown immediately to another LZ to try again.

During these "hunting" operations, which were physically demanding and dangerous, our objective simply was to engage and destroy the enemy. This is what we did best. The problem was, we were doing it in the backyards of the little villages and hamlets of a culturally civilized agrarian society, and destroying people's lives in the process.

The army gave me an Air Medal for taking part in these assaults. An Air Medal was new to infantrymen, but airmobile was our game in this war. To qualify for an Air Medal, you needed twenty-five heliborne combat assaults under hostile conditions. My average flight time was certainly not greater than ten to fifteen minutes, and I had a lot more than twenty-five flights in hostile conditions. On a full day with limited enemy contact, we would execute three or four eagle flights alone.

Nothing was more exhilarating and intense than an airmobile assault into a potentially hot LZ. This is a helicopter insertion of a combat platoon into a rice paddy where we expected to immediately engage the VC. The operation required approximately eight transport choppers and two gunships, and I usually flew in the lead slick. The choppers flew with the side doors wide open. All slicks had door gunners next to the openings on each side manning M-60 machine guns mounted on fire-fan spindles.

Usually six troops rode inside each chopper; they were seated on the steel floor, strapped in with safety belts to keep from falling out the doors. Often the chopper seats had been taken out to give us more room. I usually rode near the front, right behind the pilot's cockpit, so as we approached the objective, I could see the LZ activity and terrain through the chopper's windshield. During the flight approach, the rhythmic sound of the chopper's whirling blades, and the men's own escalating, numbing fear, seemed to mesmerize them. Gaunt, distant looks covered their faces as they stared blankly into space. There was no horsing around now. This was serious business, and they knew it.

Typically, in the distance up ahead, the artillery prep barrage pounded the LZ area unmercifully, particularly the adjacent wood lines. As the troop transport choppers got closer and began to drop in altitude, the artillery stopped or the chopper pilots veered off. Extremely fearful of being hit by an artillery round, the pilots would not fly in an area where we were shooting artillery and always approached the LZ from a direction that was not remotely close to the artillery trajectory.

When the slicks lost altitude on approach, the gunships, armed with miniguns and rocket weaponry, streaked by to soften further the VC positions, searing the surrounding wood lines with intense firepower. We then would contour-fly just over the treetops parallel to the ground. When the choppers broke over the trees and down into the open paddy, the slick door gunners would open up on the wood lines with the M-60s.

When the choppers were only a few feet off the ground, the troops would quickly exit (unass) the slick, flying out the side doors. They would hit flat on the paddy surface, then rapidly crawl to clear the Huey, which was an easy VC target that attracted intense enemy fire. This was more terrifying than any amusement park ride you can imagine. Sheer terror pounded in our hearts, filled our throats, and gave us bone-dry mouths.

One day I was looking out the windshield at the artillery prep a few miles ahead, then turned around as the choppers were dropping altitude and discovered that my troops all had their helmets off. I yelled over the roaring chopper engines and blades to ask them whose party they were going to and what their helmets were doing off. I soon learned they were sitting on them, theoretically to protect their butts from ground fire as we flew low over the trees. Once the choppers broke over the treetops and down into the rice paddy, the men quickly returned the helmets to their heads; no order from me was necessary.

In the jungles and swamps, we were the hunters by day; the VC—swift, silent ghosts—were the hunters by night. They controlled the night because they were familiar with the terrain, and because darkness reduced the effectiveness of our weapons, particularly the helicopter gunships. Sunrise was always beautiful. The dawn meant we had survived yet another long, anxious night.

It didn't take long for the war to get very personal and very nasty. It had to be difficult for the enemy, particularly because we were fighting the war literally in their backyards. But in return they used extremely brutal psychological warfare methods, such as grotesquely dismembering the bodies of American dead occasionally left on the battlefields. One seemingly routine night, 2d Battalion's Bravo Company was overrun while on a combat mission. The VC caught the three listening posts (LPs) positioned outside the company perimeter, killed all six men, and cut them into pieces. We lost eighteen men that night and had some forty wounded. Although this created morbid fear and a profound horror, it also fed our hatred of the enemy and propagated angry, inhumane retaliation. We learned from Charlie to be mean and vicious.

A major element of guerrilla tactics is psychological warfare. The VC wrote the book on psychological warfare and in this war took it to a higher, more bitter and brutal level. I can easily understand why countless men who returned home experienced severe mental problems readjusting to normal society. Many soldiers were mentally and emotionally destroyed by the horrors of the Vietnam War.

During the war, it was difficult for our soldiers to determine who was the enemy who was everywhere yet nowhere. The very nature of guerrilla tactics is to blend in with the indigenous population and to become invisible. The enemy used the local population base for their intelligence, communications, resupply, food, and shelter. Our primary objective was pacification, winning the hearts and minds, but it was impossible for U.S. soldiers, giant white and black men to the native Vietnamese, to fight a guerrilla war in a completely hostile environment on foreign soil and still build friendships with small Asian farmers who spoke a language totally alien to us.

The entire pacification concept seemed absurd. In practice, it meant attempting to make friends with one Vietnamese while simultaneously trying to kill his best friend and neighbor. In combat, U.S. conventional troops did kill large numbers of VC and NVA soldiers, but many civilian lives were lost in the process. American conventional troops, tactical infantry units, alienated whatever support might have existed for the South Vietnamese regime and weakened the South Vietnamese Army, because it had learned to rely on us to do its fighting.

We were trained for conventional combat, to search and destroy, not to fight a protracted guerrilla war for a cause and in a land we knew nothing about. It was called a war of counterinsurgency, a type of attrition warfare that the conventional U.S. soldier had not been trained to fight. We were not sophisticated enough or trained enough to engage in this psychological type of war. Most American infantry soldiers sent to Vietnam had been in the army a year or less before seeing combat. What training they received was oriented toward fighting European armies in a conventional war. Vietnam was far from conventional.

The vast majority of the South Vietnamese were only simple farmers out in the rice paddy and jungle boondocks. They knew nothing of political philosophy or the difference between capitalistic democracy and communistic totalitarianism, or the significance of either economic system and ideology. They had never heard of Thomas Jefferson or Karl Marx. Through an interpreter, I once asked a peasant about communism. He had no idea what it was. Never heard of it or Marx. Neither had the interpreter. They could have cared less about Jeffersonian democracy. These people just wanted to grow rice, raise their children, have more children, and be left alone.

Many of the South Vietnamese Popular Forces (PF) soldiers (similar to our National Guard) and the Army of the Republic of Vietnam (ARVN) with whom we worked were undependable, lacked courage, and were apathetic; they had no intensity or focus. To them the war was not a serious endeavor, and they seemed to have no vested position in the outcome. During joint operations, we learned to place little confidence in them.

One afternoon in early March, after almost eight weeks of in-country operations, Charlie Company was starting to understand clearly the true nature of this war. We were on a security sweep operation through a dense, marshy, heavily jungled area outside Tan Tru, and we had a local ARVN unit covering our left flank. It was late afternoon when we finally pushed through the dense underbrush area into an open, dry rice paddy, and much to our surprise the South Vietnamese soldiers on our flank were gone. We soon discovered that they had tired of fighting the dense undergrowth, called it a day at 1700, and gone home. They had not even told us by radio that they were leaving. Because it was my flank they were supposed to be covering, I was particularly upset, and I let Captain Monahan know it. These were the people for whom we were risking our lives.

We soon learned that the South Vietnamese worked hard at avoiding the VC, so we understood why the VC dominated this geographic area. If the South Vietnamese knew the VC's location, they went somewhere else. If they engaged them by accident, they would *di di mau* (split) at the first opportunity. The ARVN units in our area just were not serious about the war. The VC knew this, were not concerned about the South Vietnamese soldiers, and often ignored them because they represented little threat. When we were not around, the VC did whatever they wanted. We tried to avoid joint operations with the South Vietnamese soldiers, whom we considered to be cowardly and inept. This was not true of all ARVN; there were some effective, courageous units that proved to be equal to American forces in battle.

The American troops grew to hate the Vietnamese and began to see them all as the enemy. They learned not to trust any Vietnamese and resented the sacrifices they had to make for these strange and alien people whom they began to see as something less than human. Contempt toward them soon became as strong as our distaste for the climate and countryside. Unfortunately, it made it easier for us to prosecute a war that became increasingly more confusing and brutal. We destroyed their land, their crops, their culture, their community, their homes, their families, and their lives. We were a cancer in their country. They grew to hate us too.

The American soldier quickly learned the "proper" disparaging names for the South Vietnamese ("slants," "gooks," "slopes," "dinks," "zipperheads," among them). Disregard for the Vietnamese people was not taught to our soldiers; it infected them only after they had endured endless frustration, only after they had developed feelings of distrust and disgust for these people, and only after they had learned to hate everything around them. The VC, on the other hand, were always "Charlie," and they definitely had our respect.

Yes, the war was frustrating for the young American soldiers. Eventually, their attitude became, "Kill them all and let God sort them out." Pacification nearly evolved into an attitude of liquidation, which had to be stringently controlled. This became an extremely difficult situation for young line officers.

Some American field-grade officers used to be fond of saying, "It's not much of a war, but it's the only war we've got." The war was a chance for many of them to participate in activities for which they had trained their entire lives. It also created promotional opportunities for field-grade and general officers that did not exist in a peacetime army.

American policy makers and the Saigon government had established guidelines for how the war was supposed to be fought. These guidelines, called Rules of Engagement, determined such things as what types of weapons we could use, and where, when, and how. A free-fire zone was an area where anyone and everyone was considered hostile and could be fired on without verification or authorization. In a village that was designated "friendly" by the South Vietnamese government, only small arms could be used, and then only in a definite hostile engagement with the enemy. This required something more serious than mere sniper fire. Such rules were designed to prevent collateral damage, property loss, and civilian deaths, which occurred more readily with area destruction weapons such as artillery, air strikes, and gunships. It was frustrating for us when the clever VC shot at us from these essentially protected areas.

We usually worked seven days a week. Many a time I did not even know what day of the week it was. We did not recognize Sunday. Every day was just like the one before. They all seemed to run together after a while. My time measurement was based on the length of a field operation. Every day on a combat operation was an exercise in extreme risk taking. During every minute in the field, every helicopter flight, every river crossing, every patrol, we were in danger. The next step, hesitation, mental drift, or moment of relaxation was a situation of high risk and potential death. The intensity level for the decision makers, namely the officers, was unfathomable. However, the heroic American troops had great tenacity and courage, and made it through each day on nothing but grit and pride.

We were soldiers in the wrong place at the wrong time with the wrong task. Few men served in Vietnam simply because they wanted to participate in the war. American soldiers were in Vietnam because their country asked and ordered them to endure the physical and mental hardships of war and be willing to sacrifice their lives for this alleged "democratic" country of South Vietnam. Our troops were not foolhardy or fearless, but they learned to deal with fear and anxiety. These beleaguered soldiers, the line grunts or doggies, soon became disillusioned and confused young men, but they were not quitters. Few gave up. They just learned to endure, to cope, and to survive.

* * *

There were many wars in Vietnam. The "morality war" between right and wrong in the actions and decision making of the American officers and soldiers. The "race war" between American blacks and whites. The Vietnam "race wars" between the Vietnamese and the Montagnards, the Cambodians, the bizarre religious sects, and the ethnic Chinese. The "arrogance and ego war" between American and North Vietnamese politicians and generals, an extension of the cold war between the United States and the Soviet Union. The "philosophical, power, and control wars" between North and South Vietnam. And finally the "economic war," which was based on little more than personal greed.

Body count became the great joke of the war. The American command came under so much political pressure to produce dead bad guys that the field rule became if two troopers see a VC or an NVA fall, he is declared dead, even if the body and weapon are not recovered. We were sometimes encouraged even to count blood trails as dead VC. Body count symbolized the lack of character integrated into the war's purpose, direction, and execution. After a firefight came the ludicrous task of trying to work out the body count. It just added to the enormous credibility problem of the entire war. Our politicians wanted favorable reportable statistics, but body count procedures trivialized the risks we were taking.

The Vietnam War was about control and money, driven by the nationalistic passion of a civil war. Caught up in all of this was a bunch of poor Vietnamese agrarian peasants who knew nothing and cared nothing about what was happening outside the distance they could walk to and from in a day. The American soldiers were essentially poor, dispossessed urban and farm kids. No one really cared about these people.

They were all merely pawns. Victory in Vietnam for both groups was simply surviving.

This war was only about killing—us killing them and them killing us. That was the only thing that seemed to matter. It was all about the body count.

2/60TH INFANTRY SOLDIERS

Our soldiers were honorable men committed to the ideals of the great American democracy and willing to do most anything for our country without question. We were raised to believe in our country's principles. The 2d Battalion had a courageous, adventurous spirit. In retrospect, when you balance our mission with the limited training and preparation and the poor support we had on the home front, it is surprising how we all were so willing to execute our brutal and painful responsibilities. The line officers and men bonded with a spirit and sense of purpose that cannot be found in normal life, because we were committed, as in our motto, "to the utmost extent of our power."

We were in an important and dangerous military area of operation (AO). The VC units operating in this Southern Front area were active and capable because the war here was about who controlled the rice paddies and the food production. The marines and army soldiers had much tougher battlefields fighting the better trained and equipped NVA in I Corps, but we could get killed just as easily in the rice paddies north of the Mekong Delta if we were not careful. Living close to death was a way of life.

Death came close many times in Long An Province, from the Rung Sat Swamp to the "rat's nest" around Doi Mai Creek near Rach Kien to outside Tan Tru and south down around the "testicles" to An Nhut Tan and up the "bowling alley," a huge rice paddy west of An Nhut Tan. The hamlet of An Nhut Tan became a permanent company outpost and forward operating base (FOB) at the fork of two major rivers. This was an occupied fishing village and river port, allegedly under our protection because our defensive perimeter encircled the village. The inhabitants took as much of our money as possible selling products and were reasonably friendly. However, the outpost was nothing more than bait to encourage the VC to attempt to overrun the position some night. It was an indefensible position with no avenues of retreat. We knew that it would be overrun and just hoped it wasn't on our watch.

I later learned that the army had an artillery battery registered on An Nhut Tan and intended to blow it into oblivion when the VC overran the position. We were nothing more than the cheese in the trap waiting for a horde of rats to show up. When they did, most everyone there was doomed to die. In January 30, 1968, about seven months after my last An Nhut Tan mission, the company-strength outpost was overrun in what was part of the now famous Tet Offensive.

A huge rice paddy extended for miles out from An Nhut Tan and paralleled a river to the north that moved west to east. On the paddy's other side was a small tidal river that also ran west to east. Both rivers ran into another river that ran south to north. An Nhut Tan was right in the middle, surrounded on three sides by these rivers. Scattered down the paddy on the high ground were many Vietnamese hootches. Adjacent to the rivers in pockets was the mangrove swamp terrain endemic to this geography. We called the paddy, which was infested with VC, the "bowling alley." On any patrol up the bowling alley, chances of engaging the VC were very good indeed. This was the killing ground—the death paddy. These were our battlefields. It is hard even to remember all the enemy engagements now, but they were often—almost daily.

The 2/60th First Battalion commander was Lt. Col. Angus Mundy, a bright, polished man and true gentleman. But Mundy lacked the command presence and hard-charging demeanor needed to drive an infantry combat battalion. When Alpha Company's Lt. Jim Scott was killed on February 5, 1967—the first 2/60th officer killed in action (KIA) and the first KIA whom Mundy actually knew, the colonel went outside the battalion headquarters and vomited. Colonel Mundy did not have the tough skin needed for this brutal conflict and responsibility.

Major Moss was our battalion's executive officer (XO). He had impressed us when he first arrived at the 2d of the 60th at Fort Riley. Moss had great military bearing and presence and the jut-jawed, leather-skinned, chiseled image of a seasoned infantry officer. The guy just looked and sounded like a tough, rock-hard soldier. All the young lieutenants were intimidated by his presence. He had already completed one tour in Vietnam, and in the States seemed to us rookies quite knowledgeable. But as time passed and we saw him in action, we began to realize that the man was lots of bravado, not particularly courageous, limited in guerrilla warfare knowledge, and not very decisive.

We had been impressed early because we lacked experience and could not see his limitations, but whereas the rest of us gained experience and grew, he simply never changed. He could not function well in pressure situations that required quick decisions. This was a good lesson for us in first impressions. He liked First Lieutenant Bredleau, our CO, because he was also a bit of a blowhard. Moss kept some girl's underpants in his helmet liner for luck. That should have been a strong clue regarding his intelligence.

Major Moss's claim to fame was dropping from a hovering chopper into a loose sampan floating down a not very dangerous local river. The sampan was empty, but Major Moss tried to put himself in for a Bronze Star for Valor. He rationalized by saying there could have been VC in the sampan. It became the joke of the battalion among the junior field officers.

Major James Robinet, the battalion operations officer, was a sharp, bright man. He seemed to run everything in the battalion, keeping us organized and operating under a reasonably intelligent and coherent plan of action. Colonel Mundy usually did whatever he recommended. Robinet was our saving grace; it would have been chaos without him. He was the antithesis of Major Moss. Not the great image—what the army called command presence—but a solid military thinker and planner, and helpful in integrating Colonel Zastrow, our next battalion commander, into the command position. Serving under these officers made it clear to me that a man's skills in this environment were more important than his rank.

A week after the Doi Mai Creek battle, where Lieutenant Bredleau was wounded and Capt. Dan Monahan took over as the Charlie Company CO, we went on our second Long An Province search-and-destroy mission. Here Colonel Mundy's orders caused my platoon to be caught in a VC ambush. We were the point platoon on a company operation, conducting a routine search-and-destroy sweep, negotiating the rice paddy/nipa palm/mangrove terrain intelligently by varying our march direction every forty-five to sixty minutes and shagging down the wood lines. At about 1500, Colonel Mundy, circling high overhead in his command chopper, ordered me to hit the objective rendezvous point by 1700. He told me to stop fighting the wood line terrain and get on a direct azimuth.

This took my platoon into the middle of a wet rice paddy with less than fifty yards on each side, making us very vulnerable. The only way we could move was in single file down a dike. A half hour later as the platoon reached a dry paddy, began approaching a wood line and small village, and started to spread into a wedge formation, we waltzed right into a VC ambush.

The first round fired exploded by my right ear so closely that I could feel its wind; the crack brought significant pain, and my hand immediately went up to my ear. The bullet had smoked by probably within two inches of my head. A lucky split second before the VC sniper squeezed the trigger, I had turned my head toward the shooter, so instead of hitting me square in the side of the head and blowing my brains out, the bullet cracked by my ear. I had been noticeably motioning with my arms and hands to change my platoon's formation. At first I thought the soldier behind me had fired a round by accident, but seconds later all hell broke loose, and we were taking blistering, heavy automatic weapons fire. We immediately fell to the ground and positioned behind the rice paddy dikes. Sergeant Ronnie Bentley, a handsome, fun-loving prankster from Kentucky and one of my fire team leaders, fell to the ground not more than four feet away, looking right at me and laughing, as if this was some sort of a game. A few moments later a round ripped through his jaw. I heard a sickening, hollow thud as his head snapped around 180 degrees. When he turned back toward me, his face was ripped apart and blood was splattered everywhere. The bullet had torn through his face—flesh, jaw, teeth, tongue, teeth, jaw again, and out the other side.

Instinctively, he fell to his elbows to let the blood drain down, so as not to drown. Blood oozes in face wounds and does not spurt, but Ronnie's face looked as though it had been hit by a chain saw. His strong hands were shaking, and he was in excruciating pain. Tears and profound fear filled his eyes. Fear that I had never seen before—complete and utter terror. He tried to talk to me, but only blood came out. The smell of fresh human blood permeated the air. It was a smell I will never forget.

I was in shock, scared to death, completely petrified, and had no idea in which direction to fire. Bullets were hitting the dirt all around me only inches away. All I could think of was a children's Bible song, "Jesus loves me this I know, for the Bible tells me so." I started singing the song under my breath.

My platoon was pinned down in the open. By watching bullets hit the dry ground, beating up dust, I finally figured out that we were firing in the wrong direction. We were on the wrong side of the paddy dike; the VC were at our backs. They must have thought we were idiots. I told Sergeant Bentley not to move, that I would get him out, but he did not want me to leave and tried to grab my left arm. I yelled that I had to get to the radio or we would all die and reassured him again that I would not leave him there to die. He collapsed to the ground, his bloody face lying in the dirt, and continued to paw at me.

I rolled over the adjacent dike onto the safer side and screamed for my RTO, Gary Boyd, to crawl over to me. He was pinned down about twenty-five feet away in the open by savage automatic weapons fire and wouldn't move because bullets were kicking up dirt all around him. He had his head down and held on to his helmet, pushing it down tighter on his head with his hands clasped together on top. I looked for Colonel Mundy's chopper, but he was gone. I screamed again to Boyd that he had to make it to me or we were all going to die. I felt completely helpless. He finally jumped up and ran the seemingly long distance to the dike crouched over, with a hail of bullets hitting the dirt all along his path. He crashed to the ground with a bulky thud right next to me.

I felt guilty about leaving Bentley in such an awful condition and asked Pvt. Leroy Webb, who was close by, to help him. Webb hesitated momentarily, then leaped from his safer position onto the other side of the dike into the direct line of fire to help Sergeant Bentley. I turned to Boyd. His eyes were rapidly blinking and his hands trembled and shook with fear. I called for immediate gunship support and was happy to hear they were already on the way; a few minutes later they arrived. Before the gunships wreaked havoc on the crafty VC, my young fire team leader, Sgt. Mark McCowan, also had figured out the VC's position and started to fire and maneuver, with his fire team returning automatic weapons fire in the right direction. The experience was terrifying, but we survived, and we all got smarter and better from having gone through it.

After the gunships pulverized the wood lines and small village, Lieutenant White, who was one of the many 2d Platoon leaders and Lieutenant Ray's replacement, led the reaction force that swept through the nipa wood line to my right, charged through the village, then crossed the tidal stream behind it. After the 2d Platoon sweep around the wood line and roll through the small village ahead, we broke from our defensive reaction positions and followed them.

They had torched and killed everything the gunships had not destroyed. I sent my platoon on through and stood in the middle of the little hamlet with everything burning around me. There were no people here now. All the animals were dead—chickens, pigs, water buffalo, everything.

The heat of the fire was so intense that it created a powerful, swirling updraft. The dry, wood-framed, palm frond–covered hootches made loud, crackling noises as they burned. It was a searing, hair-singeing inferno. I can remember standing in the turbulent wind, billowing smoke, and scorching heat, thinking, This is terrible; this place is hell. I was being tortured in a human hell before dying.

After we crossed the stream, we could see that the 2d Platoon was still under intense fire. The VC had retreated but had not broken contact. Lieutenant White was lying partially protected behind a rice paddy dike. While he lay there under enemy automatic weapons fire, he was hit. This was his first firefight. A VC round went through his helmet, creased his forehead, then exited through the muscle in his upper left arm. When he was hit, my platoon was not far from him. After we chased off the VC, I went back to see him. He was a bloody mess but relatively happy. He had missed death, or being a vegetable for the rest of his life, by a quarter of an inch. Life and death was often determined by only fractions of an inch.

Even though I thought Colonel Mundy's orders were extremely dangerous, I had followed them. Mundy's decision had been based on expediency rather than sound judgment, and the VC made us pay. I told Major Robinet, the battalion operations officer, and Captain Monahan, my company commander, in a hard, frustrated voice to never let that happen to me again. I was furious with Colonel Mundy.

In late March 1967, Colonel Mundy was replaced by Lt. Col. Richard Zastrow, who had a much stronger command presence and capability, was much better organized and more decisive, and possessed a more analytical, tactical mind. Zastrow brought a more aggressive approach to the game and was also an honorable and good, decent human being.

I had a good point man and fire team leader in Sgt. William Joseph Price. In appearance and mannerism, Billy Joe reminded me of a young Gary Cooper. He was a tall, good-looking, grayish blue–eyed, slow-talking Kentuckian, twenty years old, with a dry, play-dumb farm boy sense of humor, yet he was one of the most courageous men I have ever known. He had good instincts in the field. Depending on the terrain, I always positioned myself to maintain visual contact with him.

Billy Joe would tell me almost every day how much his mother loved him and how it was really going to hurt her if he was killed. I would laugh, and he would say with his deadpan expression that he was being serious. I always told Billy Joe that every Vietnam soldier's mother loved her son, and we were not in a position to make decisions based on a mother's love for her son. Once I told him that my mother even loved me. He just laughed and shook his head in joking disbelief as he walked away.

Often I would ask, "Billy Joe, you don't want the point today?" He always wanted to walk the point. That's where he felt most comfortable. He had superb peripheral vision and reflexes, and he knew we were a stronger and safer unit with his skill and fire team up there. Billy Joe never whined even though he did not want to be in Vietnam, and he put his heart into every mission. He was fearful, but he possessed a noble quality of character with a sense of responsibility that gave him the courage to face death every day.

Another one of my troops, Pvt. Ray Perkins, a sandy-haired kid from Omaha, Nebraska, was your average draftee, fulfilling his military obligation to his country. We had settled in for our night position after a long, hot day search-and-destroy mission in early March when I noticed that Perkins's foxhole was too shallow and asked him to dig it deeper. He threw a temper tantrum and said I worried only about my career and that was why I pushed everyone so hard. I took him over to my platoon sergeant, Sergeant Dilley, for him to act as a mediator and explained to Perkins, "I'm only trying to save your life. I don't have a college degree and have no career in the army. I'm here only as Christmas help, just like all you young troopers, but the army gave me the responsibility to take care of you and the other guys and execute in the field, and I intend to do it to the best of my ability.

"If I survive this war, I do not want the guilt from knowing one life was lost because I did not give it my best, or I was lazy, or trying to win a popularity contest in this platoon. My only interest is to get you guys through this alive, and I don't give a damn what you all think of me. I'm just like you, and when this war is over, I'm going back to the streets, and I want to be able to live with myself."

There was never another problem with cooperation in my platoon. The formerly grumpy Perkins became a strong, positive supporter and major contributor. He became downright enthusiastic after our discussion. He became a leader. I always felt great satisfaction in helping build another leader. Once these young men developed a higher sense of responsibility, a positive attitude, and self-confidence, their leadership ability developed, and they began to grow as men of character.

My radio operator, Sp4 Gary Boyd, a sharp-looking horse of a man and a draftee from Van Nuys, California, was assigned the commo man RTO slot before I arrived at Fort Riley. He was strong enough to carry the twenty-five-pound PRC-25 radio and did fine in Kansas, but in Vietnam during firefights his hands shook badly, his eyes blinked continually, and sometimes he stuttered on the horn—not good for a radioman. This concerned me at first, but he always managed to do his job.

Boyd loved to talk about his son, whom he affectionately called Tiger, born shortly before we departed for Vietnam. Army training had taken Boyd away from his young family almost constantly for an entire year. After we were in-country nearly two months, Boyd's letters from his wife stopped coming, and a month later he received a Dear John and divorce papers. Jody, the GI's fictitious name given to the guy back home, beat his time. Boyd was distraught but continued on with relentless courage. He worried about his son, and I worried about Boyd.

While on a routine patrol in mid March, Specialist Boyd stepped on a small pressure-release antipersonnel mine. He was only ten feet behind me. I had luckily stepped over it, but he stepped directly on it. When it exploded, a piece of shrapnel smoked right past my head. Another piece lifted Boyd, ripped through his leg, broke his femur, and cut his sciatic nerve. I turned so quickly that I saw him in the air. After he hit the ground, he actually seemed happy lying there in the blood and dirt in excruciating pain. He knew he was finally getting out of this brutal, hellish place and going home alive.

I stood there and watched as my medic, Sp4 Peter Nero, cut Boyd's fatigue pants to apply a tourniquet. The limb gushed blood from a cut artery. As Boyd lay there in agony, he asked Nero first to check his crotch, then give him a shot of morphine and put him on the chopper home. Boyd waved an ecstatic, smiling good-bye to us from the floor of the medevac chopper as it lifted off the ground. The loquacious Sp4 Phil Hilowitz volunteered to take the RTO position.

While on this simple security sweep patrol outside Tan Tru, I managed to pay back my fire team leader, Sergeant Stanfield, for trying to protect me from Agent Orange up around Long Binh. Of course at the time I didn't know how much I owed him. About forty feet more down this trail, Stanfield became hung up on a booby trap. While he was frozen with the taunt trip wire pressed against his leg, I searched through the adjacent grass and found the hidden and potentially deadly device. The VC had tied the trip wire to a Chinese ChiCom grenade's pin and handle. Fortunately, the hand grenade's handle was rusted, and even though the pin was pulled, the handle did not pop loose and detonate the grenade. I picked it up from the grass, cut the wire, and tossed the grenade into an adjacent rice paddy. Talk about luck!

On the next patrol I helped save Stanfield's good buddy, Sgt. Gary Blaylock, who was somewhat at home in the Vietnam terrain because he was from the bayous of Louisiana. Young Blaylock, another one of my fire team leaders, was wounded and in the "beaten zone" of VC automatic weapons fire near An Nhut Tan. Bullets were hitting the ground all around him from two directions. He was so frightened and, I thought, so hurt that he could not move. He was dead meat. Blaylock should have crawled into a nearby ditch, but sometimes a soldier gets so frightened that he just freezes where he is.

I saw Stanfield trying to get to him, but he would have had to run directly into the heavy heat. I had a safer approach across the line of fire, so I ran over, got a solid blazing base of return fire from some of my troops, and flipped Blaylock into a safe location in the ditch. When the firefight was over, Stanfield thanked me, and Blaylock was appreciative. He was only shot through the thigh muscle, a minor wound that sent him to the hospital for a month.

Lieutenant White finally came back after a few weeks in the hospital. He was somewhat of a hero due to his close brush with death. Everyone wanted to see his scars, particularly the jagged scar across his forehead. We were all happy for him. He had kept the helmet that the bullet went through, which was quite a trophy. On his first day back, we went out on a company search-and-destroy mission, and within a matter of hours he was shot by a VC sniper clean through the thigh and sent back to the cushy hospital. But two Purple Hearts also meant no more combat duty for Lieutenant White, who spent only a few days with a line unit and a total of about eight hours in the field during his entire tour of duty. The second time he was hit, my platoon was on the point as usual. I walked back to White to hassle him about his ability to get shot so easily. Because White was in the field only a few hours each mission, I ribbed him unmercifully. I called him a freaking malingerer who had hired some VC to shoot him every time he left base camp. He had a big grin on his face. White was a very happy and lucky man. It was a clean wound—missed the bone and nerve and didn't bleed much because it also missed the artery.

Captain Monahan and I had never called in a napalm air strike, so we decided to give it a try on the VC sniper who shot Lieutenant White. It was an experiment; we wanted to see how this air support worked. We soon discovered that the reaction time for this type of air support was too slow for our rice paddy war. Artillery support response time was usually immediate, if you knew what you were doing. Helicopter gunships assigned to support your mission were also quick to respond.

For an air strike, first you needed a bird dog forward air control (FAC) plane to direct the tactical air command (TAC) air fast movers, F-105s and F-4 Phantoms. However, because the FAC had to reach the battleground first, it was hard to get an air strike in less than thirty minutes, which was usually far too slow to do any good; your entire unit could be dead and buried in thirty minutes, and the VC could be in the next province. This was the only napalm air strike I called during my entire Vietnam tenure as a rifle platoon leader. It was a spectacular show—a huge, rolling, explosive, firey mass—and the troops loved it. They even cheered, but it only burned up some jungle. Monahan and I briefly discussed how much money we wasted. He said it was worth it because the troops enjoyed the show.

I soon realized that I could think quickly and function well under extreme pressure. Horrifying fear kicked your adrenaline production into hyperdrive. In a firefight and, in particular, on hot LZs with all the slicks and gunships in the air buzzing around, the tremendous emotional high got to be almost addictive. I would get in a functional zone and, in the worst of situations, manage to think quickly and clearly, but everything always started to move slower. Firefights were like powerful adrenaline drugs, and soon you started to like the high. Life came into focus and was not complex, only simple, competitive survival.

I worked hard at communicating with my troops and keeping them informed. By educating them, helping them understand what we were doing and why we were doing it, I facilitated their development and made them more comfortable with my decisions.

I found I could be very good at this war business. I became good at calling in artillery, understanding the battlefield, anticipating enemy actions, and executing field tactics. My troops respected me because of my courage, intelligence, and value structure. But most important, they knew I truly cared about them. I tried to never let my underlying fear bother me.

However, my fear was so great in the field at night that I would wake up from a short, deep sleep and within two seconds be completely aware and coherent. It was always hard to sleep. The stars became my friends and were a celestial blanket of bright, glittering diamonds that covered me. The Vietnam night sky was not polluted by artificial light, as was the darkness over the American population sprawl, so here the stars were strikingly brilliant and engaging, and every cloudless night I admired their incredible beauty. They took me away from this evil, painful Vietnam world. The contrast between the magnificent heavens and my dirty, smelly, bloody Vietnam existence was a dichotomy I lived with every day.

All my courage grew from concern for my troops and not from my ego. The more I got to know my men, the more important they became to me, the greater my drive and commitment to protect them. After a few firefights, I realized I was sent to Vietnam to take care of my soldiers. This was my stand in life, and if I died doing it, so be it, but I was going to do this one thing to the best of my ability, no matter what the consequences.

When I took over my platoon at Fort Riley, Kansas, we knew we were going to Vietnam, and I worked my soldiers extremely hard for long hours. I broke their chops, and my troops always complained. They felt I worked them much harder than did the battalion's other platoon leaders in training their units. I was tough on my young soldiers and certainly made their lives miserable. Many of my men didn't like me for that reason. I did not have any idea what Vietnam was like, but I had a premonition that it was going to be bad. It was the unknown that killed soldiers, and in the summer and fall of 1966 they were coming home in body bags every day.

After we arrived in-country and my troops began to see what we were up against, my relationship with them began to improve. As the enemy engagements got worse and the men realized how important I was to their survival, they actually began to like me.

My men often complained because on most company operations we were the point platoon, but I felt more comfortable as the lead platoon. When not on point, a platoon was used in a reaction force position to clean up another platoon's mess. I had a higher level of confidence in myself and my soldiers than in other Charlie Company units. The point controlled the battlefield until you lost control to the enemy. Also if you did not give the VC a tactical advantage, they wouldn't attack. We had to avoid the VC ambush and establish defendable nighttime positions.

However, it was a complex leadership problem to motivate our troops to face death and control their behavior when we were so inexperienced ourselves. Platoon leaders had no idea what was going to happen on any given day, or the time and place of the next battle. We had to be prepared all the time, for anything and everything. As an infantry rifle platoon leader I had to bring hope to my troops, and they had to have confidence in my leadership. I was never going to give up in life again, as I had in high school and college, and I was not going to let my men be butchered. I was painfully aware that bad military leadership can send young men quickly to the slaughterhouse.

The troops had to believe that their platoon leaders were smart and strong enough to do this dangerous and demanding job, or they would look for reasons not to be a team player, not to cooperate and participate. They had to know you cared about them. You had to learn the personalities of your troops and be able to communicate with them. You had to motivate the men into willing action through positive leadership.

The power of officer status lost its leverage on the battlefield. The troops would follow you only if they had confidence in you and believed in you as a human being. It was impossible to inflict a punishment that was worse than what they did daily in Vietnam. Jail would have been an escape, almost vacation duty. You had to coalesce their pride, character, courage, and concern for one another to get them to focus their energy and ability into positive teamwork. You wanted your men to prove to you that they were as tough, as courageous, and as capable as you. A group of young men with these qualities would follow you into a Vietnam hell, work together as a team, and learn to take care of one another.

I watched officers come and go in Charlie Company: Johnston, Torres, Bredleau, Ray, Monahan, White (twice wounded), Gray, Kelly, McClain, Michelson, Delgado, and Hilderbrand (blinded by shrapnel). Some were relieved, some were wounded, and some were killed.

A few infantry officers were obsessed with a fantasy vision of gallant heroism. I used to call it the "princess syndrome." They must have watched one too many John Wayne movies when they were young. We were the first generation of soldiers brought up on TV and movie fantasy and certainly were influenced by the subtle World War II cinema propaganda. It had a negative effect on some of us. In infantry officers, there seemed to be a direct, inverse relationship between IQ and the need for heroism: The lower the IQ, the greater the need for heroism. Some of the young officers were starved for recognition and wanted to create it through battlefield glory and decorations. If they survived, they could walk around with those heroic battle ribbons on their chests for the rest of their army careers.

In Vietnam, I quickly learned about my most dangerous personal limitation—a slight case of dyslexia. Sometimes under extreme stress, it caused me inadvertently to reverse at least two consecutive numbers when calling in the coordinates for an artillery mission. I had to learn to compensate for this in the execution of my responsibilities. If we had time to plan ahead, I would establish predesignated fire mission coordinates before the operation, then call in the artillery fire mission preplots with a code such as fire mission or checkpoint 1, 2, 3, and so forth, then shoot an azimuth and adjust the artillery off these coordinates.

I told only my RTO about the problem, and I instructed him always to ask me twice for the fire mission coordinates. When Sp4 Phil Hilowitz took over the RTO position after Boyd was wounded, he was surprised when I explained the problem. Maybe even a little nervous. His concerned comments were appropriate. "That's just great. A lieutenant who screws up the artillery coordinates." If we had time, Hilowitz would double-check me by asking, "Are you sure?" This would irritate me, but usually I appreciated it.

I often became so engaged and focused on how we were functioning in the field and analyzing the terrain and potential battlefield that I would put down my M-16, walk away, and temporarily lose the rifle. I always relocated the weapon, but it would have been embarrassing to simply lose a weapon that could be recovered by the VC enemy and used against us. I carried only the M-16, to make me look like one of the troops. Seldom did I find myself in a position with a need to fire the rifle. With all our firepower resources, a tactical objective was to avoid those extremely stressful and critical situations.

As time went on, and I got better and better at leading my men, there was always an internal struggle between doing things that would give me individual recognition or doing things that were in the best interest of my platoon's welfare. I could never rationalize undue risk just for praise and glory. I just kept getting better and so did my troops.

In early April 1967, a situation in which I was a primary participant made the front page of the *New York Times*. It occurred when my platoon captured a .30-caliber machine gun in the rat's nest at Doi Mai Creek in a major 9th Division and VC battalion battle. The rat's nest was a geographic area so called because of its heavy concentration of VC units. After we cleaned them out, they always came right back. Many American soldiers and many of my friends, including Roland Ray, Johnny Scoggins, and Little Gonzales, had been lost in the rat's nest on previous operations. On this day my platoon landed first to secure the LZ, which we did successfully. The 2d and 3d Platoon choppers dropped in the secured LZ and landed safely.

Captain Monahan asked me to take the point. As my platoon started moving west along Doi Mai Creek, we quickly made enemy contact and were pinned down by withering automatic weapons fire. We were one of three company-size units approaching the rat's nest from different directions. It was a cordon-type operation, trying to box the slippery VC into a defined area, and it was literally raining bullets. I told my RTO, Specialist Hilowitz, we needed to move forward to get a better view. He responded with, "What for? We can see fine from here. They're right up there. What more do you need to see?"

Phil Hilowitz and I moved ahead of my point squad, crawling the last twenty yards behind a dike, looking for a better view of what was happening. My vision of the enemy's position was still impaired by foliage. The VC were laying down a powerful base of fire through the brush, and that made it difficult for us to move. We were lying prone behind a rice paddy dike with our heads down. Hilowitz was about eight feet away from me. The .30-caliber machine gun was in a reinforced bunker up ahead and smoking big-time heat, and there was at least a VC infantry platoon with automatic weapons in the surrounding wood lines. I lay there and hugged the ground.

The fear was like nails driven into my brain, but I caught the relaxing adrenaline buzz. I turned, looked over at Hilowitz, and yelled to him about the microscopic world you could see in the dirt when your nose was pressed to the ground. In the next breath I asked him how good a shot he was. Concluding that I wanted him to go with me to get the Viet Cong, he yelled back, "What, are you crazy?"

"No," I yelled, "I want you to shoot the snake off my leg." A three-foot snake had crawled up the side of my leg, and I couldn't jump up without getting my head blown off by the machine gun.

He screamed, "Now I know you're fucking crazy."

The snake lay on my fatigue pant leg from my foot to just past my knee. It lifted its head about five inches. Now alert to my presence, I think it was as surprised as I was. I looked right into his cold snake eyes, not more than three feet from my head, and concluded he didn't see well. His pitch-black shiny eyes bulged slightly beyond metallic-like, scaly dark gray skin, and his forked tongue quickly worked the air.

I thought, What a stupid snake. I have kerosene all over my jungle fatigues, and he crawled right up my leg. Can't he smell? I stared intensely for a few seconds at the shape of his head, trying to determine if he was poisonous and mentally preparing to be bitten. Fortunately, the VC's blazing fire stopped for a minute. I jumped up and rolled over, and the snake dropped off and disappeared down the hole on which I had previously been lying.

I expected to be overrun by the VC any minute. They had so much firepower and were so close. My men were returning fire, but no one wanted to move or stick his head up too far with that machine gun barking up ahead. The VC's bullets were riveting and tearing up the underbrush adjacent to the dike.

We hit the fortified positions and machine gun with artillery, then followed up quickly with two gunships. Chopper pilots' fear of being hit by friendly artillery caused us to shut down the cannons. But we briefly pounded the VC hard with an artillery battery's 105mm howitzers until just before the gunships arrived. The cannons couldn't penetrate the machine gun's reinforced bunker position, but they froze movement of the surrounding VC infantry soldiers, and this may have saved our lives.

I popped a smoke grenade to mark our position, and the gunships came in hot, shredding the adjacent vegetation. The action was so close that the gunships hit one of my men by accident. On the initial pass, the pilots may have been confused and thought we were the VC. They strafed my platoon, and I yelled at them over the radio. It was remarkable that the pilots did not hit more of us, including me. Many gunship bullet holes marked the dirt between Hilowitz and me. We found nine dead VC when we finally got to the bunker. One of the gunships had made a direct hit with a rocket into the machine gun bunker. Combat assault? No way. We were very lucky.

The sun was going down quickly, so division HQ told Captain Monahan to set up a company night perimeter in the middle of a huge, dry rice paddy adjacent to Doi Mai Creek, right where the battle had taken place. Headquarters did not want us to put out night security patrols, however, which made us nervous, given the close proximity of a major VC battalion. Division HQ was also concerned that the VC battalion we were pursuing would reverse its direction and overrun Charlie Company that night.

Fortunately, division HQ supported us all night with Spooky, a heavily armed old air force DC-3 dragoon ship the troops called Puff the Magic Dragon. The slow-moving fixed-wing aircraft was a weapons platform armed with three 7.62mm Gatling miniguns, as I recall, firing about 1,800 rounds a minute. It offered devastating support when we were in a static defense role. Tracer rounds—ammunition containing a mixture of chemical compounds to mark the projectiles' flight by a blazing trail—were fired throughout the night and made Puff look like a giant fire-breathing dragon.

Spooky's withering firepower sounded like an enormous searing whine. The aircraft went into a slow circular orbit, laying down a wall of bullets around our perimeter that stitched the ground, pounding and pulverizing the surrounding wood lines and preventing the VC from engaging us that very long night. As each Spooky ran out of ammunition, it was immediately replaced by another one. The next morning we were physically and mentally exhausted but experienced yet another beautiful sunrise. We gave thankful homage each morning to dawn, the first light of the rising sun, which was the rebirth and pillar of our courage.

The official report for the two-day battle at Doi Mai Creek was 207 Viet Cong KIAs, although in my section of the battle I counted only nine enemy soldiers. There were lots of body parts scattered around the rice paddy, so I just counted heads. We captured the .30-caliber machine gun, which was a great trophy and the reason why Charlie Company was specifically mentioned in the *Times*.

My wounded trooper hit by the gunships won the Vietnam lottery. It was his first day in the field; he was so frightened he didn't even fire his weapon, and the bullet only nicked his ankle, but it released the joint's lubrication fluid. So the cherry soldier went home with a minor but debilitating wound, a Purple Heart, and a Combat Infantryman's Badge. Everyone was envious.

Sometimes it was hard to pass up the glory, particularly for someone like me with so little previous success. Down deep inside, at the time, I really wanted recognition, but I was not willing to put anyone's life at risk because of my own interests. I was gradually winning my own personal battle, or maybe I had already won it. I was certain that my life would never be the same if I survived Vietnam. I was now tough and strong-willed and knew I would be able to do anything I wanted in the future. Nothing could ever be as bad as Vietnam.

From the first moment I met Phil Hilowitz, I liked him. He enjoyed making us laugh. His lighthearted, clever manner could make anything funny. About two months before we left Fort Riley, I was assigned the company payroll officer responsibility and had to pick up approximately $15,000 in small bills at the Fort Riley finance office on Friday afternoon for the troop's Saturday payday; I selected Phil to be my payroll guard. The finance office was going to be closed Saturday. We soon discovered that there was nowhere to safely store the money overnight, and we certainly did not want to run around during the evening carrying that much cash. We both had better things to do on Friday night than baby-sit greenbacks.

Finally, I came up with an idea. We went back to my BOQ and hid the money in my refrigerator freezer. Later I went back and stuffed the bills onto the glass shelves of my medicine cabinet behind the mirror door, then rigged a smoke grenade booby trap inside to detonate if the cabinet door was not opened with extreme caution. Phil ultimately told this story to about every soldier in the battalion and embellished and stretched it to the point of having me almost burn up the $15,000 payroll.

When we returned to Tan Tru after the Doi Mai Creek battle, I asked Hilowitz why we were the only suburban young men in this company, and what we had done to deserve this character-building opportunity. He suggested that we were just lucky. Then I told Hilowitz he was the only Jewish guy in this entire battalion. "In fact," I said, "you might be the only Jewish soldier in Vietnam. You are unique." I asked him if he had any Jewish friends in the army.

He said, "No, they're all back home becoming doctors and lawyers." Phil reflected with his characteristic wry wit that he must be the dumbest Jew in America.

Phil partied so hard at Fort Rilcy that he was happy with the few hours' sleep we got each night in Vietnam. He always appeared well rested when everyone else was tired. He also started to gain weight when the rest of us were losing it. He had been living on nothing but alcohol at Fort Riley, whereas in Vietnam he was eating meals on a regular basis. Phil was actually living a healthier life here. The troops called him "weasel," which had something to do with his being so skinny at Fort Riley, or because he could talk most of the troops into just about anything, but he had the heart of a lion.

Hilowitz had ice for nerves and never shook the way his predecessor did. He was extraordinarily dependable and was always where he was supposed to be—not too close to me, yet not too far away. The weight of the radio did nothing to impede his ability to move quickly, so his skinny legs must have been stronger than they looked. He once said, "When the shooting starts, I'm so scared I don't even know the radio is on my back." I asked him why he volunteered for the dangerous and strenuous commo man RTO position. He said, "I wanted to know what was going on." Phil often gave the field activity situation report (sitrep) to Six, the company CO, which kept me from having to use the radio frequently, giving me more time to concentrate on the action in the field and less time for the VC to zero their sights on me. One of the brightest guys in my platoon was always the RTO; I wanted to be able to yell instructions to him from a distance without having to run to the radio. As soon as the VC saw someone go to the radio, particularly if he carried a map, they knew whom to kill.

Hilowitz just liked talking, which was another reason he volunteered for the RTO position. He was a nineteen-year-old with engaging personal communication skills who helped keep the troops in good spirits. If Hilowitz was comfortable with my decision making, he had a unique ability to convey his confidence to the platoon. Phil's personality and positive attitude made us a stronger combat unit and me a more effective platoon leader.

HAZARDOUS DUTY

Whatever relief we enjoyed in the field quickly turned to tragedy. A few days after the Spooky night, a horrible situation occurred that I could do nothing about but will always regret. It was the day I wounded a Vietnamese girl about seven years old.

My platoon was crossing a large, dry rice paddy about a thousand yards long and five hundred yards wide. On the left was a small village, maybe forty hootches, and on the right was a river and a wood line of nipa palm along a mangrove swamp. I was concerned about sniper fire from both directions, so I put the troops in a wedge formation to spread them and ensured that my artillery support knew my coordinates. Once the troops were properly dispersed, we proceeded down the middle of the paddy.

About halfway through, we started taking sniper fire from the village. We got down, waited a bit, then started to move again. Once more we took sniper fire. Down again. I was beginning to get a little upset, so I thought I would send the sniper in the village a military message.

I called an artillery mission, registered with a smoke airburst spotter round, then quickly called for a variable timed (VT) fuse with a hundred-foot airburst. This was accomplished within seconds. I expected the artillery round to scare the sniper and put holes in the roofs but not hurt anyone, because every Vietnam hootch had a bomb shelter inside. The shelters were about two feet thick, made from mud and logs. Anytime shooting started, the Vietnamese villagers immediately ran into these shelters.

Using the VT fuse airburst was much safer than putting a round on the ground, where a direct hit could blow a hootch bomb shelter and its occupants into oblivion. The airburst basically said, I have artillery, I know how to use it, so back off, turkey.

After the airburst, which was dead center over the village, the sniper stopped firing and we started to move. In about five minutes, a bunch of Vietnamese women came running across the paddy. One was carrying a little girl who was bleeding badly. She had been wounded by the artillery airburst. I asked my medic, Sp4 Peter Nero, to help her. She looked awful, particularly because her white pajamas (instead of the standard black garb) were obviously bloodsoaked and shredded. All the Vietnamese women were screaming.

Her mother tried to come after me, but my troops stopped her. Fortunately, there was no major tissue damage, and no bones were broken. The little girl's wounds were superficial. It was as if her skin had been sliced with a razor six or seven times over different sections of her fragile little body. Her crying and screaming were traumatizing. It overwhelmed your emotions—anger, sadness, and frustration. It was hard to believe she had not been more seriously hurt and that so many pieces of shrapnel could have hit this child without striking a critical part of her body. It was a terrible, incomprehensible scene. What were we doing?

Nero lost his cool as he was taking care of the girl and started yelling at me. He said it was my fucking fault and my fucking war. After I had the girl and her mother medevacked by chopper to one of our field hospitals, I grabbed Nero by the fatigue collar, took him aside, and told him it was not my fucking war. I said I had nothing to do with making this war, and I did only what I was supposed to do to protect my men. I explained that the girl's mother should have put her in a shelter as soon as the sniper started shooting. They had to anticipate we would shoot back. I told Nero if we had continued across the paddy we would have lost a couple of men, or if we chased the sniper we would have lost even more. I told him to pick two men from the platoon, and we would just shoot them right here and now. I said, "Go ahead and pick the two. Pick the worst. You can be responsible." He dropped his head and apologized to me.

Nero became a medic because he did not believe in killing people. The young man was fearless and continually risked his life to help wounded soldiers. This task made him an incessant nervous talker, a constant litany of chatty jive, particularly after casualty losses. His devotion to relieving the pain or saving the lives of the wounded gave him his incredible courage. His passion ran deep. He always worried about the troops, and they loved him for it. Nero, or "Doc," as the troops often called him, worked in extreme danger and never received the recognition in Vietnam he deserved.

I was once ordered to execute a VC prisoner we captured hiding in a spider hole, a one-man camouflaged enemy fighting position. We reported the prisoner, who was already wounded, and the M-2 carbine rifle we captured. I asked my RTO, Hilowitz, to call the CO, Captain Monahan, for direction. Hilowitz called, then turned to me and said, "Shoot him." Even though we were in a high-risk situation in the rat's nest around Doi Mai Creek, we had time to stop and evac the prisoner. The prisoner appeared to be a medic, and I saw no justification for the order.

The responsibility was mine if it had to be done. I had always hoped to avoid a situation like this, but here it was, staring me right in the face. I could not delegate it to anyone else. I wanted to make it difficult for myself, so I decided I had to look right at the victim and not do it from some detached distance. This was personal, and I felt extremely uncomfortable. It was entirely my own decision whether to obey an order with psychological and legal consequences that I would have to live with forever.

I took my medic's .45-caliber pistol and put it to the VC's forehead, right between his eyes, but I couldn't pull the trigger. This was no Alabama steer; he was a human being. I understood that even in such a violent, lawless world, execution was morally wrong and illegal. I could not find enough hatred within myself to kill this man. I looked into his eyes, and he looked kind. In his wallet, we had found pictures of his family. I saw a reflection of his family's love. He was on his knees, at my feet, pitifully begging for his life.

The whole pathetic, frightening scene disgusted me. I did not want this kind of power. He did not look like some evil monster, and no matter how angry I was with these people, for all my friends they had killed and for all the suffering they had brought to my life, I could not find the hatred to take willingly another man's life when there was no justifiable reason. I am so introspective and reflective that if I had pulled the trigger, I may as well have put the next round through my own head, because I could have never lived with the guilt.

One of my men, a private, came over and said, "If you can't kill him, then I will." He saw the situation as a failure of courage on my part rather than a moral issue. I told him very clearly to wait until I had talked to the CO directly rather than through my RTO. As I walked to my radio, the blast of an automatic M-16 ripped behind me. This private said the prisoner tried to run, so he cut him in half with his M-16. He had put his selector switch on automatic and, in the troop's jargon, rocked 'n' rolled. I will never forget the Vietnamese victim's grotesquely distorted face. He was crawling toward me with his bloody intestines dragging on the ground as he died.

Peter Nero, who was facing me and looking over my shoulder, saw the event and said, "He'll be sorry for that someday." Nero was disgusted, turned his back, and walked away. The CO had not given an order to execute the prisoner. I learned that the execution directive was issued by the first sergeant, who is not in the chain of command and cannot give me any order. It was just deadly confusion and mean hatred on the battlefield.

From the VC's position on the ground, it looked as though he had tried to run to me, as if he knew I was his best chance for survival. Many of my men were cheering, celebrating his death. I knew my platoon's moral structure was starting to collapse. This place was destroying their humanity. I did not believe that the VC was trying to escape. There were at least forty American troops spread throughout the general area. If he ran, it was because he knew he was going to be executed. His chances for escape were zero. It was clear to me this private wanted the power to kill someone without risk or consequences.

The private told me himself that when he was seventeen, a New York judge gave him the option to enlist in the army or go to jail. As he stood over the dead VC, I almost shot him myself, but I turned and walked away and cursed the judge who gave him to me. Society made a mistake. This private did not belong here. He liked the killing.

The courts stuck us with this sociopath. Thankfully, the military no longer accepts the judicial system's former practice of dumping society's problems into the service for correction. In a war environment, where our actions challenge morality, where decisions of the highest order are made under the worst of conditions, where the consequences of those decisions last a lifetime, and where every combat soldier literally has the power over human life and death, we must insist that the young men charged with this awesome task are trustworthy and of sound character, fully prepared mentally and physically to handle a soldier's responsibilities.

In another incident, I learned that two of my soldiers had raped a young Vietnamese girl. I remember seeing the girl during a combat search-and-destroy operation. She was a pretty nursing mother. I told the soldiers to leave her alone, then had to leave the area on an emergency. My point squad was hung up in a mined area, and we stopped our movement for a while to work out a safe route. About a week later Phil Hilowitz told me the troops were talking about how two of my men had raped the defenseless Vietnamese girl in a hootch bomb shelter after I left, so I started asking questions and learned that the reports were true.

I was responsible for the actions of my men, so these beastly murder and rape incidents really bothered me. Even though I was too young and naive to anticipate the events, I still agonized over the heinous crimes and considered them to be my personal failure. I did not see them occur and therefore could not prove anything. My predicament was complicated. If I brought the three men who participated in these two incidents up on charges, it would tear my platoon apart. It would require soldiers from my platoon to testify against one another, and it would destroy the teamwork fabric that made us strong and helped us survive.

As the weeks passed, my anger and bitterness grew. Every time I looked at these three men, it disgusted me. I began to hate them for what they had done. I looked for a solution to the horrific situation. The law here was hard to determine and enforce. The difference between murder and everyday work was not always clear. There was no concept of justice. In the worst situations, only power and violence were respected.

I still had a basic understanding of what was right and

wrong, no matter how much civilized existence deteriorated, but I had no functional means to bring about justice. In my darkest moment, I considered taking these three men out on patrol and killing them myself.

Ironically, the only people I ever thought about wanting to kill in Vietnam were three of my own men. The people I loved the most. I have ever since agonized over these horrible, haunting events and never fully forgiven myself for letting them happen.

During these soul-searching days and between continual firefights, Capt. Dan Monahan, who had replaced Bredleau after the February 26 Doi Mai Creek battle as the Charlie Company CO, became a refreshing guiding light. Dan had a good-spirited nature and a unique feel for people, and he enjoyed the leadership responsibility of motivating soldiers to stretch themselves to do better and achieve things they never thought possible. Dan brought new energy and courage to the company, and we all suddenly began to like one another instead of intensely competing. Dan's presence and demeanor stopped the junior officers, including me, from jockeying for power. He created a renewed spirit of teamwork.

As a joke, Dan made up little cards with clever, droll notes and signed them "the Phantom." With great stealth, he or some accomplice secretly dropped them where I would find them, usually on my gear when I was somewhere else. Naturally, this caused me to try to catch him in the act, but I never did. I always made a big deal about the event, even though I knew who was doing it. Dan always denied his involvement, but I know he engineered this little stunt to distract me because he felt I was too intense.

Dan's creative notes always made me laugh. It was ridiculous that out here in this macho, brutal life, he could resort to such a silly, almost childish game, yet it had such an important purpose. He must have made up these notes ahead of time, because they would show up on combat operations, usually after we started to set up the night defensive perimeter, and I had dropped my web gear. It had to have been Dan. The notes stopped coming on April 14, 1967, the day Dan Monahan died.

April 14, 1967, was the worst day of my life. That night, Capt. Daniel Francis Monahan died in a Vietnamese rice paddy, along with 2d Lt. David Arthur Gray, our artillery forward observer, and one of my troops, Pfc. Robert Earl "Bruce" McKee. It was a bad night for Charlie Company.

Dan Monahan was one of the best men I have ever known. We worked together only seven weeks, but in the environment of South Vietnam it was more like a year, and we got to know each other well. Dan was a burly, bearlike man with an elfish twinkle in his eyes, who constantly tried to make me laugh. He had a wonderful Irish humor and always enjoyed creating a funny joke. Although he said I was too serious and worried too much, he always showed great confidence in my judgment. We would still be good friends today had he lived.

Dan's daughter, Maureen, was born a few days before he was killed. After her birth, Dan became even more concerned about his life. Maureen seemed to give Dan new purpose. He was concerned about our upcoming combat mission, and as we sat in his base camp tent one night a few days before his death, he specifically asked me to get him out if he was wounded. He also ordered me to take over the company if anything happened to him, even though I was outranked by Lt. Larry Lawrence, who replaced White as 2d Platoon leader. Lawrence had no field experience, and mine was significant. Dan clearly wanted me in charge if he had to be medevacked.

Late in the afternoon on the fourteenth, after Dan selected the company night defensive perimeter, I argued with him over the location and configuration. We were in the dry season and set up in cracked, concrete-hard rice paddy terrain. A river made a snakelike loop around the entire area, including our position. It also made an identical loop about a half mile downstream. We called this region south of Tan Tru the "testicles."

There was dense undergrowth choked with nipa palm and mangrove swamps adjacent to the riverbanks, and high ground in some sections, where a few Vietnamese hootches were located. I was uncomfortable with the defensive alignment because we were essentially on a peninsula that was accessible to the Viet Cong, and it gave them a number of convenient escape routes. I was very uneasy, almost apprehensive. The Viet Cong could infiltrate a major force into our area quickly. We were almost challenging them to come after us. Our position was precarious.

Our company defensive perimeter was set up in an approximate twenty-five-yard square behind the dikes in a middle section of the rice paddy. We dug large but shallow foxholes about every three to four yards. The deeper we dug, the damper the holes became. The water table was shallow in this area, only about twelve inches down. We got wet just sitting in the holes. The troops not on watch slept outside their foxholes on the dry, hard surface of the rice paddy and behind the surrounding eighteen-inch-high dikes.

Dan set up night ambush patrols in the adjacent wood lines to cover the easy river access routes on each side of the peninsula. We had open fields of fire and artillery support on call, so Dan said there was little cause for concern. He may have been ordered to establish the night defensive perimeter in this location by battalion headquarters. Sometimes it seemed they intentionally put us in vulnerable positions to entice the Viet Cong to attack. Usually I preferred the high ground in the wooded areas along the riverbanks, where we could dig in better. The fields of fire were not as good, but our troops were not as easy for the enemy to locate in the night, and the nipa palm, mangrove swamps, and river limited quick, quiet enemy access to our perimeter.

Dan's CP was too vulnerable. He wanted to take some pressure off the exhausted troops, who had been in the field nine out of the last ten days, so he set up his CP foxhole to pull a guard position on the company defensive perimeter. He should have established his CP in a more central location within the perimeter. I wish I had argued harder.

At approximately 2200, we began taking sniper fire from the wood line in the 3d Platoon's area on the opposite side of the perimeter from my position. I was lying down with my back on the ground, looking straight up at the stars and listening to Dan and Lieutenant Gray call in an artillery fire mission on the sniper. This was Lieutenant Gray's first real nontraining fire mission, and Dan was helping him. It was fortunate for me that I didn't go over and try to help Lieutenant Gray. Again the difference between life and death was often only a matter of luck.

The airburst registration round appeared to explode outside our perimeter. It was an extra safety precaution, because they had already preplot-registered the artillery before dark. I started to get concerned because the next round would be live and on the ground. A misplaced artillery round can be a deadly mistake. From about thirty-five yards away, I could hear Monahan and Gray talking. Although I could not hear the details of their conversation, I knew that there was too much talking for the task at hand. The longer they talked, the more nervous I became.

A few days before in base camp, I had questioned Dan regarding Lieutenant Gray's tough-mindedness, attention to detail, and technical capability to handle this dangerous responsibility. This was Lieutenant Gray's second combat mission. On our first mission with Gray, he didn't appear to have the physical endurance to withstand the sweltering heat, negotiate the tough terrain, and still function effectively. Monahan told me how proud Gray was to be working with us, to be part of this great adventure, and assured me he would be OK. Dan said he would be personally responsible for him. Monahan planned to build Gray into a great soldier. That was the essence of Dan Monahan—building better people. I cautioned him that it takes only one mistake with artillery and how lethal the consequences of one simple mistake can be.

Lieutenant Gray was young in physical maturity—chubby, almost boyish in appearance—but a nice, bright, and likable young man. Until an officer had earned his spurs through performance in this environment, no one had any confidence or trust in his ability. The rite of passage was demonstrated execution capability. Lieutenant Gray had been with us only about a week, and there was nothing more dangerous than an inexperienced new guy, especially a butter-bar second lieutenant.

Suddenly, a tremendous lightninglike flash and deafening explosion filled the dark sky. A large piece of shrapnel whistled past about four feet over my head and struck the ground within earshot about fifteen yards outside the perimeter. It was deathly silent for about thirty seconds, then everyone started desperately yelling for a medic. Someone was hit in my corner foxhole position down to the right at the end of the dike. From that direction, I heard a soldier screaming for a medic.

Our medic, Sp4 Peter Nero, the best in Charlie Company, immediately sprinted to the call. I checked my line on the perimeter to ensure the troops were alert and ready to defend their positions, then went down to check my wounded soldier. Nero was already working on him. He used a flashlight for illumination and covered himself and the light with a poncho to keep from being seen and picked off in the night by a Viet Cong sniper.

I asked Nero a couple of times how the soldier was and got

no response. He worked with great intensity. I barked again more sternly, and he came out from under the poncho to tell me the man was dead. I asked who it was, and he said, "McKee." I felt immediate and crushing emotional pain, then asked him if he was sure.

He pulled back the poncho and used the flashlight quickly to show me McKee's face and wound. I said that was only a small hole and there was no blood, so how could he be dead. Nero stuttered and replied that McKee had no pulse. I told him to try to save him. Nero was very frustrated and said, "What can I do?" I told him to try something, anything, but keep him alive.

I thought, They do it on TV all the time. Nero repeated that McKee was already dead, that his heart had stopped beating.

We could hear the company first sergeant, "Top" Johnson, yelling for Nero, exclaiming that Captain Monahan was down and needed help. Nero asked me what to do, and I asked once again if he was sure McKee was dead. He again said yes, so I told him to go help Monahan.

Then I personally checked Private McKee, because he just didn't look dead, only a little pale and asleep. I tried to wake him up, but he was gone. I asked God how he could let this happen to us, McKee and me. It seemed so unfair and completely beyond my control. I didn't even have a chance to try to save him. I stood there in the night with a feeling of absolute hopelessness and despair, and thought about his parents and how emotionally distraught and destroyed they would be.

I yelled to my troops to stay alert, then went over to check out Monahan. His chest was torn apart and his lungs were punctured. He was drowning in his own blood. I could hear my friend gasping to get oxygen into his lungs, but he could only suck in more blood. Nero was working frantically to keep him alive, but there was little hope. There was nothing I could do but stand there in the dark and say the Lord's Prayer as he died.

I watched this good man die with Nero desperately wrapping his chest in bandages trying to stop the bleeding. Nero was talking to himself as he worked on Dan. He kept repeating over and over that he could not stop the bleeding, and mumbling that Monahan was drowning. The gurgling stopped. Dan passed on, but Nero kept working. First Sergeant Johnson told Nero to stop, but he continued. Eventually, Johnson put his huge hands around Nero's shoulders and pulled him away.

Someone momentarily used a flashlight, and I caught a clear, unforgettable glimpse of Nero. He was almost in shock and stared without expression directly into the light like a deer caught in a spotlight. His skin was a ghastly ashen gray except for his bloody hands. Nero did the best he could, but the task was impossible. Only God could have saved Dan, and he wasn't going to do it that night.

Lieutenant Gray lay nearby and had the top of his head blown off. Dan and Lieutenant Gray had been just standing outside their foxhole inside the perimeter calling in the artillery fire mission on the VC sniper when three banjo-type Chinese claymore mines detonated simultaneously. It was incredibly bad luck, particularly for Private McKee, who was quite a distance away on watch, just sitting in his shallow foxhole vigilantly doing his duty. It all happened so quickly. In one instant they were all dead, and there was nothing I could do to change the painful losses.

In November 1966, I had pulled Bruce McKee from his parents' arms at Fort Riley, Kansas, as we got on the buses to begin our trip to Vietnam. His mother was so worried. You could see the love and fear in his parents' faces. I looked them straight in the eyes and told them I would take good care of their son. He was a handsome, likable, unassuming young man, eighteen years old, with piercing blue eyes. At times he seemed almost shy, but he was always dependable.

McKee's parents had traveled from Kentucky to Kansas to spend the last few precious minutes with their son, their only child, before he shipped out. In the years since, whenever I picked up one of my son's friends to go somewhere, I have felt that same instinct to reassure their parents by saying, "I will take good care of him," but I have choked on these words every time.

After the bodies were dusted off (evacked by chopper), I went back to my defensive area, very downtrodden, looked up at the stars, and tried to cry all alone in the dark where no one could see me. But I could not. Although my grief and sadness were overwhelming, my ability to cry was gone. I felt great remorse but had no way to express it. I felt lost and helpless, almost hollow. The only important thing was to be prepared to engage the next problem.

There was no time or place for remorse in Vietnam. To stop and think of your lost friends was not an affordable luxury. You had to concentrate completely on the task at hand and be totally alert to the immediate situation or you would put everyone's life in jeopardy.

Because we were unaware of the claymore mines, initially everyone thought these men had been killed by the artillery fire mission, that Second Lieutenant Gray had called the artillery round too close to the perimeter. The artillery battery denied firing the round, but no one in Charlie Company believed them. The timing had been such that it seemed to be the obvious cause—the only plausible explanation. The explosion seemed to have been almost inside our perimeter. We felt the air displacement.

I was very angry with Lieutenant Gray. First Sergeant Johnson, who had organized the night dust-off, was noticeably demoralized and also thought it was Lieutenant Gray's artillery. We knew that Gray was a rookie, and it was easy to blame it on him, but something did not seem right to me.

Monahan's multiple wounds and McKee's wound were smaller than would be expected from artillery shrapnel, and the entry angle on McKee's wound looked as though the shrapnel trajectory was down rather than up. His wound was below the level of the foxhole in which he had been sitting. I had noticed this when I checked him to determine if he was dead. In addition, the shrapnel that went over me seemed to have been moving almost on a downward angle, because I heard it hit the ground not far outside my defensive position. This seemed to be an unusual dispersion pattern from an artillery round that appeared to explode so close, almost within our perimeter; I asked First Sergeant Johnson if Lieutenant Gray had called for an airburst round, but he didn't know. I kept wondering why he would call in an airburst round so close to the perimeter. It made no sense.

I couldn't sleep, kept mentally reviewing everything that happened, and anxiously awaited the sunrise to investigate further. When the sun's first light cracked the horizon, I went outside the perimeter in the 3d Platoon's area and found the remnants of three Chinese claymores that had been tied to a small tree and positioned only seven yards from our night perimeter, right in front of a corner foxhole. The det line, a wire that connected the electricity from the ignition trigger to the blasting caps, had been left behind. Someone in the 3d Platoon had to have been asleep on guard duty to let the VC position their claymores so close.

Our battalion commander, Lt. Col. Richard Zastrow, flew out in his chopper about an hour later that morning. When I explained what had happened, he was upset. Second Lieutenant Lawrence took over the command on a temporary basis because he outranked me in date of rank. I resented this even though I knew it was not permanent. After Zastrow left,

Maj. Gen. George O'Conner from division headquarters arrived, and we went through the explanation again. He was also disturbed by the events of the preceding night. The army didn't like losing men—in particular, a commanding officer—with nothing to show for it.

The general spoke disparagingly about our haggard appearance; his last comment before leaving was to tell us that we should all immediately shave. This didn't go over too well with anyone, because the company had been in the field for a few days and had no water for shaving. We needed what water we had to just stay alive. The general's callous, disengaged remarks infuriated me. As General O'Conner turned and walked away, First Sergeant Johnson had to stop me from telling the general what I thought of his orders and heritage.

Shortly after General O'Conner left, a chopper brought in our new artillery forward observer (FO) to replace Lieutenant Gray. I was excited when I saw that it was Lt. Kevin Kelly, a New York young man who graduated from St. Johns University. He had been in my basic training unit at Fort Dix and later had visited my parents' home in Connecticut. I hadn't even known he was in the 9th Division.

It seemed to me Lieutenant Kelly had no courage for line action. He was scared to death. Who could blame him? This was extraordinarily dangerous work. He kept saying over and over that he had not trained for this type of duty, and he would not be out here long. Later that day most of Charlie Company returned to base camp, and in a couple of days Kelly was gone and I never saw him again.

I did not feel comfortable with most FOs and always preferred to call in my own artillery missions even with my dyslexia issues, particularly because I already had so much experience. We never had another artillery FO while I was in Charlie Company. Seeing Kelly, however, made me realize how much I had progressed since basic training and how much more I had grown, by virtue of my responsibilities, than he had.

The bad news continued on April 15. The day after Dan was killed was the next worst day of my life. Around noon that day my good friend in Alpha Company, Lt. Bob Florey, chased a sniper and led his platoon into U-shaped ambush in the "bowling alley." His platoon was caught in the open in a VC automatic weapons cross fire, and Bob and seven of his men died. We had a cardinal rule that you never chased a sniper. I still cannot understand why Bob did this, particularly in the bowling alley, where the risks were so great. Bob was a smart soldier, and to make this fundamental mistake made no sense. Some surviving soldiers said he was ordered into the area by his commanding officer, but we never truly knew. Bob had a wonderful sense of humor, and everything he did made us laugh. He was a funny, kindhearted guy.

When we were at Fort Riley, Kansas, Bob had bought a horse. The purchase was typical Bob, completely impulsive and totally illogical. In the late 1800s after the Civil War, Fort Riley was a major frontier cavalry post and base camp from which the United States Cavalry conducted the brutal Indian Wars. Colonel George Armstrong Custer, demoted from his Civil War general rank and relegated to the demeaning duty of chasing Indians, rode and patrolled these plains with his pony soldiers. Bob wanted to ride the same plains on horseback, just as Custer's 7th Cavalry did and establish a link with history.

It was at Fort Riley that Bob gave me the nickname "Wrong Way" Callaway as a good-natured joke because I became lost on my first training mission. He razzed me about it constantly. However, he always conveniently elected to forget the civilian car he almost hit at Fort Riley with a mortar round when his platoon fired in the wrong direction. I learned of his death over the radio while I was on patrol in the "testicles." Bob always said he would die in Vietnam. I thought about his silly trademark Clark Kent glasses, his crazy laugh, and his goofy smile. We would never see them again.

I had to force myself to think about the search and destroy mission we were conducting. My mind was overburdened with grief and wanted to drift. I yelled at my troops for diddy boppin'—the term used to describe screwing off on a Vietnam patrol. It was a vicious berating filled with expletives. They were dragging ass and their execution was sloppy. They were also laughing at stupid things. It was probably a stress reaction on everyone's part. I was ripping mad. My friend First Sergeant Johnson heard me and came up to the point to console me and calm me down. The risks were extraordinarily great, and the penalty for failure was high. I felt so sad and tired, so exhausted.

Later that day, because Charlie Company had to regroup under a new commanding officer, most of the company went back to the Tan Tru base camp. My platoon was sent to 3d Brigade headquarters base camp in Tan An, a major Long An Province city, to pull security on the army airfield. As we got off the choppers and started down the tarmac, we could see something piled in the distance. As we got closer, the normally boisterous troops, now experiencing the tremendous stress relief soldiers feel when they first get out of the battlefield heat, became quieter and quieter.

Soon I could hear only their feet moving and the noise of their equipment. They were dead silent. We were approaching eleven body bags; my friends were stacked up in them like cordwood. I stopped the platoon and asked my platoon sergeant to align the troops in their defensive positions around the airfield, then stood there and stared at the body bags for about an hour. Among them were Monahan, Florey, Gray, and McKee.

I asked myself to explain this cruel world. I thought about going through the body bag stack to look for my friends. I felt so lost and empty. At times my mind went absolutely blank. There was nothing in it. It simply started to erase. Eventually my platoon sergeant, Sergeant Dilley, came back to get me. He said, "Sir, if you stay here any longer, you're going to go crazy," and he pulled me away. The evening light began to fade. I looked back once and never looked back again.

I thought I was already a hardened soldier before these days, but this made me a lot tougher and even more distant. I tried to detach myself from the pain and death that was around me every day. I lost so much weight from not eating and sleeping that in my last weeks in the field I looked like a skeleton. I was so emaciated that no one from home would have recognized me. Nonetheless, my physical endurance and mental strength grew as I reached within myself to find the will to keep going.

You need a strong will to press on and a strong ego and concern for your fellow man to rebuild your will as it is systematically destroyed every day. The horrifying events sucked the life out of a man before it killed him. A soldier's worst fear, besides being shot in the crotch, was to suffer through this grueling experience for a year, then die his last week in Vietnam.

A few days before Dan was killed, he gave me a pocketknife as a gift. At the time I did not know it was a Special Forces knife. A week after his death, the company completed a short mission back in the "testicles" and was being extracted from the boonies by chopper. As the first slicks arrived, I accidentally dropped the shiny silver knife onto the dry rice paddy. It fell into an eight-inch-deep narrow crack in the concrete-hard mud, and I could not force my hand into the crack to get it. No knife or even the muzzle of my weapon could loosen the dried mud.

In the extraction the LZ was smoking hot. We were the security platoon for the first two platoon extractions. As usual, we were the last lift out. First in, last out every time. That is where the intense enemy heat was. The last group always took the most fire from the VC in the wood lines, because they came out from hiding to shoot us in the back. The last lift was the most vulnerable to enemy aggression and required precision in execution. A poorly managed extraction could cost many lives.

The 2d and 3d Platoons were safely extracted despite the enemy fire. I set up in a way similar to the previous two lifts, positioned the troops correctly, popped smoke where I wanted the lead slick, and gave them the approach azimuth. The eight choppers came in on the wrong azimuth. We were set up north/south, and this time they came in east/west. We were taking automatic weapons fire on the LZ, and this direction error by the aviation unit created mass confusion.

As our gunships strafed the adjacent wood lines, I waited in the rice paddy until I was sure all my men had gotten into choppers. Men were running in all directions to board them; it was pure chaos. Another danger in this confusion was that an excited and disoriented trooper could run into a slick's tail rotor blade and literally lose his head. I was angry with the pilots and would let them know it when we landed.

The other choppers and most of my troops had left, but I was still there in the paddy on my knees trying to get the knife. Gunships were strafing the adjacent wood lines, and the troops in my slick yelled that the chopper pilot was going to leave me. When I looked around, no one was on the ground but me. That little silver knife was all I had left of Dan. I didn't want to lose it, but I had no choice.

The lead slick pilot started to lift, so I needed to jump for the aircraft. I ran and dove into the chopper, and my men caught my arms and pulled me in. My rib cage hit the edge of the steel floor of the rising chopper; the pain was excruciating. I grabbed on to a single safety strap with one hand as the aircraft moved upward. Despite the pain, I hung out the open chopper door to look for the knife, but of course I couldn't see it. Even after we lifted into the sky and soared away, I continued to focus on the spot in the paddy where the pocket-knife lay. As we rose higher and got farther away, I lost sight of the location but remained hanging precariously out the door, almost five hundred feet above the ground that raced by beneath the chopper.

Then I noticed the magnificent sky, which was a vibrant, bright blue with a few mountainous snow-white clouds in the distance. The sky seemed so peaceful and far from the evil world below, inviting me just to float out into its comfort-able, crisp, and billowy beauty. I was enveloped by the clean, cool freshness, vast dimensions, and feeling of freedom. The rhythmic rotation of the chopper blades and humming grind of the engine mesmerized me. I felt free from all the mental pain and suffering. Suddenly, I caught my delusional digres-sion and moved to a safer position in the slick.

My troops did not understand what I had been doing in the paddy or why I was hanging out the door. Nero, my medic, looked concerned, asked me if I was OK, then quizzically looked at my RTO, Sp4 Phil Hilowitz, who stared blankly, tilted his head back a little, then rolled his eyes up. I confi-dently reassured them, but my mind drifted back to the fresh-smelling wind on my face, and again I gazed out the chopper door into the open, cool blue sky. When I was hanging out the door they were thinking I was going to let go. All I had to do was let go of the safety strap, my umbilical cord, and peacefully float away, leaving this misery. I quickly hooked up my safety belt, smiled at my men, and told them I had lost my pocketknife. I was left with the memories, an impish eye twinkle, a pleasant smile, and an Irish chuckle. I said farewell to Dan.

When my chest hit the edge of the door opening as the chopper was rising, a left rib broke into two parts. I could have received a Purple Heart for the broken rib, but I did not want to get taken out of the field, so I never reported it. The broken rib showed up clearly in a bone scan I had after being diagnosed with lymphoma cancer in 1993. I explained to the doctors what had happened, but they still took about ten X rays from different angles to be sure this was not cancer in my bone structure because there was so much calcified bone at the break. Sometimes it still hurts when I take a deep breath and always hurts if I press on it. After the break, it was extremely painful for about a month, and for that period, in extraction situations, I always wore a flak jacket to protect my ribs.

The army tried to give me a Purple Heart for a broken hand, which fractured when I punched a VC prisoner on another mission into the "testicles." My troops were hung up in a mined area, and I was trying to elicit information from the prisoner through my Vietnamese interpreter on how to traverse safely through the area. Being nice was not working, so it was easy to get a little mean in this environment.

My right hand held the M-16 with the muzzle pressed hard against the VC's head, and my index finger was lightly squeezing the trigger. My left hand was around his throat, almost collapsing his windpipe, and I had him pressed against a palm tree. As he gasped for air, I asked him nicely again. Platoon sergeant Dilley, who knew this was all for effect, came over, tapped me on the shoulder, and asked if I knew that my weapon's safety was off. I snapped the M-16 down and looked. He was right.

The entire time, I had thought my safety was engaged. I could have killed this man by accident, and that really frightened me. The VC started to laugh, that indefinable, stupid Vietnamese laugh the American troops learned to despise. Who knows why or for what reason he laughed. I had almost killed him by accidentally blowing his brains out, which would have destroyed my life. This was not an appropriate time to laugh. It angered me so I threw down my M-16 and punched him. He ducked, and I hit him square in the forehead, causing his head to bounce off the palm tree.

I could hear the bone break in my right hand. It snapped, just like a dry stick breaking, and hurt badly. After a couple of days, the pain was still severe and the swollen hand stopped working; I had to be medevacked from the field for a half day to have a plaster cast put on.

A Purple Heart is given for a broken hand or a bullet through the head. It did not seem right. I did not want a Purple Heart for punching a VC, and after the orders were cut and I was asked to pick up the Purple Heart, I told the battalion adjutant, Captain Jones, I would not accept it. Everyone thought I was crazy, but I loved my platoon too much to let a broken rib or hand keep me away from my responsibility.

I had trained my rifle platoon in Kansas and deployed with them as a unit to Vietnam. We had worked together for almost a year. They were like my children. My troops were so important to me, I went back into the field with a cast that covered my right hand and arm almost up to my elbow. Later, with a knife I cut it back to halfway up my forearm. Only two fingers and the thumb worked. I had to put a plastic bag over the cast when we crossed rivers and streams, and my troops always had to help me. The bone never healed straight, a frequent reminder of that day.

A few firefights later and on patrol out to An Nhut Tan, our company crossed a small tidal river. It was only about twenty-five feet across but had an extremely strong current. My platoon secured the area and set up the safety rigging adjacent to and downstream from a partially submerged, inoperative steel bridge. A young trooper from another platoon that crossed first was afraid to get in the water and make the crossing. We had the standard river crossing rope safety rigging set up and two stripped lifeguard swimmers in the water helping the troops, but this young man would not cross because, he said, he could not swim. I asked him how he got here without being able to swim.

I told him we were not going to bring in a chopper to get

him across the river, that it was too dangerous for the chopper. It was an easy river for him to cross, and we had to move quickly because the VC were moving along these rivers with the tidal current. He could cross using the rope rigging, or we would leave him. I told him he did not need to know how to swim but advised him not to let go of the safety rope.

The soldier was a small, slightly built young man, but this was an easy task. My safety swimmers took his helmet and M-16 rifle across. He was in full combat gear, wearing a web harness and pistol belt, ammo pouches, and bandoliers carrying about ten magazines (a few hundred rounds of ammo), some frag grenades, and so forth. The kid panicked in the crossing and let go of the rope. His fear even caused him to fight the safety swimmers. He went down, and the swimmers pulled him up; still he fought them as they tried to save his life.

My broken right hand was in a cast; I stood on the riverbank no more than thirteen feet away, and he looked up at me, right in the eyes, and said, "God save me."

I thought, You've got the wrong guy. I'm not God. I'm just a lieutenant. He went down a final time and drowned, disappearing in the muddy water's fierce current. Everyone in the area stared without any facial expression hoping to see him surface, but he never came up again. We looked at one another and shook our heads in disbelief, but he was already a statistic. We moved on. I never even knew his name.

A few days later a patrol found his naked body about a half mile downriver. It had been staked out on a tether line adjacent to the river by the local Vietnamese so the tide wouldn't continue to move the body, and we could find it. They had stripped the soldier of all his gear and clothing. The decomposition process had blown him up like a balloon. All the kid had to have done was hang onto the rope or just let the safety swimmers take him with the current to the opposite riverbank and safety. His fear was too great, and it killed him.

Lieutenant Lawrence, who took over the company after Monahan's death, was soon replaced by Captain McClain, who talked incessantly in a nervous, whining southern drawl about meaningless information and told self-aggrandizing stories. He was the Charlie Company commanding officer for about fifteen minutes in the field and a couple of sniper rounds. In McClain's first week of command the company had moved to An Nhut Tan. We had crossed the river east of An Nhut Tan, south of where the rivers forked, and we were conducting a routine search-and-destroy sweep.

McClain was not even close to the sniper activity, but as the shots were fired he fell down on a dike. He claimed he injured his back, had to be medevacked out, and could no longer operate in the field. I stood there with my right hand still in a cast and looked at him with disdainful disbelief as he lay in the paddy disgracefully waiting for the medevac chopper. By the rules, he got his combat command, a Combat Infantryman's Badge (the coveted CIB), and a Purple Heart on two errant sniper rounds.

A few days later in the Tan Tru base camp, trying to sound positive, I expressed confidence to Captain McClain that he would soon be as good as new and back to duty. But he said when his back went out like this, it took at least six months to recover. I asked him what he was doing in the infantry if he had such a bad back; he said he just wanted to give it a try. McClain was walking around base camp pathetically humped over, and shortly thereafter the army transferred him back to Bearcat and out of the line combat soldiers' sight.

I worried about how to explain this to my men; what if this apparent character failure influenced them, and some decided to develop their own medical problems? The situation was disheartening, but the troops seemed to ignore it, almost to the point that it never happened and the captain never existed. My soldiers refused to give in to their fear, to capitulate, to quit, and I was proud of them. McClain was not of that ilk. His dad was a lieutenant general, and I thought he would be very disappointed.

Finally, after months with no platoon leader other than Sergeant Byron, the platoon sergeant, Pete Michelson, took over 3d Platoon after Delgado (leadership problems) and Torres (bar grenadier) were relieved from the position. Michelson was an unusual Charlie Company officer in that he was a Stanford University graduate. I asked him how a Stanford graduate wound up in a place like this. He said he volunteered because it was his duty. He believed it was not fair that the poor kids got stuck with this war. He once told me he would trade his Stanford degree if he could get his men to respect him as much as my men respected me. I told him he was crazy. I tried to help him, and he listened carefully, but it wasn't long before he stepped on a land mine and went home severely wounded.

Lieutenant Herman Howard "Chuck" Payne, a platoon leader in Bravo Company, was a good friend of mine. We always had lots of laughs when we got together. The guy had a great smile and a relaxed, charming personality. We were once briefly in the same firefight with a VC unit, and in our discussions he reenacted the events as though it was Normandy. He would laugh and laugh about how lucky we were to have survived so long in this dangerous environment. The VC would shoot at the officers every day because we were usually out in the open, especially in the rice paddy terrain.

In late April 1967 Chuck Payne was killed, and I began to realize finally that my chances of surviving Vietnam were not good. Chuck killed himself accidentally by shooting a ChiCom hand grenade booby trap. A dime-size piece of shrapnel from the explosion ricocheted off the brim of his helmet and struck his forehead. A quarter inch was the difference between life and death for Chuck. White's quarter inch was life and Payne's was death.

At the time, Charlie Company was positioned at the remote An Nhut Tan hamlet, north of Tan Tru and south of Rach Kien. The 2d Platoon's Sergeant Marshal and First Sergeant Johnson came over to my CP to give me the bad news. They knew that Chuck and I were friends and that this would crush me. At first I thought they were visiting just to play a silly joke on me, but I soon could tell by their somber faces that something was wrong. Before walking away, they each put an arm around my shoulders and told me how sorry they were. I was touched by their compassion and concern. Vietnam was a sad place. You had to be able to live with tremendous emotional pain, despair, and depression to survive.

I asked everyone around to leave me alone for a while, then I walked to the edge of the An Nhut Tan hamlet defensive perimeter. I sat down, leaned against the sandbagged front of a bunker, tilted my helmet back, lit up a cigarette, and stared across the open rice paddy terrain and reflected. Chuck had died a few rice paddies over so I looked off to the southwest in the direction that Chuck had died. All I could see was activity in the paddy just outside An Nhut Tan. It didn't look dangerous out there. In fact it looked quite peaceful. Directly across the paddy, a little Vietnamese boy carrying a switchlike stick walked along with a massive surly but obedient water buffalo. They were all belligerent creatures but amazingly could be controlled by little boys.

The sun was setting. The pinkish hue bled through the distant silvery gray clouds and deep blue sky, and these gorgeous rich colors behind the wood line framed the tall nipa palms, giving them a regal countenance. There was an unusual warm, gentle breeze, which I mused was Chuck's spirit bidding me farewell. Although the Vietnamese lived here, it was where we came to die. It didn't look like a place to die and was far from our homes. It did not seem right that we should have to die so far from home. I said good-bye to my friend Chuck Payne. He was a fine man.

Just the night before, I had relieved Chuck's platoon at An

Nhut Tan, and we stayed up and talked half the night. Chuck was a rawboned, rangy man with a pleasant, caring disposition. He was extraordinarily happy because he was being pulled out of the field the next day to report for a headquarters job and getting out of the line combat heat. Several of Chuck's men had given him their day's single beer ration because he was leaving. It was their personal tribute of respect for him. Chuck shared his four beers with me, showed me pictures of his two young sons, and said he never believed he would survive Vietnam. Tears filled his eyes as we sat there alone.

He had lost two men that day and was as distressed as he was happy. Vietnam hyperextended your emotions in all directions. As Chuck's platoon had burned down the two-foot-high dry grass in front of their positions to establish better fields of fire in their section of the An Nhut Tan defensive perimeter, two American claymore mines had exploded from the heat of the fire and killed the two soldiers. The directional antipersonnel projectile mines, armed and ready to fire, had been left there in the tall grass by another American unit. The Viet Cong had turned them around toward the American troops, so they would explode in the faces of our soldiers if they were ever fired. Chuck had no reason to anticipate this situation, but he still blamed himself for not checking the grass more carefully. It was a tragedy of negligence caused by someone else. An irresponsible squad leader from another American unit hadn't done his job, and two men died. We reviewed the events many times. I tried to console Chuck, to help him through his grief and anguish, and prevent him from torturing himself.

The next day, April 26, 1967, all Chuck had to do was cross two miles of rice paddies with his platoon, then be picked up by truck and taken to the battalion base camp. Chuck became cavalier, lost focus, and made a silly mistake. It cost him his life.

Until that time, I had totally concentrated on day-to-day requirements, my missions, and my troops. My own death was not something I even considered. But Chuck's death somehow made me recognize that my dying could be imminent and certainly far beyond my control. I finally understood that although I didn't feel I was going to die in this war, I probably was, no matter how good I was or how hard I tried. All the platoon leader lieutenants were dying around me. The percentages were overwhelmingly against me. All you had to do was make one little mistake. I prayed to God, "I have never been very religious, so I am not going to pray for my life, but I will, if you let me live through this war, raise some kind kids who will help this cruel world." That commitment has been the direction of my life. I try never to vary from it. It made life simpler after Vietnam.

Many of the men who died in Vietnam had a clear premonition of death. I have never come up with a logical explanation for this phenomenon. There were too many examples for this to be a mere coincidence. I do not know if their psychological tendencies made them more vulnerable or if they had advanced intuitive knowledge.

After surviving almost six months in a combat line position, I was pulled out of the field. This was standard practice for officers, because insanity started to take over if you stayed on what we called "the line" too long. Few platoon leaders lasted six months in a combat field position. Ironically, despite all the missions I led, Private McKee was the only trooper I lost in combat under my direct command. He was the one kid I promised to protect.

In early May 1967, about two weeks after Lt. Chuck Payne's death, Charlie Company's 1st Sgt. Edward Johnson was recalled from the field to the battalion base camp. He became intoxicated one night, went over to the battalion headquarters, and appealed to Lieutenant Colonel Zastrow, the battalion CO, to take me off the line.

He told Zastrow it was only a matter of days or, at most, weeks before I was killed because I had been under such extraordinary pressure, and my willingness to risk my own life was getting significantly greater with each passing day.

First Sergeant Johnson thought I was approaching the point where you accept death as a better option than living through the torment, suffering, and death of others. Simultaneously, you completely pass through the fear barrier and begin to believe you cannot be killed. The behavior ultimately becomes "kill me if you can, but so what if you do because I do not care." It is merely an honorable way to commit suicide.

This delusion, the result of physical and mental exhaustion, is called battlefield fatigue, and it will get you killed quickly. Johnson got angry with Zastrow and asked him, "What are you going to do, just leave Lieutenant Callaway out there until he dies?" I still had a cast on my right wrist and arm.

Actually, in my opinion, it was First Sergeant Johnson who started to unravel, but he definitely saved my life. Although he had not liked me when I was a green second lieutenant during training at Fort Riley, he grew to respect me and became my friend in Vietnam. In the field, First Sergeant Johnson and I had been through significant pain together.

Johnson had a strong fatherly admiration for Darrell "Gus" Gustafson, our company clerk and Johnson's right-hand man. Gus was a capable administrator and quite brave; he occasionally went on combat missions with us. But Gus's greatest contribution, after I left, was engineering administrative magic by getting Charlie Company soldiers who were beginning to lose their sanity pulled from the field. He moved some longtime combat survivors into safe positions within the battalion base camp.

Phil Hilowitz gives Gus full credit for his Vietnam survival. Gus somehow got Hilowitz pulled off the line and hidden in the company armory during his last few months in Vietnam. Phil said he took a low profile in the armory and was quiet as a mouse so he would not be noticed. Believe me, that was hard for Hilowitz to do.

A few weeks after First Sergeant Johnson complained to Colonel Zastrow, near the end of May, I was pulled out of the field and given the headquarters job that Chuck Payne was scheduled to get had he lived. I was not given the option to refuse. Because of the experience with Payne, I was also given no notice of my assignment change. While out at An Nhut Tan, I was ordered to get on a chopper immediately and return to base camp for reassignment. I was not given the opportunity to take one last risk, as was Chuck.

I will never forget Private Moore, one of my best soldiers, running up to me as I was getting on the chopper and asking me how I could leave the platoon like this. He said, "I thought we were all going to be together through this war." I told him I had been ordered to leave and had no option. Gustafson was also standing there as I boarded the chopper. I tossed him two grenades and said, "Hold these for me." Initially, I felt extreme joy about being forced to leave, about getting out from under the incredible responsibility, about leaving the awful living conditions, leaving behind the fear, the hate, and the specter of death. I was also proud that my men had confidence in me, but most important I was proud because my men had great pride in the 1st Platoon.

I owe my life to my soldiers. At one point before Monahan was killed, the army sent in a film crew to shoot a motion picture training film of my platoon in action. I never saw it, but my father, Joe Callaway, Sr., contacted the army back in the States and arranged to see the film. I was proud of the platoon and, with some exceptions, truly miss them all.

After I left, my platoon, forty-two men strong, was split up and many were put in leadership positions throughout the brigade. The squad and team leader positions were, with the

exception of Sgt. Ron Bentley, still intact, with the troops
who originally went to war together. After six months, they
were experienced combat vets, technically functional and extremely confident. They were a superb group of young men
who worked as a team and did their jobs exceedingly well.

When I returned to the Tan Tru battalion base camp, Colonel Zastrow told me what a great job I had done and that he
was concerned about losing me, which is why he pulled me
out of the field. Zastrow then sent me on R & R. After a thor-
oughly enjoyable five-day furlough in Bangkok, Thailand, I
returned to witness essentially the destruction of Bravo
Company as they were ravaged by the VC.

That June night, Bravo Company lost eighteen men and
had forty wounded—the result of major tactical mistakes by
the company field officers. The regular company commander
was on R & R, and some inexperienced captain had been
flown in to take charge for a few days. The platoon leaders
were all experienced. They had established their night defensive perimeter on the grounds of what appeared to be an
evacuated estate house or perhaps a Vietnamese religious
pagoda. The building was large by Vietnamese standards,
was made of solid materials, had lots of adjacent trees, and
was positioned in the middle of a huge rice paddy. A rectan-
gular dry moat about four to five feet deep surrounded the
structure and the adjacent grounds.

When the VC came late in the night, they immediately
killed all six men stationed in the three listening posts about
fifty yards outside the perimeter. The LPs screamed as the
VC butchered them. The VC then began mortaring Bravo
Company's position. Because the moon was full, it was easy
for the VC to register their mortars on the area and its distinctive silhouette. They also strafed Bravo Company with
automatic weapons fire from behind the surrounding dikes.

Bravo Company had dug no foxholes. The troops were
without protection and had to jump into the moat, which was

so deep it was impossible to aim over to establish flat fields of fire. They had to shoot up at a thirty- to forty-five-degree angle or jump up to fire. This enabled the VC to crawl up to the corners of the moat and rake the defenseless men in the ditch. Our soldiers could not defend themselves. If the VC had used grenades, they could have killed the entire company by merely lobbing them into the ditch. Fortunately for the Bravo Company survivors, the VC broke off the engagement early.

This was a major tactical error by the company line officers in selecting the location of the defensive perimeter and in preparing the troops. Generally, success by the VC required the American field officers to do something incredibly stupid. The Bravo Company commanding officer was relieved from duty. What he allowed to happen was a flagrant violation of his command responsibility. The clever, patient VC always waited for us to make a mistake, then capitalized on it. Officers' errors in judgment were costly in Vietnam.

I was so upset about Bravo Company that I asked Colonel Zastrow for my platoon back, told him how good they were, how important they were to me, and how I did not want anything to happen to them. After three weeks out of the field, I felt rejuvenated. During our conversation, I seemed to be trying to convince him I was sane and told him I was fine and ready to go again. I also hated working in the battalion headquarters listening to the radios at night and doing fetch-it work.

Zastrow said the platoon was strong but was going to be split up, and some of the leaders would be sent to reinforce weaker units in the 3d Brigade. He told me he knew how effective I had been as a platoon leader and was proud of me because I volunteered to go back, but he thought I needed more than just three weeks out of the field and off the line.

In addition to the Bravo Company tragedy, one of the worst errors in the 9th Division that brought about significant loss of life occurred some time later when an air force liaison officer took coordinates from the 3d Brigade TOC tact board for the night arc light, a harrowing and ground-leveling B-52 saturation bombing strike. It turned out to be the defensive perimeter location of a major ARVN unit. We carpet-bombed our allies by mistake.

Many of the tactical execution problems in Vietnam were directly related to limited and improper training, and inexperienced and unsupervised leaders. When Americans were killed, it was most often because we had made a series of mistakes in execution or a major error in judgment. An officer needed quick analytical ability and a strong will to measure the risk in every decision and tactical action, and he needed this capability even when he was extremely fatigued and operating in horrible living conditions.

The 2d Battalion, 60th Infantry, had some exceptional junior officers, among them Lieutenants Jim Lehne, John Hulka, Ernie Parker, Steve Franke, Pete Johnson, and Gary Woodring. They were bright leaders and men of principle. Even with limited training and experience, most, although unfortunately not all, junior military officers with whom I served were intelligent, capable, hardworking, and admirable leaders.

Vietnam was full of courageous and self-sacrificing men. Most infantry soldiers were heroic people, yet what they did, they did because it was required, not because they were looking for a medal or glory or personal recognition. The men of true courage far outnumbered the others with whom we had to work. Most of the courageous officers were motivated to serve the needs of others and save the lives of others. They put the needs of the many before the needs of the few. They were not self-indulgent egomaniacs.

There was a final retribution for the self-aggrandizing, high-risk-taking line combat leaders. They were usually bagged and zipped quickly. They made themselves too easy to recognize in the field, and the VC were good at picking out a hot dog officer. I learned after my first firefight to become invisible, and my troops functioned so well that they enabled me to look like just one of the guys. An officer needed to be able to control and direct activity without standing out.

Many American field-grade officers, majors and colonels, let the line company–grade officers, captains and lieutenants, bear a disproportionate risk in Vietnam, leaving these inexperienced officers with the important and crucial battlefield decision making and, therefore, the true burden of the war. If you had power in Vietnam, it was an easy war in which to hide, particularly for the many field-grade staff officers. The Vietnam War meant career development and enhancement for the senior officers. Killing communists was just a task mission. Few senior officers showed motivation from overwhelming patriotism or a righteous cause. Most knew that this was a meaningless conflict, and except for personal advancement most showed little passion for the war.

Some field-grade officers worked on the macho nature and ambition of the unknowing, inexperienced, and gullible young junior officers. These senior officers on occasion awarded themselves medals while sending junior line officers into the breach and often to their deaths. In my experience, the senior officers usually took little risk themselves. In all fairness, the war was a series of small unit battles that did not warrant a field-grade officer's participation. The junior line company–grade officers had to learn the combat game and the art of survival on their own.

In Vietnam we eventually learned we were nothing but human bait sent out to make contact with the VC and NVA so we could respond with overwhelming artillery and airpower. Vietnam infantry grunts were sometimes used as expendable people—just part of the strategy.

Medal distribution in Vietnam was directly related to status and the attitude of the headquarters command. Lieutenant colonels could be given a Silver Star just for flying low over a battleground or landing shortly after the battle was over. When Sergeant Bentley was severely wounded, I asked Pvt. Leroy Webb to help him while I called in our gunship support. I moved to a more protected position to use the radio, while Webb had to move out of his safe position and directly into the line of fire. Webb exposed himself to withering automatic weapons fire, and without regard for his own safety put his life on the line to help his badly wounded team leader.

I recommended Webb for a Bronze Star for Valor, but the battalion adjutant, the portly black Captain Jones, refused to approve it because he said Webb was supposed to be returning fire. I told him that Webb did what I told him to do. He responded, "Well, it was not heroic if he did what you told him to do; he was only doing his job."

This administrative drone had no idea what he was talking about, and had only read some guidelines in an army manual. It was what you would expect from an officer who never left the security of the battalion base camp, never came into the withering battlefield heat, never endured the brutal life on the line. I told the captain to kiss my fanny and walked out. I told Webb how proud I was of him and thanked him for demonstrating so much courage. The distribution of official recognition in Vietnam was sometimes as phony as the war.

War can bring out the best of character within an individual, but it also destroys many. For the pain it brings to those who are wounded, or to the friends and family of those who die, there is no justification. If you are ever faced with the decision whether this country should go to war, you must ask yourself if it is worth your son's life. If you are not willing to give up your own son for the cause, it is not right for you to ask someone else to give up his son. Always remember, every soldier who dies is somebody's son, husband, father, brother, or friend. They love him as much as we love our children, relatives, and friends.

In late June, shortly after the 9th Division was given responsibility for the Thai army regiment that would be op-conned (operational controlled) to the 9th when the unit deployed to Vietnam, I was offered one of the attractive tactical adviser assignments. I was extraordinarily lucky to have survived as an infantry platoon leader. In that position, I learned the meaning of what I once thought in OCS to be a hokey army slogan. "Follow Me" should never be taken lightly. It is an enormous and dangerous responsibility.

A junior officer in Vietnam combat had to be lucky early to live long enough to learn what he needed to know to survive. The only way to learn was through experience. The probability was, he would be killed or wounded before he learned enough to be a leader and before he learned enough to survive. My infantry combat experience in Vietnam had been a miracle. The medal citation, a simple Bronze Star, I am most proud of says, "Although on the line for over six months, Lt. Callaway's platoon, through his superior leadership, lost only one man and had very few casualties." The casualties comment is relative. I had about thirteen men wounded in action (WIA). My good luck was that many were just flesh wounds. Charlie Company and the battalion sustained a substantially higher killed in action (KIA) and WIA casualty rate than my platoon. And I mean substantially. The battalion had been easy prey in the beginning.

Vietnam brought about the metamorphosis of my confidence, character, and ability. All my courage evolved from my concern and love for my men. Except for my family, I have never loved anyone more. All my character grew from my personal courage. All my ability to succeed developed from my character. This personal growth helped me find my lost soul.

THAILAND:
THE QUEEN'S COBRA

I was selected to go to Thailand in mid June 1967 as one of the operational trainers and combat advisers to the Royal Thai Army's regiment, which deployed to Vietnam in September of that year. The Thai unit was called the Queen's Cobra, and the troops were all Vietnam volunteers. These soldiers, the queen of Thailand's personal regiment, split between two bases: Chonburi, south of Bangkok on the Gulf of Siam, and Kanchanaburi, northwest of Bangkok near the Kwae River.

The dispatch of Thai combat forces to Vietnam marked a shift in Thailand's policy. These Thai troops would be under the operational control of the 9th Infantry Division in Vietnam, and I was responsible for educating, training, and introducing to combat two Thai infantry companies (four hundred men), which was half their combat contingency. My counterpart was Major Surin. The company commanders were First Lieutenants Charlard and Suthep.

I spent ten weeks in Thailand. The Thai prime minister's son, Maj. Narong Kittachachorne, was the regiment's operations officer. Being in Thailand as Narong's guest at Prime Minister Thanom Kittachachorne's family birthday party in his home, with only our six-man officer advisory team and his immediate relatives, was hard to juxtapose and completely incongruous with the mud and blood of Vietnam.

Narong's father was also the commanding general of the

Thai army. Earlier that day, we had attended his formal birthday celebration in downtown Bangkok, located at the northern point on the Gulf of Siam straddling the Chao Phya River, the Thai equivalent to the Mississippi or Nile Rivers. In Thai, Bangkok is called Krung Thep, which translates into "the city of angels" and is their center of power and commerce.

Narong never paid for anything. If he had lunch in a hotel, no matter how many people were with him, he would just say, "Please send the bill to my dad." That was all he ever had to say, in any situation, anywhere in Thailand. Everyone in the country knew him. I do not know if the bills were ever sent to his dad. Everyone always seemed happy to see him, so maybe they quadrupled the bills before they sent them. But most likely the Thai people were exploited and never got their money, because it was obvious that power at the highest levels in Thailand preempted the law.

It was here I met Special Forces (SF), specifically the 46th Special Forces Company (ABN), whose primary focus was training counterinsurgency forces in Thailand. The 46th SF Company was originally Company D, 1st Special Forces Group (ABN), out of Okinawa, but most of the soldiers used to staff the unit deployed from Fort Bragg. Special Forces were the fabled airborne (ABN) Green Berets. They had an extensive complex of training operations throughout Thailand and were headquartered in Lopburi, which was also the location of the Thai army airborne operations. I worked with Special Forces officers 1st Lt. Jim Duncan and Capt. Walt McDonald, and eventually replaced them, but for about a month we had a good time working together with the Thai army.

Jim and Walt, unfortunately, did not like their Thai training mission. They originally were assigned to set up guerrilla operations to be launched from inside the Thailand border to harass the Ho Chi Minh Trail from the back side. The trail was a clandestine supply and troop movement route that ran from North Vietnam through Laos and Cambodia to South Vietnam. However, President Lyndon Johnson called off the mission because he was afraid it would expand the Indochina War into Thailand. Jim and Walt had a strong background in counterinsurgency guerrilla training, but I had much more actual combat experience. In Kanchanaburi after work, we used to hang out at a little restaurant overlooking the Kwae River (Khwae Noi) and drink Mekhong, the Thai rice-based alcohol beverage, or Thai Singha beer (9 percent alcohol).

Our Thai advisory team was on temporary duty in Thailand, so we had to fly back to the 9th Division headquarters from Thailand for one day in July to get credit for Vietnam duty for the month and to maintain our combat pay. We picked July 4, 1967. As I walked down a Bearcat road, I ran into my most noble point man and team leader, Sgt. William Joseph "Billy Joe" Price, who just happened to be in Bearcat. He thanked me for teaching him to lead from the front and for getting him promoted to sergeant, but he registered concern that the responsibility was going to get him killed on his next mission. The mission would be his last before moving to a division job conducting long-range reconnaissance patrol (LRRP) training. I told him, "No way, you are too good and experienced now." But I was wrong. The kind, amicable, and courageous Sgt. Billy Joe Price died on his last combat mission two days later.

Billy Joe was ambushed and killed by a small VC unit as he led a patrol in the "bowling alley." Our mutual friend, Phil Hilowitz, who had been with us in the 1st Platoon since Fort Riley, was there to medevac Billy Joe. Putting the bullet-riddled Price on the medevac chopper was an awful task, and a few minutes later the pilot called to say Billy Joe had died. He was such a pleasant, irreplaceable young man and a true hero. I still miss him. There will always be a special place in my heart for Billy Joe. He was one of America's best.

I learned about Billy Joe's death a week later back in Thailand from some Charlie Company personnel on R & R. I just wanted to cry and needed to find some peace, so late one July afternoon I sat alone on the Kwae restaurant's balcony, sipping my Singha and watching the endless, tranquil flow of water down the river. It was one of those youthful moments when you stop to take a breath. Life seemed to be moving so quickly, and some new unimaginable development occurred so often that there was seldom time for peaceful reflection. The river water moved along too. Like time, it could not be stopped or controlled. Occasionally, a foreign object popped up in the water or a boat passed, changing the picture, but these influences were short-lived. They moved on and the unrelenting river continued. Not more than a month ago, I had been in the Vietnam battlefield heat; in Thailand my life was a fantasy that could never have been anticipated. The exciting activities each day distracted me. This Thai adventure temporarily turned the Vietnam horrors and pain into distant memories. But Billy Joe brought the horrors back. I knew I would never escape from these awful memories.

On the weekends, Special Forces guys from around the country and some CIA officers met at Tiger Lilly's in Bangkok. At the time, there were many representatives from both organizations in Thailand. I am told that some of these guys still meet at Tiger Lilly's and celebrate New Year's there every year. A few minutes after New Year's Eve midnight, some start the race from Bangkok to Los Angeles. Because time starts at the international date line, in the middle of the Pacific, and moves west, they race against time and one another to see who has the fastest transportation support and can make it from Bangkok traveling east across the Pacific to Los Angeles before time moving west around the world—across Asia, Europe, and America—and celebrate New Year's Eve midnight in Los Angeles, as well, more than twenty hours later.

In mid July 1967, the training of the Thai units became

solely my responsibility; Jim and Walt would soon be leaving, expecting to perform recon work in Laos and Cambodia. As part of the transition, we took the companies on a two-week field training operation; Jim and Walt phased out during this exercise. Our first task was to conduct a river crossing, so we used the Kwae River farther to the northwest of Bangkok in Kanchanaburi Province, near the location of the famous World War II Japanese railroad bridge that British prisoners built and was later made famous by Hollywood in the movie *The Bridge Over the River Kwai*. Hollywood was not accurate in its presentation of the events. The famous bridge was not wood; it was not blown up by sabotage explosives but by an aerial bomb; and it was not on the Kwae River but on a parallel river. Hollywood even spelled the name incorrectly. During World War II the Japanese wanted to develop a direct connection between Bangkok and Rangoon, Burma, to move troops and supplies over land. So, using Allied war prisoners and indigenous conscript labor, they began the construction of the railroad, which required building many bridges and laying about 250 miles of track through incredibly ruthless jungle terrain. I walked through these soldiers' nearby graveyards. Thousands of men died building this railroad.

Once we crossed the Kwae River, I discovered that the Thai soldiers were carrying live ammo. They told me that drug trafficking, poppy fields, snakes, and tigers presented serious risks. You never knew when you might accidentally run into something extremely dangerous in the jungle terrain of Thailand.

The training exercise execution took us through sparsely inhabited areas deep into the canopied Thai jungle near the Burmese border but not quite in the mountains. I participated as an observer/adviser and let the Thai soldiers know when they did something wrong, which was about every hour or so, or whenever they made their next tactical decision. They often became lost because the maps were so poor, but we gradually managed to work our way through the rugged terrain and back to Thai civilization.

The Thai liked to celebrate and used any occasion for a party. When we finished the two-week training, the four Thai companies joined to set up a regimental base camp where the jungle and civilization met. Thai army trucks came rolling in with countless cases of Singha beer, two steers, two large pigs, and assorted supplies and foods. They dug two huge pits, used selected pieces of wood to start fires in the bottom of each, then fed the fires until they had about three feet of smoldering coals. They laid some type of special, almost flame-retardant palm leaves over the coals, then added more dirt and another layer of palm leaves. They put the butchered animals into the pits and piled more palm leaves on top. Finally, they covered the pits with tarps and buried everything under more dirt. Hollow bamboo poles with corked bottom ends were driven into the pits; when the ends burned off, the bamboo served as air vents.

Four hours later, we had a major barbecue. It was a festive occasion and a grand party. The Thai were happy that the two weeks were over. But Vietnam would be significantly tougher than this training. The difference between their field exercise and Vietnam was the difference between a summer shower and a tornado. I tried to conduct a summary review to explain again the differences between their little field exercise and Vietnam, but they wanted only to celebrate, so I gave up and joined in the fun.

In August we finished our final three weeks of training at the Queen's Cobra base in Chonburi. In this intense training, we drilled the Thai in the exact tactics and methods of operation employed by the Viet Cong. For me, the highlight of these three weeks was living in a little bungalow right on the Gulf of Siam. It was a beautiful location. The only thing I did not like about my bungalow was the Thai toilet, which was porcelain but practically flush with the floor with small depressions on each side for your feet. To use the toilet, you had to squat over it. No sitting here. This required a good sense of balance.

During the final three weeks of training, we had increased the intensity level and proposed another two-week field exercise, but the entire Thai regiment took an unannounced two-week leave instead. The advisory team was upset because we were running out of time. We had nothing to do while the Thai were on vacation but hang out in Bangkok for a relaxing and pleasant two weeks. However, the advisory team was starting to get frustrated and was disappointed in the Thai's progress. Apparently, the Thai failed to understand the magnitude of the danger in their future.

Captain Larry Waala, a former company commander from the 3d Battalion, 60th Infantry, 9th Infantry Division, who had been responsible for training the other two Thai companies, and I had both already concluded there was no hope, that these Thai troops were going to get slaughtered. We tried to impress upon them the VC's war skills and capabilities and tried to push the Thai to be tougher and quicker. They were attentive, but they simply did not know how or want to work hard. Their country was proud of them, but they were going up against the toughest, most experienced light infantry in modern warfare, and we knew the VC would tear them to pieces.

The Thai were courteous, sociable people and had a relaxed, carefree charm, but as soldiers they were just too nice. They did not have the competitive, in-your-face nature of Americans. They realized the absurdity in trying to establish certainties in the ever-changing, fluid existence we all face daily. The Thai were also masters at compromise. They were not fighters. Because of their political philosophy, which is to bend but not break, their country has not been occupied

Capt. Daniel
Francis Monahan

Lt. Chuck Payne.
A good friend.
He had a great
smile. April 25,
1967.

Gary Boyd and
Peter Nero.
Noble warriors.

Sp4 Darrell "Gus" Gustafson and First Sergeant "Top" Ed Johnson. Gus was the company clerk, but he went on some combat operations.

Lt. Bob Florey. One very funny guy.

Lieutenant Callaway

Private McKee, Sergeant McCowan, and Private Odom. Bruce McKee was a crushing loss.

Sgt. Billy Joe Price—a true hero.

Painful reflections. Sp4 Phil Hilowitz. The heart of a Jewish lion.

Sp4 Peter Nero was a great medic, with incredible courage and a wonderful soul.

Sergeant Rasch—1st squad leader, 1st Platoon, Charlie Company. He had a close call. Note the bullet hole in the smoke grenade.

Lieutenant Callaway and Lieutenant Colonel Zastrow. Early morning, April 15, 1967. It was a bad day.

Billy Joe Price and Joe Callaway—April 1967, Battalion LZ, Tan Tru. I had lost some weight.

Lieutenant Callaway and Vietnamese children.

A child's disrupted life. Our task was terrible.

We created awful fear for families. They were only rice farmers.

We conducted war in their backyards. Sp4 Phil Hilowitz

Reading mail in a dry rice paddy. Kind words from home.

Lieutenant Callaway. My friend Sergeant Marshal.

Thundering artillery fire mission shakes the ground.

A soldier's view from behind a dry rice paddy dike.

Vietnamese casualty evacuation. Battalion CO's chopper.

1st Platoon, Company C, 2d Battalion, 60th Infantry, 9th Infantry Division, South Vietnam, 1967.

Chopper aerial view. Typical rice paddy terrain.

and controlled by a foreign invader for nearly a thousand years.

They even worked a deal with the Japanese in World War II. The Japanese occupied parts of Thailand but never took control of the country. The Thai's most significant military campaign occurred about two hundred years ago when they repelled a Burmese invasion. It was the Thai army's most glorious moment, and they talked about it as though it took place only a few years before.

It was not the nature of the Thai to be disagreeable, argumentative, or confrontational. It was difficult for us because they were almost too polite, and it was hard to determine if we were all on the same page during training discussions or operational meetings. They tended to agree when they really disagreed, then would go ahead and do what they wanted rather than tell us ahead of time that the agreed-upon action plan was diametrical to what they intended to do.

If two Thai families were discussing the possible marriage of their children and the host family served inconsistent dishes, such as bananas and pickles, that meant the marriage was not going to happen. Everyone was polite and understood, and no one's ego was hurt. There were always subtleties in agreed-upon actions, and we had to learn to read the signs, including the Thai's tone and body language.

This was the way they treated people they respected, and they expected them to be able to figure out what they really meant and intended to do. To the Thai, everything was clear. Working with this cultural quirk was complicated in a war training environment. As it turned out, they were easier to work with in Vietnam. The fear factor made them much more direct.

The Thai form of Buddhism, called Hinayana, which is based on reincarnation, contributed to their gentle nature. The Thai troops were always respectful of their officers because they believed a general could come back in the next life as a private, and a private today could come back as a general, and each would then expect the same respect they had received in the previous life.

The Thai men were, however, extremely tough on women, who were relegated to a secondary role in their society. Married Thai men engaging in sex with a female prostitute was an acceptable and standard practice, but any promiscuous behavior by married Thai women was strictly forbidden. The economically poor Thai actually sold their daughters into bondage and prostitution. I guess the males never considered they could come back as females.

The Vietnamese form of Buddhism, called Mahayana, on the other hand, is a more aggressive, religious-based philosophy, and the people were not so gentle. The NVA and VC were significantly tougher and better soldiers.

In late August, before the regiment, the advisory team, and I deployed from Bangkok to Saigon, the Thai king and queen gave the entire regiment a spectacular farewell party with the best Thai food and entertainment. I watched the merriment and activities but could not shake my concern that these Thai troops were not combat ready.

A few days later in early September, we sailed from Bangkok on a Thai troop transport ship. I was the only non-Thai on board. I remember standing in the wind and misty sea spray on the ship's bow as we crossed the Gulf of Siam and went around the Indochina peninsula and up the South China Sea to Saigon. I was thinking about this past year. My life seemed far away from my adolescent problems and the failures of my youth.

The rest of the advisory team and most of the Thai headquarters staff flew to Vietnam. As our ship docked in Saigon harbor, a number of senior American officers boarded immediately and told me to be sure not to tell the reporters who lined the docks that these Thai troops were not ready for combat. General Westmoreland was there to greet the Thai soldiers, the regiment commander, Col. Sanan Yuttasaphrasit, and Maj. Gen. Ban Cha Minetrakinetia, the Thai ambassador to South Vietnam. The Thai general said that Thailand wanted to unite with other nations in the collective effort against communism. A welcoming Vietnamese band played "Colonel Bogey's March" off key. A petite Vietnamese actress, Miss Pham Mai, placed a garland of roses and carnations around the neck of Colonel Sanan. As the troops stepped down the gangway, General Westmoreland said, "Boy, these are sharp-looking troops, aren't they?" We made the second page of the *New York Times*.

Later I was told that U.S. politicians paid Thailand $100 million and gave this Thai unit our state-of-the-art combat equipment and weaponry as an incentive to deploy this Queen's Cobra unit to Vietnam. No wonder we were invited to such fine parties in Thailand. As a commemorative gift, the Thai officers gave me a Queen's Cobra ring, which is not of great economic value but is something I have always treasured. The Thai troops also gave me a Buddha necklace to protect me on our combat operations.

On my first real Thai combat mission in Vietnam, after the transport choppers had dropped us off in a III Corps jungle in Bien Hoa Province, I noticed lots of opened C-ration cans with food residue littering the terrain and footprints made by U.S. jungle boots everywhere in the area of our operation. The comparatively large-foot boot tracks and the C-ration can remains seemed fresh, so I called to check with division because I did not want to run into an American infantry unit by accident, especially with these two Asian companies. Much to my amazement, I learned that the army had sent a 9th Infantry company to sweep the area the day before to be sure all the VC were cleared out prior to the Thai operation.

We soon figured out that the presence of the Thai army in Vietnam was a ploy by the United States to show support for our war effort in Vietnam by another Asian country. There was no real intent to put these Thai troops at great risk. The United States did not want the bad publicity of a major Thai defeat. The American commanders made sure the areas to which the Thai were sent were occupied only by small VC forces. The Thai army did not know they were being sheltered. The Queen's Cobra deployment to Vietnam was an expensive U.S. public relations sham that cost our citizens a fortune—a fortune the Thai government did not share with its people but distributed only within the country's power structure.

When we completed our participation in the Thai indoctrination into Vietnam, Col. Sanan Yuttasaphrasit, the regimental commander, representing the queen of Thailand, gave each member of the advisory team a lifetime honorary membership into the Queen's Cobra and the Royal Thai Army. We were given a document with the queen's seal formalizing this award. I have recently been told by a Thai U.S. citizen who saw the document that no more than fifteen to twenty Americans have ever been given this recognition by the queen and the Royal Thai Army.

We lost very few Thai on combat operations. Captain Larry Waala lost two Thai on patrol because a soldier forgot to crimp a grenade pin; a bush branch caught the ring and pulled the pin, killing the negligent soldier and the buddy to his front. Another Thai soldier was shot in the chest, but one of his Buddha necklace amulets stopped the bullet from driving into his body. The Thai felt that was a positive sign from Buddha that he was looking after them. I thought the 9th Infantry Division CG must be related to Buddha, because he was giving the Thai such easy missions.

During September and October 1967, I continued to work with the Thai, integrating them into the 9th Division and continuing their in-country training, but basically it was an uneventful time. When we arrived in Vietnam, our assignment designation was changed from advisers to liaison officers. American politicians and the U.S. Army wanted to present a more competent image for the Thai troops. They wanted to create the impression that the Thai were a capable and combat-ready unit that could perform at least at the same efficiency and image level as the supposedly more aggressive and brutal South Koreans.

Later in the war, Special Forces recruited and trained an eight-thousand-man Thai mercenary army. They moved the Thai into the Laotian mountains near the North Vietnamese border and used them as a counterinsurgency force to assist the CIA's existing Montagnard (mountain people), Mnongs, and Mco tribal mercenaries in Laos. The Thai reportedly proved to be effective, worthy soldiers on this expedition.

In October, after my last mission with the Thai troops, Lt. Col. Edwin Chamberlain, former commander of 3d Battalion, 60th Infantry, and then my Thai advisory team commander, tried to give me a Silver Star—a decoration I felt was undeserved. The action was minimal, and I told him I had been involved in many situations a hundred times worse. He said, "You know, if a colonel writes your recommendation, you will get the medal." He added, "We want you to get this for all your missions over here. You know that every time out, you were the first person they were trying to kill. Don't you want people to know what you did?"

I told him, "The only person who needed to know what I did was me, and for all the missions you guys sent me on, I really never put the mission before saving my men's lives, which was against primary orders."

Colonel Chamberlain's eyes started to water. He said, "Son, you are the real hero over here. If you live through this war, you will have a good life."

To get the Silver Star, I had to file my report to say we were in a firefight, but I just could not do it. It was a tough call, but ultimately the principle was more important than the medal.

During this same minor skirmish, Colonel Chamberlain had been in the Thai headquarters when the Thai staff officers, listening to radio reports from my two Thai companies in the field, became convinced their soldiers were in a major firefight. Chamberlain immediately requested that an American infantry company be deployed as backup. The U.S. infantry company moved to the Bearcat tarmac to wait for choppers. Chamberlain got on my radio frequency to talk with me, and I surprised him by calling off the deployment of the reaction force.

Chamberlain and Major Walker, our team's logistics executive officer, both got on the radio, very upset, and said they could hear significant small-arms fire over the airwaves. I told them it was all outgoing, and if the Thai did not stop shooting soon, I was going to be in the jungle with four hundred Thai troops without ammunition. I had to stop the Thai from firing because they were killing only trees.

They said, "How can you be sure the weapons fire is all outgoing?"

I told them, "Experience. You can tell by the crack, and we are taking no casualties." Walker questioned me again regarding how I knew the weapons fire was all outgoing. Now I was angry and I yelled, "Major, because I am standing up."

That was the end of the conversation. Chamberlain later thanked me for not letting him overreact.

In Vietnam, I developed self-confidence and strong character, and did not want them to be stolen from me by either my need for recognition or the army's need for positive, favorable publicity. By then I had learned that self-esteem is never given, it is earned.

In late October 1967 our Thai responsibility was complete, and I had a week left in Vietnam. I located the 5th Special Forces recruiter in Long Binh and signed up for a six-month extension in Vietnam. I liked the men in Special Forces, and I was interested in Special Forces missions. Then I decided to go back to Tan Tru and the 2d of the 60th Infantry, my old battalion, to visit for a day. I ran into Sgt. Lonnie "Tall Man" Caldwell, a young black soldier from Charlie Company, 2d Platoon, and a protégé of Sergeant Marshal. Caldwell had been promoted shortly after McCowan. Caldwell thanked me for promoting McCowan and said, "It opened up promotional opportunities for young blacks throughout the battalion."

I told him, "There is no reason to thank me. I just put the best man in the slot, and that was my job."

He replied, "That's why I want to thank you, sir. Because you had the courage to do that. You made a difference, and I want to shake your hand and thank you. Before we got to Vietnam, the troops all thought you would be the first lieutenant killed, and in the end you were the only one left. We were all wrong. You were the best."

I will always treasure Sergeant Caldwell's comments more than any army medal and consider this to be one of the proudest moments of my life. However, what I did probably saved my life, because McCowan was so good, and his promotion facilitated teamwork between the races in my platoon. Although promoting McCowan created significant internal short-term disruption, perhaps it was the best personnel decision I have ever made.

The army gave me many Vietnam recognition medals, but I refused to authorize press releases, so no one in my hometown of New Canaan, Connecticut, ever knew about the medals, at least not from reading the papers. The army decorated and advertised live heroes partly to get more young men to enlist and to build a more positive image for the war. America loves heroes, and the army was working hard on a public relations campaign. I did not want, even indirectly, to encourage anyone to participate in Vietnam. It was not a healthy environment for anyone, including the sheltered suburban rich young men with whom I went to high school.

Extending six months with the 5th Special Forces entitled me to a month of free leave, so I headed home in early November 1967. The plane was a chartered commercial aircraft, called a Freedom Bird flight, and was filled with about 175 soldiers. I do not think I have ever been with so many people for so long—about twenty hours—who were so happy. They were friendly to one another, and overjoyed and ecstatic to be going home. I just sat and watched them in amazement. Their spirit, energy, and enthusiasm for life flowed throughout the plane. The flights were continual parties.

I spent the first night in the USA at my Grandfather Callaway's in Newport Beach, California. I arrived at his house in the late afternoon, extraordinarily tired after traveling for roughly twenty-four hours, and went to bed around 8 P.M. When I awoke, the clock was at eight again. I told my grandfather it was unusual for me to sleep so late, and he laughed. It was 8 P.M. I had slept twenty-four hours. It was a great relief to be home and wonderful to be back in America. My next stop was home in New Canaan.

During the month I spent most of my time in solitude thinking about what had happened to me and what I was going to do in Vietnam for the next six months. Sometimes I asked myself why I was going back. On the few occasions where I saw my old friends, the "Huck Finn" crowd, I was disappointed. Some still behaved like self-centered adolescents. They thought they were tough guys, which I found amusing. It was hard to relate to them; I felt like an old man among children.

My life of the past few months was difficult to integrate into life in affluent New Canaan. I had left an intense and demanding environment in Vietnam, where I was respected, and returned to New Canaan, a hometown that had no respect for me. People treated me as if I was still the same person they once knew. No one could relate to my experience, change in character, or maturity. It did not occur to them that I might have performed capably at a high level of responsibility in Vietnam. They did not ask, and I did not volunteer. It was impossible for me to talk about the war; I was not willing to expose my complex emotions regarding Vietnam. The only person who seemed to care about me was my faithful friend Bobby Stewart.

The highlight of my month home was the rehearsal dinner and wedding of Bobby Stewart's identical twin brother, Dickie. These were happy events, and I felt honored to be included. This was a part of normal life and, although I had issues with some of the Huck Finn gang there, it was important for me to see and participate in this joyous ceremony. It was the only time during this leave that I actually separated from Vietnam.

My friends knew something had happened to me—that I was different—and it seemed to make them uncomfortable. Oddly enough, some of them unknowingly had helped save my life in Vietnam. Near the end of my rifle platoon leader duty, during those dreadful moments when my spirit hit rock bottom, when I had nothing of me left but the shell of a man ready to collapse from the pressure and heartbreak, I reached into the past and found the memory of my friends and used the best personality and character strengths of each individual to give me the will to continue. During these dark moments, I thought of the personal characteristic I needed the most, selected the friend who had the greatest strength in that trait, and integrated my actions with that memory. I used these borrowed characteristics to help me behave and function effectively when everything seemed hopeless.

One of the few nights I ventured into the suburban social world almost ended in disaster. As I sat on a bar stool in a local tavern, the guy next to me asked if I was a soldier. I told him I was and had just returned from Vietnam. He asked me what I did. I said I served as an infantry platoon leader for about six months and as an adviser to a Thai regiment for the rest of my tour. He looked straight at me and, slurring his words, said that if I survived I must be a coward and that all good platoon leaders get killed. I looked this miserable drunk right in the eyes and contemplated crushing his head on the bar. I thought about it long and hard, actually calculating how many times I would have to drive his head into the hardwood surface before cracking his skull. Then I thought how angry the army would be if I killed this guy. So I got off the stool and walked away.

After a month at home with nothing to do and few people with whom to talk, I was ready to go back to Vietnam. In New Canaan, what I thought of myself and what others thought of me were no match, and there was no way to reconcile the disparity other than beating up a few people. I wanted to go back where people respected me and where I could be responsible for something. The army must have known that a free month's leave would drive a soldier crazy. I had no regrets about getting on the plane to go back to Vietnam.

THE 5TH SPECIAL FORCES GROUP (ABN)

My Green Beret friends in Thailand had encouraged me to join Special Forces. Because I had nothing better on my agenda, it seemed like a good thing to do. When I had returned to Vietnam from Thailand, my initial discussions with Special Forces in October 1967 were focused on Thailand, but in the army it was next to impossible, for some reason, to go from Vietnam to Special Forces in Thailand for a permanent assignment without first going through training at the Special Warfare Center in Fort Bragg, North Carolina, and the army was not going to do this for me.

The Special Forces recruiter I met in Long Binh convinced me that my best opportunity to help in the war effort was with the 5th Special Forces Group (ABN) in Vietnam, so I did my six-month extended Vietnam tour with the 5th Special Forces Group in Nha Trang, located on the coast, east of the central highlands in II Corps.

Before his assassination, President John F. Kennedy strongly supported and funded Special Forces, the elite army paratrooper Green Beret unit with the motto *"De Oppresso Liber."* Kennedy was the Special Forces' political champion and believed that this type of military unit was best suited for the guerrilla warfare struggles the United States would be facing around the world in the future.

Because I was not airborne qualified when I reported to the headquarters in Nha Trang in early December 1967, Special

Forces made me the area defense coordinator for the Special
Forces headquarters complex until they could put me
through parachute jump school. This was not a difficult job,
and it gave me the opportunity to move around all the government organizations in the Nha Trang area. I had two senior master sergeants (E-8s)—Sergeants Fernandez and
Overfield—and three radio operator buck sergeants (E-5s)—
Sergeants Rand, Love, and Smith—working for me.

We had a comfortable, sandbagged, metal-reinforced, air-
conditioned radio communication and coordination bunker,
which was practically next to my concrete-walled office and
living area in the A-503 Montagnard compound, adjacent to
the 5th Special Forces Headquarters complex (SFOB, or
Special Forces Operational Base). The senior sergeants alter-
nated twelve-hour shifts and the junior sergeants worked
eight-hour radio monitoring shifts. I moved around Nha
Trang at will, talking with and observing all the military and
government operations and activities. I went into the CIA
operation in downtown Nha Trang and talked with them
about the Civilian Irregular Defense Group (CIDG) program, then over to the air force base to talk about their security operations.

In my area defense coordinator function, I was invited to
all major intelligence and operations meetings, which covered not only Nha Trang but the entire country, and collected
significant knowledge regarding Vietnam. I went from the
platoon leader micro world to the Special Forces headquarters macro world. This also gave me the opportunity to learn
a great deal about Special Forces operations. I became familiar with highly classified (at the time) Special Forces–related
projects, such as MACV-SOG (Studies and Observation
Group), Phoenix, C & C (Command & Control), Delta (Detachment B-52), Omega (Detachment B-50), Gamma (Detachment B-57), and 403d SOD.

I went to the almost daily 5th SF Group intelligence briefings, which reviewed all enemy activities and engagements in Vietnam. At that time, the United States was also running what were referred to as "Black Ops" out of Vietnam that went all over the world. Some teams never even came to Vietnam. If you were assigned to Vietnam and were killed someplace else, no one would ever know the difference. You were listed simply as a Vietnam KIA or MIA (missing in action).

Major Carlos Carlos, from the Cuban Bay of Pigs group, and I became friends soon after I reported to the SFOB in December 1967. He was in transition to an MACV assignment. The United States bought the freedom of the Bay of Pigs Cuban officers from Fidel Castro and integrated them into Special Forces/CIA to keep them out of Alpha 66, the Cuban renegade brigade staffed with expatriates training in the Florida wilderness during the mid 1960s.

Carlos and I talked often about the war and the developments in Vietnam. He was reluctant to talk too much about his Cuban experience, particularly his prison time after being captured during the Bay of Pigs, because it was so gruesome. Many captured Cubans starved to death. The Carlos I knew was not the infamous Cuban assassin. My Carlos was a handsome, sensitive man of reason, with philosophical depth—very different from his friend Felix Rodriguez, who was torn, sardonically bitter, and almost fanatical about the loss of his homeland to the villainous Castro and evil communism.

Felix Rodriguez had been sent to Bolivia in October 1967 to hunt and identify Che Guevara. I was never sure whether Rodriguez was in Special Forces or the CIA, but he was definitely from the group of Cuban officers captured in the Bay of Pigs. I do not remember him having a rank insignia on his collar, so he was probably CIA, but he dressed in fatigues and was assigned to MACV.

According to Rodriguez, he had sighted the sniper rifle to be used against Fidel Castro and was the last Cuban assigned and trained by the CIA to assassinate the Cuban leader, but President Johnson had called it off after a policy change against this type of government-condoned murder. Johnson had decided that assassinations were bad policy, primarily because he was concerned about personal retaliation against himself. It was not a sudden moral awakening.

Felix talked about his assigned mission to execute Castro. He would have enjoyed pulling the trigger. Rodriguez was present when the Bolivians tracked down and executed Che Guevara, and this depressed him. The Bolivians apparently cut off Guevara's hands and sent them back to Castro. Rodriguez liked Che but hated Castro. Why he differentiated between the two was probably related to how the Cuban counterrevolutionaries were treated in prison after the Bay of Pigs debacle. Rodriquez also considered Che to be a patriot with a bad philosophy, and Castro to be a brutal, ruthless tyrant.

One day when Carlos, Rodriguez, and I were having lunch together in the 5th Special Forces officers' mess, Rodriguez brought up the Castro assassination. I asked him if he was proud to be an assassin, and told him I saw no valor or courage in shooting a defenseless man with a high-powered rifle from the bushes. He said, "Why? The VC do it every day."

I answered, "That's soldiers at war. Assassinating Castro is political murder. There's a difference."

I told him he did not look like an assassin. He was a squatty guy. He said, "What is an assassin supposed to look like?"

With nothing better to say, I responded, "Like Carlos." Then Felix went into a highly emotional extended diatribe about the evils of communism as justification for assassination. I asked, "Where did you get a name like Felix? Are you guys making up these names? Carlos Carlos? The only

Felix I ever heard of was Felix the Cat, and he was a cartoon character."

Up went the table, and Carlos had to separate us. I was having a bad communications day.

In January 1968 I became friends for a short time with Lt. Lewis "Bucky" Burruss, who was in the 5th Group's Mobile Strike Force A-503 (Mike Force). Bucky was a long-faced, blond-headed, tall and skinny stretch, highly emotional with a great sense of humor, and he had a particularly uncanny ability to tell a good story. He was an animated showman after he had too much to drink. He later became an original member of the U.S. antiterrorist organization Delta Force and went on to participate in the failed 1980 Delta Force Iranian hostage rescue mission, commanded by Col. Charlie Beckwith and directed by President Jimmy Carter. Burruss was a rowdy character but an intrepid soldier when he was a junior officer. He eventually retired from the army, surprisingly as a lieutenant colonel. Because of his dedication and courage, the army apparently overlooked his behavior.

The A-503 Mike Force was a reinforced Special Forces A-team that controlled and directed, at the time, a seven-hundred-man mercenary Montagnard hill tribes battalion based in Nha Trang. The Mike Force was the countrywide reaction force for all Special Forces camps; it was an elite, highly trained unit often attached to Project Delta/Omega operations. The dark-skinned Montagnards, called Strikers or 'Yards, were excellent hunters. The battalion was made up of several nomadic tribes, including the Rhade, the Cham, and the Koho, and these tribes were divided into separate companies. The A-503 also had a company of ethnic Chinese Nungs, who were usually used in defensive positions. The operation was later expanded, had the name changed to

Detachment B-55, and split into two A-teams, each with 'Yard battalions.

The 'Yards were aggressive, tough little guys, extremely fierce and very loyal to Special Forces. Each tribe was superstitious and had its own unique and bizarre beliefs, rituals, and customs. They asked me to go through their blood brother ceremony in which they drink fresh blood from a water buffalo and rice wine while sitting in a circle chanting and singing. They cut an artery in the buffalo's neck and let the blood drain into a jar. To prepare for the ritual in their normal habitat, they paint their faces chalk white, but I do not recall face paint on this occasion. After careful consideration, I decided it was not healthy to drink buffalo blood even though it was fresh and elected not to participate, which I tried to do without insulting them. It seemed foolish to have escaped a combat bullet only to be killed by a Vietnam microorganism from a water buffalo. Completing the ceremony qualified you as a blood brother, and you were given a Montagnard bracelet. Burruss gave me one of his gold-enameled Montagnard bracelet, and I have always kept it.

Historically, Montagnards were badly discriminated against by the Vietnamese. The Montagnards in turn hated all Vietnamese, so they had no problem killing them. North or South Vietnamese on either side, it made no difference. They hated them all. The Montagnards would soon get to demonstrate this anger with the Vietnamese in the 1968 Tet Offensive.

Special Forces Projects Omega and Delta were sophisticated reconnaissance and intelligence collection operations. Omega specialized in regions within Vietnam; Delta operated over a broader base throughout Southeast Asia. Each operation had a Vietnamese Ranger-reinforced company attached as an emergency reaction unit, to be used in the event a reconnaissance team got into serious trouble or found a good target; however, the project commanders usually preferred to use the A-503 Mike Force because they trusted them more than the Vietnamese. Working on these recon teams was extremely dangerous.

The story is fascinating of how Special Forces organized all the Montagnard tribes and religious sects, such as the Cao Dai and Hoa Hao, throughout Vietnam into their personal mercenary armies. As I recall, the Cao Dai worshiped Jesus, Winston Churchill, and Victor Hugo; the Hoa Hao covered their bodies with snake tattoos for protection. For almost my entire Special Forces tour, I lived in the A-503 compound with the Montagnards and with a small contingent of Project Omega and Gamma officers.

Project Gamma conducted the most sophisticated and successful intelligence-gathering operations in Vietnam, and my friend Capt. Eugene "Gene" Schweiker was one of their operations officers. The project had a compartmentalized network of well-paid Vietnamese agents throughout Vietnam and often kept suspected double agents in a metal Conex container behind our building, using this torturous hot box in the blazing Vietnam heat as a jail cell while putting the suspects through a series of polygraph tests.

About a year after I left Nha Trang, some of the Gamma officers got into serious trouble for torturing and executing a Vietnamese double agent who compromised a segment of their intelligence network. They apparently dropped him into Nha Trang Bay with his hands cuffed and feet tied. The political repercussions led to Colonel Rheault, the 5th SF Group commander at the time, being relieved of his command and actually jailed for a short period by Gen. Creighton Abrams, who had replaced Westmoreland as the MACV commander.

The political fallout regarding this situation was the result of a rift between Special Forces, MACV, and the CIA. General Abrams's reaction manifested his extreme displeasure with the publicity surrounding the incident. Abrams, the

MACV commander in charge (CINC), had never liked Special Forces because of its unregimented and unorthodox military style, its unrestricted access to unappropriated funds, and its generally close connection with the CIA. Abrams's actions were completely hypocritical, because justified murder in Vietnam was about as common as lacing up your boots.

Project Phoenix, conducted and executed by the South Vietnamese, was organized and directed by the CIA and Special Forces. In this program, known village leaders sympathetic to the VC were identified by our intelligence operations, and under our direction the Vietnamese went into these villages at night and summarily executed the VC sympathizers, reportedly often with Americans present or at least in the area.

We learned this brutal program from the VC. They had been doing it for years with village leaders sympathetic to South Vietnam before we developed Project Phoenix. When I was in Vietnam, I was aware of this secretive program but had no idea of its magnitude; it was not discussed openly. Reports now say that ten thousand Vietnamese were summarily executed by Project Phoenix.

On January 29, 1968, the day before the infamous Tet Offensive began, the Vietnam intelligence community did not have a clue regarding the movement and positioning of major NVA and VC units around South Vietnam's cities. Everybody was preoccupied with the battle going on in Khe Sanh; the growing significant threat to the Special Forces camp in Lang Vei, near Khe Sanh; and preparation for the Tet celebration. Khe Sanh was clearly a diversion or a warm-up created by the North Vietnamese to set up the 1968 Tet Offensive. Everyone was concerned about the possibility of Khe Sanh becoming another Dien Bien Phu, and they were extraordinarily focused on preventing that from happening.

We were taken completely by surprise by the well-planned enemy offensive, and this Tet and surprise attack began the Vietnamese "year of the monkey."

Nha Trang was a big party town for Americans; in fact, many officers from all service branches were partying in downtown Nha Trang when the two NVA companies attacked. About a thousand yards across the rice paddy, in front of the Special Forces Headquarters compound, we had a small but relatively safe LP outpost with multiple foxholes in a circle connected by trenches on top of a small knoll.

The LP was manned each night by a Montagnard squad and some clerks from the SFOB. The duty was almost a joke because we had a capable Montagnard Mike Force battalion only a thousand yards away, but it gave some of the SF clerks the opportunity to feel as though they were taking a more active role in the war than sitting behind a desk in the SFOB. After accumulating ten nights of LP duty, the clerks received special consideration and the highly coveted and prestigious Combat Infantryman's Badge, which an infantry soldier is normally awarded when he comes under enemy fire.

In the early morning hours of January 30, 1968, the NVA overran this position and killed all the soldiers on duty at the outpost. The NVA overran the LP simultaneous to the general attack on Nha Trang. On the eve of Tet, January 29, and during the battle for Nha Trang, I was the night duty officer at the 5th Group Headquarters compound and also was responsible for its defense. After the attack, the NVA lobbed a few mortar rounds into the SFOB and the adjacent Montagnard compound. During Tet there was supposed to be a general truce from war activity observed by both sides, but Ho Chi Minh tried to take advantage of our announced truce and did not honor the stand-down.

The Nha Trang Tet attack by two NVA companies resulted in a near traffic jam of jeeps returning from Nha Trang back to the 5th Group compound. The NVA could

have wiped out the entire Special Forces Headquarters staff
if they had anticipated this chaotic and almost hilarious retreat from Nha Trang and had attacked between the SFOB
and the town, effectively cutting these men off from safety.
I saw some frightened Green Berets come scurrying back to
the SFOB compound. The Tet Nha Trang party had ended
quickly.

The A-503 Mike Force Montagnards and the Delta Project
Vietnamese Rangers made quick work of these two NVA
companies. The little Strikers kicked butt, killing any Vietnamese who moved. If you were Vietnamese and on a motor
scooter, even the next day, you were slated to be dead. No
questions asked. They wanted the scooter. You were presumed to be an NVA or at least an NVA supporter. I had
wanted to go with A-503 into the Nha Trang battle, but I
could not leave my post as the SFOB defense coordinator
and duty officer. I could have been court-martialed if there
was a direct attack on the SFOB and I wasn't there.

The rest of Vietnam was the same as Nha Trang. The NVA
and VC were crushed. Only in Hue did they hold out for any
length of time. This made my job even easier in my last
months, because it was unlikely that North Vietnam would
try this aggressive strategy again anytime in the foreseeable
future.

A few days after Tet, the American Red Cross contacted
me regarding a family tragedy. My sister's husband and fellow New Canaanite, Lt. Richard "Rick" Larcom, had been
wounded severely during the Tet Offensive when his unit, as
part of a reaction force, was ambushed going from Cu Chi to
Saigon and Tan Son Nhut, the city's airfield and an American
air force base. He was with the 25th Infantry Division's
mechanized 3d Squadron, 4th Cavalry, also known as the
Three Quarter Cav. My sister, Joy, and Rick had married in
November 1966 just before I left for Vietnam with the 9th

Division. Nha Trang was stabilized, so I asked the 5th Group deputy commander if I could go see my wounded brother-in-law in the Cu Chi hospital.

Most choppers in-country were committed to war activity, but I found a seat with the CIA, who flew me to Saigon in one of their fixed-wing aircraft. They dropped me off at Tan Son Nhut, the airfield located outside Saigon in a relatively uninhabited area. At least it was when I arrived. The two agents I flew down with offered to take me with them to their compound and put me up for the night, because it was getting late and Saigon was under martial law with a strict 1700 curfew. However, I wanted to report in to the Special Forces Saigon operation in case someone was looking for me.

Parts of Saigon, down in the Cholon area and out by the racetrack, were still under siege. It was beyond the 1700 curfew, and the CIA men asked me again to come with them. My concern for Rick severely impaired my judgment. I made the incredibly stupid decision to decline their offer. I told them I would find a way to get to the Special Forces Saigon compound and asked them to just send me in the right direction. They said, "OK, tough guy," pointed the way, and drove off. I started walking down the completely deserted streets toward the center of Saigon as though I was walking around my hometown.

A significant amount of gunfire was reverberating in the distance out by the racetrack, and I did not even have a weapon with which to defend myself should the need arise. After a few more blocks, it was apparent that I had done something very foolish. My fear of impending danger increased with each step and every minute, because it was now growing dark. An unbelievably vulnerable and lonely feeling came over me. I had no infantry platoon or Montagnards around me now. They were excellent security—security to which I was accustomed. There was no one on the streets, and there was nowhere to go for shelter. I had no idea how to get to the Special Forces compound and had no one to ask for directions. The ripping automatic weapons fire in the distance continued to increase. Finally, I woke up to the fact that Saigon was still under siege, and the once vibrant town was now dead.

Suddenly, speeding—and I mean speeding—around the corner on about two wheels came an army three-quarter-ton truck with three GIs aboard. There was a driver, a passenger riding shotgun with an M-16, and another soldier in the open bed of the truck behind an M-60 machine gun. The M-60 was mounted high on a spindle so it could fire in all directions except over the truck cab, and the position was heavily sandbagged to protect the soldier manning the weapon.

Mercifully, they stopped for me and said they would take me to the Special Forces compound. The door gunner politely offered me the shotgun seat because I was an officer, but I hopped in the back with the machine gunner, and we went tearing off through the empty streets at terrifying speeds, making dangerous turns at every corner for a truck this size. We never slowed down and stopped for nothing, not even stop signs. I was lucky not to have been killed by the ride, but I would never have survived the night alone on the Saigon streets during the chaos.

The next day I hitchhiked again and hopped an army chopper to Cu Chi, where Rick's hospital was located. His wounds were bad but his spirits were up, and he was happy to be alive. He had been shot several times with a large-caliber weapon and lay wounded on the battlefield for four hours before being medevacked. He gave himself morphine for the pain, but also had to stay awake and tourniquet his own wounds during these hours to keep from bleeding to death. He was all alone. Everyone around him had already been killed or was severely wounded and dying. It had to have been a night of sheer terror and extraordinary pain. If he had not had a strong will to live, he would surely have died.

When Rick arrived at the Cu Chi hospital, the lower part of his left leg was attached only with a small bit of skin and muscle. When the local taxicab driver delivered that "bad news telegram" to my sister back home, she read the army's incorrect report that Rick's left arm had been amputated due to combat wounds. Some mistake. His left leg had been cut off below the knee, the left-hand little finger was shot off, and he had major tissue, nerve, and bone damage in the thigh of his right leg. I talked to the doctor who amputated Rick's left leg and asked him if that had been the only option. He assured me there was no other choice; he showed me the X rays and went over, in great detail, the process and actions taken.

Rick was heavily sedated in the Cu Chi hospital and was conscious only for short increments. I tried to be there when he was awake and stayed with him almost two days and nights before he was evacked. On my first night there, the VC mortared the Cu Chi base camp, which made me furious. It was frustrating that even in the hospital, these wounded, defenseless men were threatened once again. I rode with Rick in a military ambulance on the trip from Cu Chi to Saigon and finally said good-bye to him the same day he left for a hospital in Japan.

Spending time with Rick in that field hospital, listening to severely wounded, frightened men moan and cry out in the night, took something out of me. I was surrounded by so much pain and fear. Those were sad, soul-searching, and agonizing nights for me. Rick was strong, but to see someone from my normal life brutalized and have to endure the pain and suffering of this rotten war especially bothered me. Rick was more than a soldier to me. He was from my hometown, my sister's husband, and a friend of my family's.

Everything that had happened before in my Vietnam experience seemed like some type of quasi-fantasy. Suddenly, when I saw Rick, I knew it was very real and forever. This was no personalized development program for me created by God Almighty. This was not some movie fantasy in which I was playing a role. I was no longer a participant/observer and could no longer distance and detach myself from the reality of this war. It just seemed so destructive, so pitifully senseless.

During the January 30, 1968, Tet Offensive, while fighting two NVA companies in the defense of Nha Trang, A-503 lost two officers—Lt. Joe Zamiara, killed in action, and Capt. Larry O'Neil, severely wounded in action. Burruss asked me to join as a replacement. He was distraught over the loss of these two men. O'Neil, who had become Burruss's friend, had also been his basic training commander.

The night I got back to Nha Trang, Bucky Burruss got drunk and ran around the A-503 team house essentially buck naked, wearing only a web gear harness, pistol belt, and steel pot with no liner. He looked like a goofy naked stork and gave everyone a good laugh. But his inebriated condition also produced a poignant confession. If he were not in the army, he said, he would be nothing and nobody and probably working in the coal mines of West Virginia getting black lung disease.

I thought, hell, I can do something besides this; I do not need this craziness. I could tell that Bucky was only trying to justify the great risks he was taking with his life, but his behavior was out of control. He got into a fight with another officer, a leg (nonairborne) REMF (rear echelon motherfucker), as he called him, and broke his hand when he punched the leg REMF. The irascible Burruss was a good man, with a good soul and highly idealistic principles, who had been in Vietnam only a few months and was already manifesting combat fatigue.

Burruss and his Montagnard unit soon left Nha Trang, but not the entire Mike Force. I saw Burruss seldom thereafter. He went off to the highlands to recruit more 'Yards. The army wanted Burruss out of the headquarters area because of his behavior, and he never knew the impact his antics played in my life. My grief for Rick and the scene in the A-503 team house told me to go home. If I joined a high-profile SF project permanently, I would never leave. It was too much of an ego trip. I decided I had done my part and just wanted to get out of Vietnam alive.

I was resigned to leaving Vietnam. Rick Larcom was in Japan or on his way back to the States. Burruss was banned and on his way to the Vietnam hinterland, and the Tet crisis was well over three weeks old. Essentially the danger had passed, except for problems in I Corps. I needed to shake out some of the mental cobwebs and decided to go over to the officers' BOQ to see my young Italian buddy, Sp4 Anthony Tagliaferro.

When I initially checked into the 5th Special Forces in December 1967, I had stayed in the BOQ for a few weeks. Anthony was an orderly who looked after the place, took care of officers passing through, made sure the Vietnamese mamasan maids did their cleaning and bed-making jobs, and also passed out towels, pillows, and linen. Anthony was vigilant about keeping track of pillows and towels. Apparently, officers took them occasionally when passing through. While I waited about a week for my initial assignment, he and I frequently played chess, and concurrently he gave me the inside scoop on everything, which always included his own colorful opinions, no matter what the topic.

Anthony was a pleasant, energetic, and personable young man, and I used my limited Italian vocabulary to make him laugh. He often asked me about my combat experiences and had, down deep inside, the glory itch; I could tell. He lamented his BOQ responsibilities. I told him he had a great job and should be proud and happy to have such a good situation. I also explained the physically grueling, fearful existence of the grunt, line doggie, infantry soldier. I made Anthony aware of the extreme and indiscriminate dangers in the field, never glamorized or romanticized line combat to him, and tried always to discourage his nagging discontent.

I told him about an unfortunate incident that had occurred when I was in the infantry to demonstrate how tragic life in the field could be. A cook, Sp5 Robert Francis Stevens—whom I knew in Charlie Company, 2d of the 60th Infantry, in fact from Norwalk, Connecticut, the town adjacent to New Canaan—had volunteered for field duty. I told him to stay a cook, that the work was tough, not glorious but safe. He used to say if a New Canaan man can do it out on the line, then a Norwalk man should be even better. I couldn't talk him out of the decision.

As a member of Sergeant Marshal's 2d Platoon, he was killed in the "bowling alley" on his first patrol, on June 10, 1967, when he was shot through the side of his chest by a sniper. He never knew what hit him. He was just walking along in a rice paddy next to a wood line when he was drilled by a VC and fell over dead. It was so arbitrary and final. It seemed that life should have more value than this.

I was looking forward to my visit with Anthony at the officers' BOQ because we always laughed a lot. When I arrived, I was surprised to see someone in his place and asked where Anthony was, thinking he might be on an R & R furlough. The orderly looked shocked, went immediately pale, then became uneasy. He stuttered. I knew the look but did not understand it. Then he said, "Don't you know? Anthony was killed weeks ago."

I said, "How could he have been killed? He was a BOQ orderly. Did a mortar round get him?" The soldier told me that Anthony had been on duty at the LP outpost when it was overrun by the NVA during Tet. I sat down in a nearby metal chair. Anthony's death took my breath away. With my elbows on my knees, I bent over and put my face in my hands. I had never checked to see who was killed at the SFOB outpost, and I was the duty officer. It hadn't seemed important at the time, just a few nameless clerks and Montagnards. Had death become that insignificant to me, or was I just that accustomed to it? This war punished me once again by stealing another friend's life.

How could death reach in here, the powerful SFOB, and strike a defenseless kid who passed out towels? No one was safe from its cruel destruction. I couldn't accept the fact that this fine young man was dead—never to speak, laugh, or breathe again. It was so indiscriminate, so unfair. I got up and left the BOQ and never went back.

I walked immediately over to the headquarters company, where the first sergeant, another First Sergeant Johnson, verified the tragedy. Overcome by guilt, I chastised him for not telling me that Tet night when I was the duty officer. Sergeant Johnson said he didn't know we were friends. I was frustrated and discouraged and tried to drink to drown my emotions. I started at the Special Forces officers' club, which was a superficial place inconsistent with the carnage taking place on the battlefields around it and an alien environment for my hostile emotions.

I watched the surrounding, comfortable life, REMF hypocrites laughing and enjoying themselves, and felt like tearing up the club, burning it down, destroying it, so I went back to my room to be alone. This sorrow could not be drowned in alcohol, and the more I drank, the more bitter and depressed I became.

I threw a half-full beer bottle against the concrete wall of my room, then turned out the lights. Using the moonlight coming through my window, I stared at the beer dispersion pattern on the wall long into the night. I focused on it and analyzed every little detail of its configuration. I felt empty inside and thought of all the lost young men and of Rick. This war was draining the life out of me, and I hated it. Finally, I decided to go to sleep as an escape. I had to stop thinking.

I had horrible nightmares that night, and awoke exhausted and drenched in sweat the next morning. It was as if I had been doing push-ups all night. My bedsheets were also torn up. Anthony had been working for the Combat Infantryman's Badge and the recognition that came with it, and it got him killed. I hoped he was awarded the badge posthumously. He really wanted the CIB, and he certainly deserved it. Then I thought, How ridiculous, a life for a little blue and silver metal badge. The NVA killed one very nice towel boy and one very good human being. We kill them, and they kill us. The insanity continued.

On my first trip to the Vietnam Veterans Memorial, I looked for Anthony's name and couldn't find it. I later searched through the books that listed the Vietnam KIAs on The Wall but still could not find Anthony's name. Eventually, I remembered that the 5th SF Headquarters Company First Sergeant Johnson had told me Anthony had been evacked to Japan, where he died of his wounds.

For a while I thought I was spelling Anthony's name incorrectly, but I have since been told that to be listed on The Wall, you actually had to die in Vietnam. All the wounded men who died of their wounds outside Vietnam are not acknowledged at the memorial. If this is true, I intend to make it a special project to see that Anthony is given his proper recognition and that his name is added. This would be symbolic of another gross inequity and error in judgment associated with the management of this war. Who cares whether Anthony died in Vietnam or Japan? He died of Vietnam combat wounds. He gave his life for his country, and he deserves to be on The Wall with the rest of these American heroes.

FIGHTING SOLDIERS
FROM THE SKY

When assigned to Special Forces, I was not airborne and therefore a man without silver jump wings. I was a "leg," the derogatory term applied by paratroopers to someone in the army not parachute qualified. You needed to be parachute qualified in a Special Forces unit. My jump school program had been delayed in December and January due to holiday scheduling, then pushed back again after the major Tet Offensive in late January.

Finally, near the middle of March 1968, Special Forces put me through a one-week program at the Vietnamese Jump School in Cam Ranh Bay, and I learned all the mechanics of parachuting, including how to pack a chute. I was in good shape, so the physical part was not difficult. Our initial training jumps, from the rear ramp of a CH-47 Chinook helicopter, were pretty simple; all we had to do was hook up our static line, make sure it was not wrapped around our neck, and step off the tail ramp. Before that last step, we took in the spectacular panoramic view from about fifteen hundred feet. As I stood on the Chinook tailgate admiring the scenery, I could see in the distance the waves breaking along the white sand beaches of the South China Sea.

Next, we advanced to the smaller UH-1D transport choppers, which were a little more difficult because we jumped from a sitting position, but we had to be sure the chopper was stationary to be able to clear the aircraft. Getting our chute caught in the chopper blades would have been a fatal disaster. Ultimately, I jumped from many different types of air force fixed-wing aircraft, including the C-47, C-130, and C-123.

I always enjoyed parachuting; I jumped at every opportunity while in the army and probably made thirty jumps in my military parachuting career. Later when in the 10th SF in the States, we had training jumps often. My confidence level in the chute's opening was always high. I particularly liked the Special Forces T-10 chutes with the orifice in the back, which gave us the capability to maneuver the chute's direction somewhat by pulling down and climbing up a riser, one of four straps that connected our body to a deployed chute. It was, however, important that we judge the ground winds correctly, because the orifice gave the T-10 forward running speed.

Riding the wind into the ground on a landing was not good unless we wanted a broken leg, because the chute speed supplemented the wind. The art was to turn the chute into the wind at the last moment, playing the chute speed against the wind speed before hitting the drop zone, then land standing. I was proud of myself after my first successful land standing, but a sergeant on the drop zone yelled at me to fall over. Because army regulations then stipulated that we could not land standing, Special Forces paratroopers would often float gently down, land standing for two seconds, then fall over. We had to do a phony parachute landing fall (PLF) to pretend we had not done the standing touchdown we just did or be given an Article 15 for violating the rules. Military regulations!

Special Forces had exceptional people. Its obnoxious, macho, full-of-bravado, tough-guy image was only partially true. Special Forces soldiers could be obscenely arrogant, sinfully vain, unabashedly proud, and on occasion insufferably self-promoting, but they were first and foremost talented. They had to be courageous, clever, and resourceful to execute the assignments they were given.

One day I met a thirty-six-year-old captain and learned he was a reserve Special Forces officer with a highly successful law practice in Florida. He had activated himself to be sure he would not miss the Vietnam show. This was in 1968, and he was afraid the war would be over before he could get into action. I also ran into SF medics who were medical school dropouts. Most of these men were so well trained, experienced, and intelligent that they were light-years ahead of most soldiers in conventional infantry units. Some Green Berets were excellent soldiers and some were masters at working the system, but generally they were both.

I met Lt. Col. Arthur "Bull" Simons one day. He later led the team that successfully rescued Ross Perot's men who had been taken hostage in Iran. Special Forces sent me to Song Be for a day to talk with Colonel Simons about his operations and tactics because Col. Jonathan F. Ladd, group commander, was not getting the reports he wanted. I was to find out politely what was going on. Colonel Simons was hospitable but considered my presence a waste of his time.

Shortly after I left Vietnam, my friend Capt. John Hulka, from the 2/60th Infantry, where we served as platoon leaders, was assigned to the 5th Special Forces in August 1968. He became A-team leader and camp commander for a Special Forces fortification in IV Corps south of the Mekong River, just a klick from the Cambodian border. John's camp was almost overrun many times by major VC and NVA units. On one occasion the enemy was in full combat assault, and sappers—enemy soldiers specifically trained to penetrate the perimeters of U.S. positions and installations—entered the camp's defensive concertina wire. John's men had to lower their 105mm howitzer artillery piece to shoot flat trajectory beehive rounds, each with thousands of tiny steel darts, into the waves of attacking enemy soldiers.

John told one of the funniest Special Forces Vietnam stories I've ever heard. In Can Tho, he was on the flat roof of the C-team company headquarters building, which had been converted into an open air bar/lounge area to take advantage of the surrounding scenery, and was having late afternoon cocktails with some other Special Forces officers. They were watching some Special Forces soldiers not far away on the airfield tarmac trying to convince a CH-47 Chinook pilot and crew chief of the need to transport a water buffalo for their local Hoa Hao mercenaries to some distant place in Vietnam. The debate continued, with the Hoa Hao and water buffalo standing around them. After much heated discussion, arguing, and negotiating, the aircraft personnel agreed, making the Hoa Hao very happy.

It was a struggle, but eventually the Hoa Hao got the huge water buffalo up the CH-47 tail ramp and restrained with ropes to limit his mobility inside the Chinook. But the chopper's engines cranking up distressed the animal, and as the Chinook started to lift off the ground the aggravated buffalo decided he wanted no part of flying. He broke loose from the restraining ropes and started rumbling about loose in the chopper. To avert a potential catastrophe, the pilot pancaked the Chinook in an adjacent rice paddy. All the Hoa Hao poured out the still open tailgate, followed by a very angry water buffalo.

The surly beast proceeded to chase them around the paddy, then turned and charged, head down, right into the side of the helicopter, leaving a sizable dent in the aircraft. Everyone on the headquarters roof got caught up in the comic absurdity. Special Forces concluded from this experience that it was not a good idea to transport water buffalo inside an aircraft. It was much safer, although still risky, to sling-load a water

buffalo under a Chinook chopper. These animals definitely
did not have the airborne spirit.

John also witnessed another humorous incident in the
Delta when one of his team sergeants mounted a 106mm recoilless rifle on a small boat. The sergeant was proud of this
innovative weapon capability, so he gathered an audience for
a demonstration run. Unfortunately, the sergeant forgot to allow enough distance for the back blast, and when he shot the
recoilless weapon, the back blast hit a bank of tall reeds right
behind the boat. The displacement force caused the boat to
spin around about twenty times, throwing the sergeant into
the water. So much for that idea.

John Hulka was critically wounded in early 1969 when his
camp came under heavy mortar attack from the surrounding
wood lines. He was driving an army truck full of ammunition away from a populated area when a VC mortar round hit
the truck, causing its load of white phosphorus (WP, or
willie pete) ammunition to explode. John was severely
burned and temporarily disfigured by the white phosphorus
and spent six months in the Houston Burn Center getting
skin grafts and recovering from his wounds. White phosphorus burns when exposed to oxygen; water will not put it out
and only accelerates the burning. The only way to stop the
combustion is to cut off the oxygen supply by smothering
the fire. John survived numerous skin grafts, shrapnel re-
moval operations, and multiple infections. He was a courageous young man.

Another Special Forces officer I knew wanted to learn to
fly a helicopter and asked a chopper pilot friend to teach him.
In the middle of a large rice paddy, they conducted flight
training exercises. The Special Forces officer caught one of
the chopper's skids on a dike, which flipped the chopper; it
was destroyed in the resulting crash. The men were relieved
they weren't injured and devised a plan to cover their predicament. They went back to the A-team camp, got an AK-47,

shot the chopper full of holes, and told everyone they had been shot down.

The Special Forces accommodations in Nha Trang were much like a resort. The officers' hootches had wooden floors and screens and at most four occupants. Vietnamese mamasan hootch maids cleaned, made beds, and did personal laundry. The camp had a movie theater and concrete tennis and basketball courts. The officers' mess and club even had attractive Vietnamese waitresses, called *coes*. These beautiful young ladies were definitely not mamasans.

The Special Forces officers' club was exceptional, and officers, including nurses, from all military services around Nha Trang visited. The club had different rock 'n' roll bands about three times a week, and slot machines. Mixed drinks were twenty-five cents. All these facilities in Nha Trang were air-conditioned. Socializing at steak barbecues was common, even on the Nha Trang beach in the evening.

Sometime after I left Vietnam, the SFOB sergeant major put up a Carvel ice cream stand near the 5th SF Group Headquarters building. He later put in, behind the SFOB barbershop, a massage parlor staffed by young, beautiful Vietnamese ladies. The Special Forces chaplain apparently discovered firsthand that there was inappropriate activity going on in the parlor; he complained to the Special Forces commanding officer that this was a disreputable, unacceptable operation being conducted within the U.S. Army facility and had the place shut down. After that, no one would talk to the chaplain.

One Special Forces A-team actually tried to jump-qualify a monkey. The monkey was a camp mascot, and they took him to the hundred-foot jump training tower at the Vietnamese jump school and had the monkey make five parachute jumps from the tower. He had his own customized parachute. They considered this sufficient for airborne qualification so the monkey could get jump wings.

The Nha Trang SFOB was easy living. It was like Disneyland, not war. I almost felt guilty about the time spent at the 5th Special Forces Headquarters and elected to live in a concrete building down with the Montagnards near my control communications bunker. It made me feel better.

The comfort in Nha Trang sometimes made me angry. It seemed unfair compared to how the combat infantry units lived or, more correctly, existed. The disparity was blatant. Most Americans did not understand that although we had 500,000 troops in Vietnam, only 10 percent—a mere 50,000—were carrying the full brunt of the war, living like animals in a line combat situation and risking their lives daily.

Life in the Special Forces A-team camps was not nearly as comfortable as in Nha Trang, and certainly more dangerous, but it was still much better than a conventional infantry unit's. Special Forces was masterful at creating comfortable surroundings. Even the A-503 Mike Force team house had a full bar, pool table, and air-conditioning. Special Forces conducted a major business trading war paraphernalia and trinkets with the air force personnel in Cam Ranh Bay for items of comfort such as furniture, mattresses, generators, refrigerators, and air-conditioning units. Captured weapons, uniforms, hats, VC flags, and so forth were all instruments in trading for merchandise used for comfort in these under-the-table transactions.

Special Forces even had the Montagnards make crossbows and arrows, jewelry, VC flags, and anything hot for trading that could be produced in their little sweatshops. These bogus items were traded or sold to the rear echelon troops as authentic war booty. It was American free enterprise and an entrepreneurial cottage industry at work.

United States greenbacks were illegal for soldiers in Vietnam to possess. The army paid soldiers and ran internally on special government issued Military Payment Certificate (MPC) scrip, which was used by all service branches and accepted in all in-country U.S. military facilities such as clubs and PXs. This was done to stop the outflow of greenbacks into the South Vietnamese economy and the black market. The color of the scrip was often changed at the military's discretion, meaning that all outstanding currency had to be converted to the new scrip within a specific period of time or it would acquire the same purchasing power as Monopoly money. This switch allowed the military to determine if an individual had a disproportionate amount of scrip; at the same time it would completely devalue illegal scrip that a crook might be reluctant to convert. This helped reduce corruption.

Some SF NCOs beat the system by encouraging the enlisted men to send their paychecks home and have their parents or families send them checks from the United States. The NCOs then cashed the soldiers' personal or third-party checks into scrip and gave them a 10 percent plus premium. To complete the scam, the NCOs sent the checks back to the United States and deposited them in U.S. accounts. This was one way that NCOs with large scrip holdings (supposedly from large gambling winnings) got all their money out of Vietnam. Some senior NCOs seemed to move freely between Okinawa and Vietnam, and a few owned bars and brothels patronized by GIs in downtown Nha Trang. Vietnam was a second home to many of these entrepreneurial senior NCOs, and they often extended their duty tours to capitalize on their lucrative businesses.

Money and merchandise flowed around Nha Trang. The black market in Vietnam was a major problem. I was told that even American weapons and ammunition were being sold on the black market in exchange for American greenbacks, and I am sure many men walked out of Vietnam millionaires. The key exchange vehicle was always the greenback dollar, because the army scrip and the Vietnamese currency (piastres, or Ps) had limited value in-country and essentially no value outside of Vietnam. The greenback was all-powerful.

I was not in Vietnam to get rich or to catch crooks, so these sub-rosa activities were of no interest to me. I was interested only in the war, so I ignored whatever was none of my business. I felt that to be too inquisitive was a good way to get myself killed, or at least sent to a place where I could be legitimately killed without any questions being asked.

About six months after I left the 5th SF, a young lieutenant in charge of the Nha Trang SF clubs and concessions was arrested for embezzlement. The bright, handsome man was a good friend of mine, but I had no idea he was involved in illegal conduct and am not sure he was convicted. Others were indicted in the scandal. I am sure that more were involved and significant other corruption existed in Nha Trang, because there were many men running around with gold Rolex watches and gold diamond rings. I expected some day to see someone drive up to the SFOB in a brand-new black Cadillac. I have always found it hard to believe that a good man such as my friend would compromise his character and expose himself to the incredible humiliation associated with larceny, but this Vietnam world was an evil place, and it corrupted and destroyed people.

In the late spring of 1968, my last months in Nha Trang, I spent significant time with the signal corps specialists in Special Forces. These men set up and managed the sophisticated communications equipment that Special Forces used to connect their operations and monitor NVA and VC radio transmissions. Major Lou Christiansen, Capt. Luke Boeve, and Capt. Bill Parker lived in a hootch together. Christiansen was in charge of all Special Forces communications operations, and Boeve, a West Point graduate, was second in command. Parker ran the 403d Special Operations Detachment (SOD), a signal intercept unit that monitored enemy radio transmissions.

These guys were like the *M*A*S*H* movie characters. They were technically competent and loved to drink and laugh. They sat around at night drinking martinis and making fun of the army and the stupid things it did. Christiansen and Boeve had extended their tours six months so they could terminate their army careers without having to return to Vietnam for another complete year and risk an undetermined environment that could be significantly worse than their current assignment and living conditions. They were hilarious, entertaining comedians who had a love-hate relationship with the army.

While in Vietnam, Boeve actually smuggled an entire radio communications system back to the States. Every day he sent home in the army mail one small component until he had all the parts for a sophisticated radio communications center sitting in boxes at his home. Luke told his wife to save the boxes for him to open when his tour was over. He did not want to get his wife involved in case he was caught. He gambled that the army mail inspectors would not recognize what he was doing. It took Luke almost a year to get all the parts home. He did this for amusement to offset the boredom that Vietnam created for these signal corps officers. Once they set up the communications system for a new operation, they had virtually nothing to do all day every day, so they looked for things other than drinking to keep themselves busy.

These officers and I had been friends about a month when late one night after a few drinks I began to tell them about my experiences in the 9th Division. I told them about Dan Monahan. They looked shocked and got very quiet. I asked them what was wrong, and they told me they knew Dan Monahan.

He had been in the 5th SF before becoming CO of Charlie Company. One night in February 1967 they were having a few drinks with him. In fact, Dan had been sitting on the bed in the same spot where I was now sitting. For some reason, Dan had pulled out a .45 pistol and shot a few holes in the hootch roof.

Some of the higher-ranking SF officers heard the shots and investigated. At the time, the 5th Group commander was Col. Francis Kelly, and he had been trying to clean up the unit's out-of-control, rowdy-bunch, cowboy image. Dan was to be made an example to the other rowdies. He was verbally reprimanded and asked to leave Special Forces. The army sent him to the 9th Infantry Division, where he became the Charlie Company commander. These guys said they heard he had been killed and wondered what had happened. I told them the circumstances of Dan's death and said, "Well, now you know. No one could give a better account than I, since I was there when it happened." This coincidence put a damper on the evening. I excused myself and went back to my place in the low-rent district with the Montagnards and thought about the shiny silver Special Forces pocketknife I lost almost a year ago.

By the time I was jump qualified, around the middle of March, I had only about ten weeks left on my SF tour and started to vacillate on my "let's just get out of Vietnam alive" position. I had good contacts and could have transferred into any number of projects, but most of them would have wanted me to extend another six months, and I did not want to spend an additional six months in-country.

I thought about Dan Monahan and the overlap in our lives. I had no interest in becoming a piece of meat for some megamacho, high-risk program such as a recon team leader for C & C, and decided to finish out my last few weeks in the comfortable luxury of Nha Trang. There was nothing left for me to prove to myself except that I could get myself killed. It was time for me to leave Vietnam.

My 5th SF time did give me a good opportunity to watch, learn, and better understand the war. By then, I knew that North Vietnam's strategy was to aggravate us in small fire-fights and skirmishes and wait us out. They were in no hurry. They had infinite patience and all the time they needed, and they knew sooner or later we would run out of both. Going home was a good decision for me, although I felt guilty because soldiers with my experience always believe they can save lives. This may be true in the short run, but eventually in Vietnam everybody runs out of good luck.

When I took the area defense coordinator job, I reported to Maj. Kevin Touhey on the 5th SF Group staff. When his tour ended in late March, I reported to the headquarters company commander, whose primary function was the administrative management of all enlisted personnel in the headquarters operation. About a month after Tet, Special Forces was given complete responsibility for the defense of the entire Nha Trang area; A-502, a reinforced A-team, was assigned the task. When my tour ended, my duties, which included just the SFOB, would have been integrated into A-502.

In May 1968, Captain Senneli took over the SF Headquarters Company. By June we had a strained relationship. I thought he was an administrative flunky. He was the consummate unidimensional military officer who had bought completely into the military rhetoric and the Special Forces image. When referring to Special Forces, he often used "we" as if he and Special Forces were one entity. The guy needed the military to define who he was. The weaker military officers always bought heavily into the authority, recognition, award symbols, military rhetoric, and structure. They needed the military to program their lives, values, character, and personality. The more intelligent officers were men with philosophical depth, analytical and elastic minds, and exceptional leadership skills.

* * *

In early June 1968, I had actually sat in the Generals'
Meeting, which included all the commanding generals in
Vietnam, conducted in the 5th Special Forces Headquarters
operations briefing room. Again I came in contact with General Westmoreland, who still had a distinguished appearance
and strong command presence. The guy just looked like a
general.

However, this Vietnam Generals' Meeting surprisingly
lacked inspiration and was downright disappointing. The
presentations and discussions were ambiguous. No one
stepped forward with an innovative idea or a strong position
on any topic. I expected to be reassured that we really knew
what we were doing in Vietnam and that there was a coherent, logical plan for victory, but I left with the feeling that although America had deployed and positioned its armies well,
it was not sure how to use these soldiers in a guerrilla war.

I am certain these great leaders were tentative and unsure
because a political firestorm was raging back in the States
over America's participation in this war, which had already
destroyed Johnson's presidency. Presidential candidate Senator Robert Kennedy and Reverend Martin Luther King, Jr.,
had recently been assassinated, and America was on the
verge of political chaos.

A sense of uncertainty, unexpressed confusion, and lost
confidence had eroded the spirit and power of the meeting,
and the absence of enthusiastic and persuasive leadership
created an atmosphere with an underlying feeling of loss and
failure. It was not until many years later that I learned our
politicians were actually making many of the tactical execution line decisions in the war. This knowledge helped me
better understand our military leadership's subdued behavior
at this extraordinary meeting.

As I sat in the back of the Special Forces briefing room
just behind all the American and ARVN generals, CIA and

other key intelligence directors, I laughed to myself, remembering how difficult it was for me to graduate from high school. It was humorous to be sitting in this small room with all these incredibly powerful and successful men, when only a few years ago I was the Lang's Pharmacy delivery boy and having a tough time with that responsibility.

I left the meeting bewildered about what direction we were going in Vietnam. I could feel the pall of death as the Vietnam political winds began to turn, and so could the army. This was the beginning of the long, final chapter to the Vietnam War. The meeting was a funeral. I didn't know it then, but these astute men knew that Vietnam was terminal. In retrospect, I understand their distant, solemn faces that gray day.

Captain Senneli was upset that I had been invited to the General's Meeting and he wasn't included. His belligerence toward me continued to increase. I had about three weeks left on my Special Forces tour when he asked me to volunteer for an allegedly special and secret mission. I asked him what it was, and he refused to tell me. I asked him to let me speak to the mission's commanding officer, and he refused. He said "we" want you to volunteer your life. I told him I could not volunteer my life unless I understood the reason and purpose for the action. He said, "That is all 'we' will tell you." He then delivered all the usual flag, country, and patriotism rhetoric. I asked him to give me until the next day to think about it, and he agreed.

I discussed the dilemma with my signal corps friends, and they considered the situation to be bizarre and highly irregular. They had never heard of a similar situation occurring before. They agreed with me and advised me not to take the assignment under these conditions, particularly because I had only a few weeks left in Vietnam.

Six months earlier, when I left my Thai assignment for Special Forces, Colonel Chamberlain had warned me that although I was friends with some Special Forces officers in Thailand, I would go to the 5th Group as an outsider, and they would not be inclined to worry about my life. He said, "Do not go to that unit and get yourself killed in some high-risk mission or project where they do not want to send their own people."

I also worried about the corruption that existed in Nha Trang. Someone may have wanted me killed because they were concerned about what I knew and what I might say when I left. I could have been taken out to Cambodia and dropped off with some suspected Vietnamese double agents on some trumped-up recon mission, which would have been sure death. Perhaps Senneli volunteered me for reassignment because SF wanted to use my head count immediately in the reorganization of the Nha Trang security forces. I never knew the answer.

I decided not to volunteer my life for this army robot. If I had been given more information on the mission or spoken with the commander, I may have done it, but under the circumstances I felt I had no other option. We were talking about the value of my life. To Senneli, my life clearly had no value. What Captain Senneli was asking me to do was entirely inappropriate and not consistent with any standard procedures in the army. This was an abuse of power and exploitation of patriotism by an administrative officer who thought he was a great military warrior because he was in Special Forces.

Tom Wood, Jr., who eventually became a gunship chopper pilot in Vietnam and was the oldest son of my Little League coach, had asked me during my month leave between Vietnam tours, while we were at a friend's wedding rehearsal dinner party, if I was just trying to get myself killed by returning to Vietnam. At the time, I ignored his comments because he had no knowledge of my past Vietnam experience and could not possibly understand my emotional connection or motivation. But his comments lingered in my memory, and as I contemplated this decision, I vividly recalled his words.

The next day I told Senneli I could not volunteer for the mission unless I talked to the mission commander. He said if I did not volunteer, he would give me a bad officer's efficiency report (OER) and ruin my career. I told him I had no career, that I was not a college graduate, and that it made no difference; my decision was a matter of principle. He gave me the bad OER, and I reluctantly signed it, even though it did not mention the volunteer requirement or our conversations. I just did not want any more issues. The headquarters company First Sergeant Johnson later told me, off the record, that Senneli's intentions were not in my best interest, and I had made the right decision in turning down the mission.

I later learned that Lt. Col. Charlie Beckwith, former commander of Delta Project (B-52) and later the original commander of Delta Force, was commanding a 101st Airborne battalion in the A Shau Valley and was looking for combat-experienced, airborne-qualified, company-grade officers to join him. If this had been the assignment, despite my negative feelings about the war, I would have been tempted by the opportunity to serve under Beckwith.

No one at a higher level than Senneli ever mentioned this sequence or issue to me. It apparently was completely driven by Senneli. Although somewhat incorrigible, Bucky Burruss represented all that I admired about the army. He was passionate, compassionate, high principled, and respected by his men and peers, and he embraced leadership. He loved the responsibilities and cared about others. Senneli represented all that I detested about the army. They both wore the same uniform but were diametrically different.

These accounts are examples of the sinister side of patriotism. It can be easily manipulated by the military or politicians to serve needs other than the apparent objectives.

Patriotism can be a general concept that obfuscates the decision-making process when addressing important issues.

A week later, on June 21, 1968, I was promoted to captain. Two weeks later, on the day I left Vietnam for the final time to return to the States, I went into the headquarters company office as Capt. *"Dai Uy"* Callaway to say good-bye. I gave my farewells to the company executive officer, Lt. Ronnie Stollings, First Sergeant Johnson, and the clerks. Then I turned to Captain Senneli and said, "What I have done in the army I did out of a sense of responsibility. You do it because you need a job." I walked out the door and headed home.

In July 1968, the Freedom Bird flight was just like my first some seven months before. The chartered commercial aircraft was filled with about 175 soldiers and was another continual party, but it was old hat to me now, and I slept most of the trip. I arrived in the States dressed in summer khakis, ribbons, spit-shined jump boots, and green beret and again went down to Newport Beach to visit my grandfather. I had heard about returning Vietnam soldiers being harassed by war protesters in the United States, but my trip from Travis Air Force Base to the Oakland airport and on to Southern California was uneventful. As I walked through Los Angeles International Airport, a man stopped me. I was somewhat apprehensive, because I didn't want to take any bunk from a civilian. He was a scruffy-looking guy accompanied by his wife and daughter, who appeared to be about twenty. She was attractive but had a disgusted, sullen look on her face and wore tattered jeans, a skinny braless T-shirt, and cheap jewelry; her hair was stringy and unwashed. Her dad told me I looked great and asked how old I was. I told him twenty-four.

He turned to his daughter and said, "Look at this guy. Why can't you find somebody like him to go out with instead of those bums you hang around with?" The girl looked mortified; I was shocked, embarrassed, and tongue-tied. This exchange demonstrated how the strain of youthful rebellion and the lack of adult understanding were creating a break-down in communication that was fracturing the American family. I thought to myself that America must be a wreck. I told the young lady that her father was simply worried about her; then I told them I had to catch a plane.

The situation was very different from what I had expected to encounter upon my return. But I was home to stay and not concerned with the civilian world. I didn't bother it, and it didn't bother me. I liked it that way. I was thinking only about my next assignment, which would be the 10th Special Forces Group.

THE 10TH SPECIAL FORCES
GROUP (ABN)

Being promoted to captain before leaving the 5th Special Forces took some of the bitterness out of my final days in Vietnam. The Special Forces deputy group commander who pinned on my captain's bars never said a word about any secret mission or lack of commitment or patriotism on my part. Regardless, I finally escaped Vietnam, returned to the States, was assigned at my request to the 10th Special Forces Group (ABN) in July 1968 at Fort Devens, Massachusetts, and eventually became the assistant operations and training officer for the group.

The army had honored my request to go to the 10th Special Forces particularly because they were going to restaff the 10th, which had been stripped of head count prior to its reforger to Fort Devens from Germany. Everyone close to transfer to a new unit was sent to his new station rather than moved to Devens, then moved again shortly thereafter. But this also gave me the opportunity to be near my brother-in-law, Rick Larcom, who was recovering from his Vietnam wounds in the Fort Devens hospital.

The 10th's primary mission was North Atlantic Treaty Organization (NATO) support. We focused on Eastern Europe, including the Balkans, but we were also responsible, to a lesser extent, for the Mideast. We trained for small atomic demolition munitions (SADM) execution and integration into the European resistance should the Soviet Union invade

195

Europe. We were trained to parachute in behind the advancing Soviet army and destroy the bridges behind them, cutting their resupply lines with the small atomic bombs we carried, then work with the underground resistance. There were many native Europeans in the unit and some real hotshot American specialists, including top-level skiers and mountain climbers. No one was expected to survive if we ever had to execute, but we never discussed it.

This was the army's glamour unit. It had just relocated to Fort Devens from the old Nazi SS headquarters in the Bavarian Alps in Bad Tolz, Germany. Part of a C-team company split off as a detachment and was scheduled to remain in Bad Tolz. We had abundant training money and our own air force wing. We ran scuba training in the Caribbean or the Mediterranean and ski training in the Alps. We actually flew troops in a C-140 from New Hampshire to Alaska and parachuted them in so they could get used to a long flight before a jump. When I was the training officer, I rented a submarine from the navy to run scuba training off Cape Cod. One day I flew to Washington, met with the Defense Language Institute, and spent $500,000 on a language school for the group.

The 10th Group trained and partied hard; Bad Tolz was a continual Bavarian *Oktoberfest,* and some of the revelry carried over to Fort Devens. The group was a close-knit unit with good camaraderie. We were a novelty at Fort Devens, which was a "leg" post, and overpowered the bar at the officers' club. Our presence put this small, sedate criminal investigation and security training post in shock. It was not a good marriage.

I joined the 10th reforger advance party at Fort Devens. My first assignment was temporarily headquarters company commanding officer. All the advance party troops, lieutenants and below, reported to me. My direct reports, who supervised all the projects preparing our Fort Devens area for the 10th's main body, were Sergeant Major Grandy and

Sergeant Major Strickmaker. Grandy was my inside organization admin guy and Strickmaker was the outside organization butt kicker. We accomplished a lot in a short time with approximately two hundred troops.

After I had been in my new job for about two weeks, Major Leets, the advance party CO, asked me if I wanted to give some of the junior lieutenants more responsibility. I told him they could work with the lower-ranking NCOs on their projects and learn something about leadership, but we did not have time to work with these kids now. They were twenty-two, and I was twenty-four, an old veteran by then. I told Leets I wanted to stick with Grandy and Strickmaker as my right-hand men because they each had more than twenty years' military experience and knew how to get things done. He said, "I just wanted to see what you'd say. You'll do fine." It was a one-question quiz, and I passed.

When the 10th completed the relocation to Fort Devens, the post had us conduct a group parade as part of the official welcome ceremony. The 10th Special Forces Group CO, Col. Richard Green, wanted me to have the headquarters company command for the parade because I had done such a good job with the advance party unit, and he wanted a captain combat veteran with a Combat Infantryman's Badge and war ribbons up front rather than some young green lieutenant.

The group commander, his staff, and the colors led the parade. My headquarters company and the three Special Forces C-team line companies followed. We wore our dress green uniforms and marched across Fort Devens, where the post marching band met us near the parade field. The band members eventually positioned themselves next to the reviewing stand and played all the popular John Philip Sousa marches, including "Stars & Strips Forever," "U.S. Field Artillery March," "Semper Fidelis," "Washington Post March," and "El Capitan."

The post came out en masse to watch and greet us. We did

a pass and review by the post commander and the reviewing stand. When I did the eyes right and saluted, I was a little concerned I would trip, but it went fine. The four companies passed the reviewing stand, marched down the parade field, turned back up the field, and came on line facing Colonel Green and his staff, who were on the parade field in front of the post commander on the reviewing stand.

My guidon bearer was just to my left and rear, and my company was behind me. We stood at attention as the other three companies came on line to our left. I peeked out the corner of my eyes to see them. It was a beautiful early fall New England day. When Colonel Green did an about-face to present the 10th Group to the post commander, I had to cheat and turn my head a little to look. It was a great cheat. I could see the C-team company commanders, Lt. Col. Martin Beck and Lt. Col. Jim Cole, standing to my left with a big grin on their faces. Their guidon bearers and companies were behind them. It does not get any better than this in the military. The parade field was filled with Green Berets. The post band was playing and the flags were unfurling in the wind. Everyone was happy, and I was proud to be there.

Then I began to think of the soldiers crawling in the stinking Vietnam mud. Fort Devens was light-years away from that army. Vietnam was very far away, yet so near to me. I thought of the wounded soldiers in Ward 21 at the Fort Devens hospital. I remembered how, as an acting platoon leader in basic training, I had marched the platoon into the barracks wall, and how I had just executed this parade perfectly and without concern. The only difference between my ability during basic and now in this parade was confidence. Then I told myself to stop thinking and, for one time in my life, just enjoy today for what it is. No guilt. No remorse. No analysis. No plans. Just embrace the joy, and let it be. It was a fine day.

My brother-in-law was in Ward 21 and would be in a body cast for almost a year to give his shattered right femur a chance to heal and mend. The stump where his left leg was amputated just below the knee healed much more quickly. Doctors had also cut off the knuckle and hand bone on the side of his left hand where his little finger had been shot off, which made it less noticeable and easier to manage. It was a difficult time for him. He had about six more months in a body cast when I arrived. But he was well cared for in this hospital, unlike some of the wounded Vietnam veterans in some Veterans Administration facilities where soldiers have horror stories to tell about their care and treatment.

I tried to see Rick as much as possible. It made me sad to be in the hospital and see all the wounded soldiers, but I always tried to put up a good front and suppress my own deep-seated remorse regarding the war and my personal losses. These wounded men already had enough baggage to carry. They did not need any more.

In early October 1968, the 10th SF sent me on temporary duty (TDY) to the three-month Special Forces Officers' Course (SFOC) at the John F. Kennedy Special Warfare Center in Fort Bragg, North Carolina. This was an engaging and challenging experience; I enjoyed the training and had a good time. There were a number of young lieutenants in the course, and I tried to give them the benefit of my combat experience and knowledge. There were also a few navy SEALs (sea, air, land), some more seasoned company-grade officers, a doctor, and an Iranian officer. The SFOC training incorporated all the skills, responsibilities, and functions of Special Forces in its principal role operating behind enemy lines with an indigenous, underground resistance army.

We were trained in communications, escape and evasion (E & E), operational techniques, survival skills, bomb building, sabotage, psychological warfare (psyops), foreign weapons, and more. We learned to build a bomb from cow manure and a thermite bomb from magnesium filings. We

fired all types of foreign weapons, including the heavy
Swedish K, the indestructible Russian AK-47, and the tiny but
powerful Israeli Uzi. The program was exciting and entertaining.

We did little actual counterinsurgency training but worked
on learning the Special Forces' primary mission. This training would not help the young lieutenants in Vietnam, but
Special Forces instructed them anyway, so they at least could
become Special Forces qualified and have some common
base with the SF soldiers they would work with in Vietnam.
The SFOC program's length would also give some of them a
few more months to live.

One of my worst noncombat army nights occurred in this
training program. To begin a two-week field exercise in the
pine-forested foothills of North Carolina on an unusually
cold December night, we made a full combat-equipped night
parachute jump, which meant we were each going with an
M-16 rifle and fifty pounds of equipment not including our
main and reserve chutes. The equipment pack, which included a rucksack, sleeping bag, food, blank ammo, demolitions, entrenching tool, and other survival paraphernalia, was
initially connected tightly to the front of our body under the
reserve chute.

Before we hit the ground, we had to drop the equipment
pack, which was attached to us on a fifteen-foot tether line.
This was rigged to have the equipment pack hit the ground
independent of our body to reduce the risk of injury. It was
important to judge this correctly and drop the pack only after
clearing all trees and just before hitting the ground. This was
no easy task at night. If the pack caught in the top of a tree,
we were in serious trouble.

We were flying in a C-123 aircraft and were supposed to
do about thirty minutes of low-level contour flying over the
treetops to simulate conditions when an aircraft is trying to

avoid radar, so the troops could experience the motion sickness this creates. Our pilot was a reserve air force officer getting in his required flight hours.

The pilot soon became disoriented and eventually lost. Thirty minutes turned into ninety minutes of flying in big circles, so we missed our resistance ground support group's light signals identifying the drop zone. At last, the pilot thought he had located the resistance group's light signals, so he put us in the door. I took the lead position for the stick, which was the army's term for the soldiers jumping.

Most everyone had motion sickness, and some had vomited. I hooked up my chute cord static line and moved to the open C-123 door as the pilot climbed above fifteen hundred feet, a safe noncombat parachuting altitude. I wanted out of the plane, and we waited anxiously for the green light—the pilot's signal to jump—to illuminate. The jumpmaster and I kept staring at the light, which was adjacent to the door. I was uncomfortable with the weight from all the equipment attached to me, and very cold and tired. It was dark below, and I stood in the airplane door for what seemed like an eternity. We already had been at this stage, with static line hookup and a man standing in the door, on two previous occasions this night, and the process was wearing down the stick.

When the pilot banked the plane sharply, I almost fell out the door and had to hang on to my hookup static line, which we are not supposed to do. The jumpmaster told me to put pressure with my hands and arms on each side of the open door frame to keep from falling out. I was too frightened and bone cold to tell him what I thought of his training at this point in time.

My apprehension was starting to increase dramatically. The jumpmaster was getting frustrated and upset, and I yelled a few unkind four-letter words for him to convey to the pilot. We were screaming at each other to be heard over the plane's roaring engines, and we kept looking down from the open door for the signal fires, but it was pitch-black below. Freezing air continued to blow in through the airplane door. My hands were numb and barely worked, and I was exhausted.

Finally, the pilot again told the jumpmaster over the phone that he had located the signal fires, and in about thirty seconds the green light went on. The jumpmaster has the final decision on a jump, but I did not care what he said, because I was ready to collapse. I was out the door about the time he gave a weak OK. At this point, I did not care whether the pilot was right or wrong. My chances were as good jumping into the unknown as landing in this plane. I closed my eyes and jumped through the open door into the dark, cold night. Geronimo.

As I counted to four, I could feel my chute open; I looked up in the dark to see that it had deployed properly, then looked for the signal fires. The chute seemed to be fully deployed, and I could see a string of fires, but they were some distance away. To ride in that direction, I turned the chute with my cold and barely functional hands by climbing the front-right riser, then began looking around for my friends. Hopefully, they had jumped. I thought I heard them go out the door after me but was not absolutely sure. There are usually just split seconds between jumpers parachuting from a fixed-wing aircraft. Even with the fast exits, the pilots always slowed the plane to keep soldiers from being spread too far across the countryside.

In the night I could not see anyone but wanted to be sure not to run into one of them. It was dark and quiet up there. I started looking for a lighter area on the ground, which would indicate a field for landing. I had stopped worrying about hitting the ground signals; they were too far away, and I was going to miss them by at least three hundred yards. I just wanted a safe place to come down.

The wind in my face told me that the chute was moving too quickly. Based on the time elapsed, I presumed I was getting close to the ground, so I started to climb my front-right riser to turn the chute again and slow down. Because I was not sure of the door exit altitude and could not see the ground, everything was a guess. It was hard to judge my distance from the ground because it was pitch-black below. Then I started to worry that the dark area might be a lake. At this point, I had to take whatever was below and just hoped it was not water. If it was, I had to be prepared to get out of all the equipment quickly or drown.

I dropped my pack a few seconds before my anticipated impact and prepared to hit the ground. Fortunately, the turn had slowed down my chute speed. My pack hit, and a split second later I hit hard. It was dirt. Wonderful dirt! I was OK but had hit *terra firma* like a sack of potatoes. It was not graceful. Not getting hurt on this type of night jump is complete luck. We had little control, and every decision was guesswork.

In night parachuting, we were sure of only one thing, which was at some point very soon we would make physical contact with some part of the earth. This was significantly more difficult than the standard daytime training jumps, which were fun in comparison. Night jumping was probably why Special Forces officers were paid an extra $110 a month.

My landing zone was a strange-looking place in which all the surrounding trees looked dead, but I was just happy to be in one piece. I had no idea where I was, but I heard people talking in the distance and started to gather my parachute. In a few minutes, shooting started. It was a massive weapons fire with live bullets and tracer rounds going through the area to my right, about seventy-five feet from my position.

For a second, I thought this was a surprise live-fire training exercise and was too frightened to be angry or rational. Immediately my reflexes took over, because this was almost like Vietnam. I got close to the ground, then started crawling. I looked for something to get behind and found a large hole about four feet deep. I thought about all the snakes in North Carolina but got into the hole anyway.

What the air force pilot thought to be our resistance group's signal fires were actually the warming fires of soldiers conducting a night live-fire weapons training exercise. The pilot had dropped us into a firing range. I was eventually rescued. Of the twelve-man stick, only one soldier had a broken arm and one had a broken leg. The soldier with the broken leg forgot to drop his pack, rode his T-10 parachute with the wind, and drove into the ground. This was a frightening noncombat-related army experience in which someone could easily have been killed. Training in the army, particularly in combat preparation exercises, can be extremely dangerous. Before the 9th left for Vietnam, during a major field training exercise, three men in our 3d Brigade were killed in training accidents. One fell into a ditch and broke his neck; another died in a jeep accident; and the last was run over by an armored personnel carrier (APC) as he lay hiding in tall grass.

The soldiers in this SFOC three-month program developed some good relationships. I became friends with one of the officers in our SFOC program, Capt. Shassoon Azzafar, and invited him to my family's home in New Canaan over the Christmas holidays. Azzafar gave me a preview of the ominous dark clouds on the distant horizon for Iran, telling me about the military threat that Iran felt from belligerent Iraq, and the constant military engagements the Iranian army had with the pesky Kurds in the border areas. He alluded to serious internal problems in Iran, particularly as they related to the shah of Iran and his rule of terror conducted by Saavaak, the secret police. The Iranian people were very dissatisfied with their government. Captain Azzafar told me he could be put in prison or executed just for telling me about these internal issues. This made me feel better about America despite all our problems in 1968.

For a great part of the Vietnam War, Gen. William Westmoreland was commander of all American forces in Vietnam. He was responsible as the principal military architect of America's war effort, and I had already crossed paths with him three times in the service. Sometime after I joined the 10th Special Forces Group at Fort Devens, General Westmoreland was recalled from Vietnam. President Johnson's popularity had plummeted because of the war, and he decided not to run for reelection. It was widely believed that the war was not going well, and Westmoreland was being unfairly blamed.

As part of his new responsibilities in the States, General Westmoreland conducted a trip to Fort Devens in the spring of 1969 to see the 10th and visit with the new post commander, Brig. Gen. John Cushman, who had also just returned from Vietnam.

I had already come into contact with General Cushman at Fort Devens because Special Forces' ability to disburse large budgets amazed him. One day he called me into his office and said, "You Special Forces guys know how to spend money." He told me to find a worthwhile project on which to spend $500,000 in two weeks because the post was running that much behind budget; he needed to unload the money quickly to justify an increase in the next fiscal year's budget. This is where we got the $500,000 to spend on the language school.

Westmoreland flew into Hanscom Field, a small airfield we used adjacent to Fort Devens. The 10th SF staged a training parachute jump to coincide with the general's arrival. Selected strack (very sharp) soldiers were standing in formation, spit-shined for the general to review. He walked the lines, inspecting the soldiers and stopped when he got to me. Noting his old World War II unit's insignia—the 9th Division patch—on my fatigue jacket's right shoulder, and the CIB over my left front pocket identifying me as a combat soldier who had served with the unit in Vietnam, he said, "Captain Callaway, I understand you recently returned from Vietnam. I would like to speak with you." He took me by the arm and we walked about thirty feet from the other troops. General Westmoreland said, "I would like your opinion about how things are going in Vietnam." He mentioned being in Vung Tau when the 9th arrived in December 1966. At first I was tentative. After all, this was a four-star general. Then I quickly consolidated my thoughts.

I told him fighting a guerrilla war with conventional troops was difficult. As I said this, I could see in his face that this was a great leader in deep anguish. He was a crushed and defeated man. I told him how the morale of the troops was good, their effort and courage were outstanding, and they all respected him. Then I really started hedging on the truth and said the troops supported his strategies. I tried to lift his spirits. Most troops did not have a clue as to what we were doing in Vietnam. Certainly, most did not even know what the word "strategy" meant.

This was one of those awkward moments when you know you didn't handle things well and forever wish you had the opportunity to do it over. General Westmoreland was an exceptional and honorable man. On an impromptu basis, at age twenty-five, I wasn't talented or knowledgeable enough to be more engaging and uplifting, and I regret it.

As the 10th Group training officer, I had a highly visible and responsible position. Colonel Green spent time talking with me and definitely liked me. This became evident when his daughter, Barbara, returned home from college in the spring of 1969 and he invited Captains Charlie Pfeiffer, Ray

Bradbury, and me for dinner. He had his daughter prepare the food and serve us. She came in to join us in orchestrated appearances but did not sit down for dinner. Colonel Green talked about how his daughter knew nobody in this area, because it was a new post for his family. It was an awkward evening.

Charlie Pfeiffer and I were already friends. We were both from New Canaan and often rode our motorcycles together. He had a Triumph 650cc, and I had a BSA 500 twin. Charlie talked without moving his lips, similar to Marlon Brando, and was a handsome, personable young man who went to secondary school at the famous Culver Military Academy in Indiana, then to the United States Military Academy at West Point.

After we finished dinner and left, I asked Charlie what this Colonel Green dinner meant, if there was some military tradition here unfamiliar to me. He said, "No military tradition, but he wants one of us to date his daughter."

"What about Bradbury?" I asked. The professional, taciturn, bespectacled Capt. Ray Bradbury was about thirty-two, much older than we, and had a master's degree in sociology. Charlie said he was a stiff, a token thrown in to set us up. I quickly replied, "She's a nice young lady, Charlie, but you have the great military education, so you handle the situation. This is your responsibility."

Charlie was a good guy and always made me laugh. On one hand, he was impressed with himself. On the other, sometimes he seemed troubled and lonely, and I was never sure if it was family problems or Vietnam. He once said, "How would you like to have spent almost your entire life away from your family in military schools and the army, and all you had to show for it was Vietnam—a war everybody hates." I will always remember him because he was an engaging person during a period when I questioned relationships. I had lost so many military buddies that I almost became afraid to make any more close army friends. I didn't want the pain of losing another personally connected soul.

Charlie and I had New Canaan and Vietnam as common ground and had a strong need to laugh. He encouraged me to leave the army and often said there is a better world out there than this. Charlie had a health problem and had to undergo frequent tests. He left the army a month before I did due to medical complications, and our paths never crossed again.

The army wanted me to do another tour in Vietnam and had already offered me, in writing, a regular army commission, which is an upgrade over a reserve commission. This was unusual given that I did not have a college degree. I asked about helicopter school, and they offered to send me. This required at least a two-year commitment to the army after flight school, and you know where a helicopter pilot went from there. They also offered to send me back to college, but in the college deal they wanted one more tour in Vietnam first. No thanks.

It was difficult for me to give up the army, but I ultimately decided that it was the best course of action for me. The army was the only place I had achieved anything, the only place I felt successful, productive, and needed. But it was time for me to move on. When the army learned that I was leaving, they were surprised. Colonel Green flew me to the Pentagon to discuss my career with them, and they tried to encourage me to stay in the army. I wasn't the only one leaving, though; at that point, more than 50 percent of the surviving officers in combat arms, including the West Point graduates, were leaving the army.

When the 10th Special Forces sent me to the Pentagon for career infantry officer counseling, the infantry branch officers mentioned what an outstanding background and record I had. I told them about the poor OER from Captain Senneli, and they said they did not count it because it was from a captain I worked under for only a short time, and I had so many excellent OERs from field-grade officers. I did not even discuss the circumstances. They told me that the poor OER would be discarded. The army was desperate to retain officers with my field experience. I stood there in the Pentagon, thought about Captain Senneli, and just smiled.

A childhood civilian friend and my Little League coach's second son, Gorton Wood, had talked to me for four hours one night some months earlier when I was in the 10th and made a strong argument as to why I should not go back to Vietnam. Gorton jokingly told me that his job was to keep the VC out of Boston Harbor and to date he was doing a damn good job. He was proud of his joke and got the biggest kick out of telling it. His real point to me was, I had done my job and now I should let it go. He influenced my decision. He had a happy, carefree personality, and it was good to see someone like him back home in a world that seemed so confused and bitter.

But far more important, I had already met a wonderful young woman, Susan Archambault, who was an Eastern Airlines stewardess, and could not justify the risk. I knew far too much about Vietnam then. In my last weeks there in 1968, Special Forces was already preparing withdrawal strategies. Although I felt guilty about it, in the spring of 1969 I decided to give up the army for Susan. She was very pretty—no, beautiful—a kind and gentle young woman who seemed very vulnerable in a very tough world. I needed to be near a kind and gentle soul. It was one of the best decisions I ever made. She became an outstanding mother to our three sons and is a major reason why our family is so close and successful.

A few weeks later, I took a day off from Fort Devens, put on my dress green uniform with all my citations, ribbons, and insignia, laced up my black corcoran spit-shined jump

boots, donned my green beret, and drove home from Massachusetts to New Canaan. I had no idea why I was doing this,
but the emotional need was compelling. I drove by my old
high school on South Avenue and saw the high school football coach conducting a phys ed class on the soccer field adjacent to the football field. I decided to stop. My 1961 class
had donated the football scoreboard to the school. Seeing the
dedication inscription brought back old and not so pleasant
memories.

As I walked across the field in Coach Joe Sikorski's direction, he walked toward me with a group of students. At first
he looked at me with curiosity. About the time I introduced
myself, he recognized me. The last time he had seen me,
about eight years before, I weighed only about 145 pounds;
now I was in exceptional physical shape and weighed between 205 and 210. I was six foot three. When he recognized
me, he just stared in disbelief. It was the weight and uniform.
As we started talking about the war, I could see the concern
on his face. He told me how worried he was for all the young
men who had to participate in Vietnam.

Less than a year before, on October 18, 1968, he had lost
Rick Bickford, his football quarterback in the class of 1962.
Bickford was in Rick Larcom's high school class. My current neighbor Pete Economos, who in Vietnam had served
with the 23d Artillery Group, as a 105mm howitzer battery
fire base commander, knew Bickford at the Military Academy in West Point. Economos had vivid memories of Bickford because during Pete's freshman year, the upperclassman
Bickford had harassed him unmercifully.

At the time, lots of young American men were paying the
price for the ravages of Vietnam, although proportionately
less in the wealthier communities. As we talked, the coach
put his arm around my shoulders and told me how good I
looked and how proud he was of me and how proud he was
of all the young men serving in Vietnam. Then he started to

cry. The coach, now the athletic director, insisted I go with
him into the school, where he introduced me to all his col-
leagues and assistants.

Coach Sikorski then took me down to the display trophy
case to show me the Olympic Gold Medal that Bill Tomey
had won in the decathlon event in 1968 in Mexico. Tomey
had graduated from New Canaan High a few years before I
did. According to Sikorski, he was not an exceptional athlete
in high school, but at the University of Colorado he worked
for ten years to develop the athletic capability required to
win the Olympic medal.

Sikorski was so friendly and engaging to me that it was almost embarrassing. He had always been considerate of me
when I was a kid, and he was one of the few people who, no
matter how bad my mistakes, always expressed some faith in
me. What made him exceptional was that he was like that
with everybody. Suddenly feeling overwhelmed, I told him I
had to leave. He seemed genuinely disappointed. I was having a hard time dealing with my emotions. It felt good to
have Joe Sikorski respect me. Everyone needs to have a person like this in his life and a moment like this.

Before leaving the school, I walked the empty halls to my
senior year locker. I stood in front of it, thought back to those
years long ago, then walked down senior row one last time. It
was strange to be in this place where eight years before I had
experienced so much failure and fear. It did not look intimi-
dating now.

I remembered what it was like to be so lost and demoralized. It was a melancholy, touching reflection. Then the bell
rang and young students poured into the halls. They were
everywhere—it was like an ant colony—and I felt like a
green giant in my army uniform as they scurried by me, chat-
tering away and laughing with one another. Although they
were too preoccupied to really notice me, I felt out of place
and left immediately. Their enthusiasm and youthful spirit

made me feel good, almost happy, and I left with a smile as I thought about their gregarious, delightfully spontaneous energy. This visit was one of the few times I felt good at New Canaan High.

I then drove farther down South Avenue to the New Canaan business area, parked my car at one end, and walked the length of the town and back. It was a warm, pleasant early June day. I clearly stood out in uniform. I stopped at the local bar, Pierre's, to say hello to Nick the bartender and look for old friends. Before going into the army, I patronized Pierre's only a few times due to my youth. Nick did not remember me, but he bought me a beer. I told him I had been on a difficult four-year journey and it was good to be home.

I looked at myself in the mirror behind the bar at Pierre's, but the reflection was not familiar to me. It looked like a Special Forces captain, but it felt like me. Close up in the men's room mirror, it looked like me. Who and what was I now? No one here knew me anymore, even if they recognized me. What would I be to these people when I took off this uniform. The person they knew no longer existed. How could I ever fit back into this environment where I had not fit even during my adolescence? Who was that guy in the mirror? Where was home?

Then I walked down to Stewart's Market to see Bobby Stewart, a noble friend, then back to my old employer, Lang's Pharmacy, to see Bill and Mae Lang. Unbeknownst to me, Bill had died of a heart attack some years before. Mae said Bill would have been proud of me because he never thought I would amount to anything. I laughed, but she wasn't joking.

It was strange to be walking around this town. It looked so much the same, yet I felt so different. I did not understand what I was doing at the time, but I knew that I did not belong here anymore. Basically, I was conducting my own parade. It was all I needed, and then I left. I felt good and was ready to move on in life.

When I had looked in the bar mirror, my introspective image was deeper than the visual reflection. Yet when I walked down the street, I saw myself as others saw me—a Special Forces captain. There is a comfort zone in a strong projected image, but by now I understood that if you want to build strong character, you must know and understand the real person in the mirror. A productive and rewarding life is structured only from internal strength.

My year in the 10th Special Forces was an important transitional step back to civilian life from Vietnam. It was akin to being part of the most powerful and wealthiest Boy Scout operation in the world. We had outstanding toys and generally a lot of fun. But even here the pain continued, as men I knew in the 10th SF, including Lt. Col. Martin "Marty" Beck and Capt. Louis "Lou" Geneseo, who had gone together to Vietnam, came home in body bags. These losses were painful and demoralizing.

A month or so before, we all had been drinking beers and socializing in the Fort Devens officers' club. Beck and Geneseo went together to Vietnam to do their duty and seek their glory, and now I was to become an honor guard at their funerals. Actually, I could not bring myself to go to the funerals. I already had so much sadness buried within and would not have been able to control my emotions had I gone. America had just put men on the moon—a giant step for mankind. I was getting married to Susan in a few weeks—a big step for me. It was all so confusing. This was supposed to be a joyful time, a new beginning, not a time for great remorse and anger.

I remembered Colonel Beck's dynamic energy, raspy voice, sense of honor, and smile on the Fort Devens parade

field. Lou Geneseo had come from the New England Reserve
Special Forces Group. He was from Maine and had volunteered for active duty when the 10th SF arrived at Fort Devens. He was a dedicated man who loved Special Forces.
These two men had not been in-country much more than a
week. They had flown out to visit a completely unthreatened,
remote Special Forces A-team camp. Their helicopter landed
outside the camp's defensive perimeter on an unsecured
chopper pad right on top of an artillery shell that the ingen-
ious VC had fashioned into a land mine. They did nothing
wrong except be in the wrong place at the wrong time. The
day I learned of their deaths, I went down to the Fort Devens
post headquarters for retreat, and later that night stood
solemn and alone in the dark at post HQ for taps.

Going to post headquarters for retreat had become something of a ritual. Every day at 1700, I had stopped, gotten out
of my car, and saluted to pay tribute to the lowering of the
American flag and to my fallen comrades. Many a day when
I was alone, I tried to cry but could not. The retreat ceremony
generally was both uplifting and a time for reflection. But after the day I went for Beck and Geneseo, I tried to avoid it
and worked my schedule to never be near the post headquarters area at 1700. I made sure I never heard taps again.

For God and country! I was tired of seeing men give their
lives for their country in this war. The phrase was starting to
sound ridiculous, almost revolting. I was angry with the
army and its proud traditions and responsibilities that left so
much anguish and sadness in its wake. And what was God's
complicity in the loss of so many beautiful, irreplaceable human lives? It all made me sick. Susan Archambault and I
were married on August 16, 1969, the same day as the famous Woodstock rock festival in upper New York State. On
September 1, 1969, I happily left the army. I was disgusted
with the wretched Vietnam War.

Vietnam was a tumbling napalm canister right in the center of my life. Few days have passed that I did not reflect on the agony of this experience. Over the years, the heartbreak has become less painful, and Vietnam seems to have drifted slowly farther and farther away. The grief and remorse over the terrifying events I experienced have become tougher to visualize and remember than they used to be. The survivor's guilt has become easier to handle. I do not get into dark closets anymore and sit alone, as I did a couple of times my first year back into the civilian, or so-called normal, world.

The anger no longer gnaws at my soul. Instead of internalizing remorse, I learned to cry again. That happened in 1995 when my second son, Casan, was diagnosed with Crohn's disease, an incurable, progressively debilitating disorder of the intestinal tract. The symptoms were frightening. My wife had ulcerative colitis, a familial disease. Casan's condition was misdiagnosed, it was later determined to be related to stress, much of which came from me.

The intensity and driven focus that grew from my Vietnam experience left me hardened and demanding. Over the years, I may have pushed my children too hard on occasion, but my vision of the world was built on surviving amid great adversity, violence, and horror.

It sometimes bothers me that my sons are going to miss the military experience. It was the best and worst of times. I have been careful never to glorify or glamorize war to them. Military training and camaraderie are great, but the reality of war is a horrible nightmare. The activities of war have no morality.

War is a catastrophe. We justify it and search for nobility and honor in its execution, but war is only a malicious attack on reason; it is social anarchy, the genocide of goodwill, and the slaughter of the soul. Major wars will undoubtedly happen again. Unfortunately, it is within our nature.

COMING HOME TO AMERICA

Most of us vets were happy just to be alive, but we returned to a world almost as miserable as the one we left in Vietnam. America did not have the bullets, the shrapnel, and the leeches, but it too was hostile. America was divided into those who supported the war and those who opposed it. It was a world of hawks and doves, depending on your Vietnam War point of view. Friends and families were divided.

The returning vet could barely hold himself together, much less deal with a belligerent and self-absorbed American public. The vets were not greeted with appreciation for their sacrifices—for doing what, by law, they had been required to do. Instead, they were ridiculed and harassed, often by rioting college students. The military selective service draft system gave the children of the wealthy escape avenues and captured the children of the poor. Soldiers suffered survivor's guilt and guilt from their actions. This was not "When Johnny comes marching home again, hurrah." Coming home for the Vietnam soldier was very difficult.

I did not have ill feelings against the antiwar protesters when I returned home. As long as they did not break the law, they had the constitutional right to demonstrate against the war. I was not even offended. What did offend me was the bitterness that existed in America.

I felt more comfortable in Vietnam than in America, but eventually I adjusted. When I left the army, I was very much

216

against the war. My position was based solely on the fact that the approach the United States was taking made the war impossible to win, and there was nothing to win.

After spending time in Thailand, I lost confidence in the domino theory and began to look for another justifiable reason for our divisive Vietnam commitment. Vietnam had striking beaches and lots of rice paddies, but that was it. If there had been a strategic economic reason, such as the massive oil reserves in Indonesia, I could have understood, or if there had been a humanistic reason, I could have understood, but involvement in Vietnam's civil war made no sense.

When I returned to the United States, I was not looking for recognition or approval, as were many returning vets. I did not buy into the Vietnam military hero program. My attitude toward Vietnam discussions was, I really do not give a damn what you think about the war, either way. Furthermore, I am not even going to waste my time to tell you what I think. I had learned in Vietnam to distance myself from what I did not like. To just step over the bodies. To make the next decision right. I was truly mission-focused, which I had to learn in order to survive the war. I felt very isolated, but I was an honors graduate of the "University of Vietnam." It was a powerful education, and it made me know that I could do most anything. However, the war's tragedies and the America to which I returned left me a very sad man.

Within two weeks of leaving the army and marrying Susan, I started college at Boston University (BU). This was August and September 1969, and I was twenty-five years old. Boston University became a bridge that helped me return to society and gave me the technical, analytical, and reasoning skills I needed to build a successful family and career.

My poor past academic record and more than four years in the army made college a challenging and almost frightening objective. But I found that if I went to class and studied, I could excel, despite my reading limitations. Most important, the Boston University experience gave me three productive transitional years in which to think through the complexities of the war. I searched for answers to questions such as how the war had impacted and influenced my life and what it did to me as an individual. Was it just or unjust? Why were we fighting this war? What was this cancer doing to America? Why was I angry? Why did I feel guilty about not going back, about surviving? I sifted through all these issues and analyzed and evaluated what I learned in the war. More than thirty-five years later, I am still searching.

Vietnam was my reality, and this nonmilitary university world was almost like fantasy to me. When I left the army, I separated physically from Vietnam. As I progressed through Boston University, I tried to bring about a mental separation as well. It proved to be significantly more difficult. Each year, as my interests and intellect expanded, I increased the mental distance between Vietnam and myself. I recognized the power and influence the war would have over the rest of my life, but I did not want Vietnam to be all of me. I was afraid of being a fifty-year-old drunk who lived in bars talking about the war. I did not want Vietnam to destroy my life after I had survived so much.

Because the war was the hot topic on campus during my college years—1969 to 1972—going to BU was the last phase of the war for me. My Vietnam experience and maturity made me a novelty on campus, and my willingness to look for the truth and not be entrenched in rigid social, political, and philosophical positions helped me grow rapidly in the university environment. Everyone, professors and students, listened to my opinions and supported me as an individual. Returning to college was a good decision, and my success there gave me confidence.

My first semester I met David Tait, and a long-lasting friendship began. In the first week of class, this young freshman stood up and lambasted our sociology professor. He basically said that sociology was pretending to be a science but was only a bunch of bull allegedly using a scientific approach and terminology to mask its insignificance and shallowness. After class, I introduced myself to this pretentious punk, and we became immediate friends. David was brilliant and arrogant, and I liked his courage. I asked him jokingly what grade he expected to get in this class. He was the grandson of the famous English philosopher Sir Bertrand Russell and the great-grandson of a former prime minister of England. He was in the aristocratic intelligentsia, but to me he was just an interesting kid I liked.

David was instrumental in improving the quality of my BU experience. We actually taught a course together, called the Radical Course, on Marxist communism, under the supervision of our leftist professor, Howard Zinn. David led the discussions and graded the students. His job was to present Karl Marx's philosophy; I just helped out from time to time, giving encouragement when needed. Initially, I participated to explore Marxist theory, but eventually my interest evolved into developing a realistic and rational opposition, if nothing else but for myself. My early relationship with David set the stage for an important responsibility in my BU years, which was to keep my other young classmates from destroying their lives with irresponsible or illegal actions. I liked them and was inclined to be somewhat paternalistic toward them.

When the Ohio National Guard shot and killed five student war protesters at Kent State University in May 1970, causing college campus riots across the country, a former army officer, then a BU student familiar with my military background, asked me to make a thermite bomb to destroy the BU records he said were secured in metal cabinets. I knew how to build such a bomb with magnesium filings but was not that radical and disillusioned. He asked if I would teach his group

to do it, but I wanted no part of this foolishness. He was
caught up in the excitement of protest. Whenever possible I
tried subtly to foster a rational balance and sound judgment
in the student population.

The extremism that called for an American socialist revolution had an expanding student support base, but it was only
the product of general discontent and disillusionment with
the Vietnam War. I told students that their attitudes would
change when the war was over; then jobs and their future
would become more important. They were the children of
materialism. They did change and have become much more
conservative, but the 1960s experience perhaps has made
them a kinder, older generation.

Boston University was an institution of ideas, concepts,
theories, and ideology. Everyone had a position on something and everything. I noticed that most were just a rehash
of someone else's ideas that had actually been stolen from
someone else, and so on. I began to recognize that you
needed intellectual free will to withstand the ideological assaults you were bound to face in life. This experience had a
strong influence on me when I became a parent. I taught my
sons that they were responsible for their own decisions, actions, and the consequences, to be willing to question the status quo or the accepted tenet, and to never be afraid to be
different. This did not mean different in the context of ear-
rings, tattoos, and long hair. I was not talking about superficial rebellion but substantive social and philosophical issues.
Standing alone was sometimes necessary.

David Tait loved dogma, but often he just set it up to bring
forth a challenge. Tait had wild, curly fire-red hair, wire-
rimmed glasses, a heavy Canadian army coat, and a smoldering anger inside, but I knew he was talented and not
threatening to his fellow man. He was intellectually combat-

ive and loved to debate ideas. He loved rhetoric and verbal altercation and had a high energy level and a more mature view of life's complexities than most people his age. He always called me "Captain," never Joe, and it made me laugh every time.

David became editor of the *BU News,* an independent weekly school newspaper with a 50,000-paper circulation. I wrote antiwar articles for David under the pseudonym Dan Monahan. They were practical explanations of why Vietnam was a bad war. Tait loved the newspaper business and was not afraid to use his paper's power to influence the student body and stir up trouble. He often used the pen name David Russell as a measure of respect and connection to his grandfather.

In 1971, John R. Silber, president of the College of Arts and Sciences at the University of Texas, became the new Boston University president, and the fortunes of BU started to rise rapidly with his vision, energy, and drive. His abrasive style seemed to energize Tait in his student paper business. Silber hired William J. Bennett, one of his former Ph.D. philosophy students from the University of Texas and a recent graduate of Harvard Law School, to be the dean of students. Bennett was only twenty-seven years old. When he was not around, some students occasionally called him "Cowboy," because he always wore his Texas cowboy boots and used to make a corny joke about them being good for killing cockroaches in the corners of Boston apartments.

Bennett formed a student advisory counsel, of which Tait and my friend Clark Furlow were members. Bennett also asked me to be on the counsel, but I declined. He knew I was influential with many young people on campus. I told Bennett that one of my university goals was to keep the young BU students from doing destructive things, including destroying their own future, but I did not want to work in a formal structure, particularly because I had just finished four years in the very regimented army. I also thought Bennett was a little pompous, and he probably thought I was a little arrogant. My perception may have been the result of the significant differences in our formal educations and life experiences. Some students placed Bennett on too high a pedestal, which made me uncomfortable. We are all fallible, and achievement should be respected but never idolized.

This student advisory group worked out of Bennett's office, and I occasionally stopped by to say hello. Bennett eventually became secretary of education under President Ronald Reagan and was President George Bush's first drug czar. He also compiled *The Book of Virtues* and a number of other anthologies. Today he enjoys a successful career as a media commentator and advocate of ethics and morality. Bennett and I were not social friends but were philosophically similar in that we had a higher regard for authority, order, and traditional American values than most students, whose discontent, unrest, and destructive activities produced an environment that frequently bordered on chaos.

When Tait was the *BU News* editor, he asked me to cover, as a reporter, a student protest being conducted at Fort Devens in support of a "free speech" bookstore operating in Ayers, Massachusetts, a town adjacent to Fort Devens. The store was allegedly distributing un-American subversive literature to the troops; consequently, Fort Devens made the store off-limits to the post soldiers. Furthermore, the local police were harassing the business. Tait knew I was once stationed at Fort Devens, but he had no idea what he was asking me to do within the context of my past. I reluctantly agreed to do it, if for no other reason than to prove to myself that I was a free man with personal courage that extended beyond combat.

Only about twenty students participated in the protest. We

first went to the store, which was nothing but a little counter-culture bookshop run by harmless hippie types and was certainly nonthreatening to the United States Army, then on to the Fort Devens Ayers gate, where, naturally, we were stopped. Soon the MPs arrived in four jeeps. It was a pathetic protest, almost laughable, and I just stood in the back and watched.

Shortly, a six-foot-four, 240-pound black MP captain walked through the crowd toward me. "Aren't you Captain Callaway from the 10th Special Forces?" he asked.

I said I was, but I was here covering this as a news event for my college newspaper. I recognized the captain as a former WIA Vietnam patient from Ward 21 in the Fort Devens hospital. The soldier had convalesced a couple of beds down from Rick Larcom for a few months.

He looked at me with disgust. "What happened to you? You were a powerful guy here. You were somebody, and now look at you." I had a scraggly mustache and, although not shoulder length, rather long hair. I told him I was a student at Boston University but still had a top secret security clearance. "I don't care," he responded. "You are not coming on this post. You are not in the army anymore."

This scene was a complex situation with extraordinary irony. Here I was being reviled by a huge black MP captain for being nobody when from a young age I had been concerned about the problems and hurdles facing the black population. I was now looked upon as being weak when my decision to return to college was perhaps the most courageous intellectual decision I have ever made. I was denied access to Fort Devens and regarded as a misfit when as a Special Forces captain I used to waste, almost criminally, exorbitant sums of taxpayer money and was revered for it.

I thought about my participation in the glorious 10th Special Forces welcome ceremony and marching across the Fort

Devens parade field with all the Green Berets, and flags un-furling in the crisp fall wind. Was I a better man then? The MP captain looked upon the students as maggots. His disdain was evident. The students looked upon the black captain as the American gestapo, a co-opted, manipulated, sellout agent of the ruling class. I was happy he had done so well and was not behind a plow stock and mule in Alabama. It was a crazy, humorous, thought-provoking scene. The captain asked me if I didn't have anything better to do with my time. I laughed and said, "You have a good point there," and I turned around and left.

I will always appreciate the excellent education I earned at Boston University. The school's activist spirit made every day exciting, and the professors went out of their way to give me encouragement and technical help. But David Tait made my university education most enjoyable, interesting, and ful-filling. His humor and activities kept me constantly amused and engaged. He integrated me into the university commu-nity and kept me from being an estranged, detached soldier going back to school in an environment certainly hostile to the military. I felt comfortable at Boston University. My only regret is that I did not attend my own college graduation in 1972. Skipping graduation was a form of rebellion against formality that was common among college students during those years.

I was proud to be the best man in David's wedding in 1976. Bennett was there, and I laughed to myself and won-dered if he knew that David respectfully called him "Cow-boy" in earlier years. At the wedding, I checked to see if Bennett was still wearing his cowboy boots, and I was re-lieved not to see them. David was at Harvard Divinity School then and today is an Episcopal priest. He recently completed his Ph.D. in history at Oklahoma State University and teaches history at a local junior college. He is now very conservative and is known as "the Reverend Doctor."

After Rick Larcom was medevacked from Vietnam and spent about a year in the Fort Devens army hospital, he returned and graduated from Harvard. In the fall of 1969, I met a young local banker, Noel Bailey, in Winthrop, Massachusetts, the town where Susan and I lived. Noel asked me to talk at a Winthrop town meeting about Vietnam. He was a recent graduate of Bowdoin College and had helped me write my first Boston University paper. I felt obligated and reluctantly complied with his request. Perhaps I looked forward to it, but I definitely had some apprehension concerning the event. Rick was going to Harvard at the time, and I asked him to participate. About ten people showed up.

The other speaker at this event was a former navy officer, John Kerry, who has been senator from Massachusetts for some time. He promoted himself through his Vietnam story, and it was evident from his speech that he intended to ride his Vietnam experience into prominence. After Kerry gave his presentation, with a little phony Kennedy accent, which he, incidentally, does not have today, Rick and I gave our presentations. When we finished, John Kerry was almost apologetic for his comparatively limited combat experience, which he had portrayed as rigorous and dangerous duty. He was being a gentleman in acknowledging the hardships we had suffered.

In June 1970, a month after the shooting of student war protesters at Kent State and the student riots that shut down many of America's colleges and universities, Vice President Spiro Agnew, on the television program *Meet the Press* (or perhaps it was *Face the Nation*) said that America did not have and has not had American troops in Cambodia. I told my grandfather, Jesse Thomas Callaway, who was watching the program with me, that Agnew was lying and that Special Forces frequently sent recon teams into the Cambodian jungles, particularly to monitor the Ho Chi Minh Trail.

My ultraconservative, patriotic, and trusting grandfather and I had a bitter argument over my statement. He said, "You mean to tell me the vice president of the United States of America would, on national television, lie to the American public?"

I reiterated that he was lying and added, "We had major infantry operations in Cambodia many times over the past two years."

My friend Capt. Steve Franke had crashed his transport chopper just the month before, on May 8, 1970, west of Tay Ninh, two miles inside the Cambodian border. He had been an infantry lieutenant with me in the 2d of the 60th Infantry and was doing a second tour in Vietnam as a helicopter pilot. He was in Alpha Company, 25th Aviation Battalion, 25th Infantry Division, flying missions out of Cu Chi.

Steve was a giant in character but not in actual height; in fact, back in the 2d of the 60th, his friends respectfully skirted any references to height unless they were looking for a hostile confrontation. For some reason, Steve didn't mind his friends calling him "Peanut," but he was one tough, combative hombre. In a bar just outside Fort Riley, I am told, Steve and Bob Florey once beat up two Kansas State football players, each twice their size. Franke's helicopter pilot call sign was, appropriately, Little Bear.

On that May day when Steve crashed his chopper, he was bone weary exhausted, having flown "night hawks" on mission alert at a forward base camp for night combat operations most of the night before and "ash and trash" (routine noncombat flying—scut work) earlier in the day. When he went down on a resupply run for American troops in Cambodia, he already had eleven and a half hours' blade time that day.

The soldiers needed the supplies badly, and they had wounded men who needed to be evacuated back to Vietnam.

The hole cut out of the jungle for Steve's chopper was too small, but he had tried it anyway. His blade hit a tree, and the chopper flipped over; it landed upside down in a tree. Steve was knocked unconscious. When he gained consciousness, he could smell fuel—JP4. He told his rescue troops to pull him out of the chopper immediately, not to be concerned with his physical injuries. He did not want to burn to death. He was fortunate to survive with only a severely broken leg—a compound femur fracture—which caused the limp he still has today.

My Grandfather Callaway said Boston University was making me soft on communism and came close to calling me a communist. His and my bitter arguments made it clear to me that he had an inflexible trust in government and was unwilling to give me credibility despite my experience and knowledge. Agnew was later indicted on felony charges for taking kickbacks when he was the governor of Maryland. He had to resign in disgrace as America's vice president.

The Agnew incident inspired me to be more open-minded and less accepting no matter how overwhelming the evidence might be or how powerful the person giving the information. Eventually, it became public information that our politicians had in fact lied about having troops in Cambodia. My grandfather could not apologize to me, but he did say sometime later, "I guess you young people may know more than we give you credit for."

The Vietnam veteran returned to a homeland that gave him little credit for his experiences, ridiculed him for his honorable support of our country's laws, and demeaned him for his courageous sacrifices. It was a confusing period for most American soldiers. Even many World War II veterans, now the so-called "greatest generation," turned their backs on

Vietnam vets, yet it was the World War II generation's representatives who initiated and managed this war. We were just the young men who tried to fight by the rules and under the conditions they established. In our society, traditional relationships began to disintegrate and our social order started to fracture. This was the America to which many Vietnam veterans returned. Our great country had developed some ugly characteristics while we were away.

POST-TRAUMATIC STRESS DISORDER

Only the dead know the end of war.
PLATO

In 1773, Benjamin Franklin wrote, "There never was a good war or a bad peace." But peace is only the end of hostilities, not the end of the war. The war complications are far from over, as the wounded, grieving friends and families, and combat survivors start the recovery process.

Returning to normal civilian society was extremely difficult for Vietnam veterans. For many American combat soldiers, particularly the small percent who were the true frontline warriors, the return from Vietnam marked the beginning of the second battle for their lives. These soldiers were dropped back into American society unprepared for the adjustment challenges they would encounter.

Combat leaves mental wounds, almost a war neurosis—emotional and moral complexities that challenge the sensibilities of sane men. Veterans' war experiences become a dominant part of their mental information base and a significant influence on their personalities. If these horrific war memories are suppressed, they can become dangerous to the individual later in life.

Written history from the time of the ancient Egyptians, Greeks, and Romans documents the postwar soldier's plight. It is not a new problem but one that America tried to ignore, and perhaps one that those in power did not want us to understand. They would prefer the population to focus on the virtues of heroism, so in the next conflict our youth will be mentally as prepared and trainable as the heroes of the past.

The American Civil War produced very visible postwar casualties. It introduced technological advances such as repeating rifles, revolver pistols, and more accurate artillery, which took killing to a new level. To compound the horror of the war, soldiers were, in essence, killing their brothers. It was hard to dehumanize the enemy. The surviving veterans often felt disconnected, particularly in the North, which had little compassion for its returning soldiers. In dismantling its armies, the North gave their frontline combat veterans free railroad passes to return home and sewed the tickets on the veterans' shirts. They were patches that said "homeward bound." Many of these veterans felt they could not go home, so they continued to use their free passes endlessly and aimlessly to ride the rails. They could not, or believed they could not, function in normal society. From these "homeward-bound" rail riders emerged the term "hobo."

During World War I, the term for war-related trauma was "shell-shocked"; in World War II and the Korean War, it was "battle fatigue." Postwar casualties during these conflicts were hidden from the American public. Frontline troops always came home after the parades were over. Those who could not adjust were stuffed away into veterans' homes or left to survive as indigents.

When our society first became aware of the negative impact the Vietnam War had on returning combat veterans, we called it post Vietnam syndrome (PVS), as if it was something unique to this war and these soldiers and not a condition endemic to all wars.

The high-level military officers and politicians who directed the war left these soldiers to struggle alone until some veterans became spokesmen and started to reveal the truth.

The American public, deceived by World War II images that painted war as a glorious and romantic experience, could not be as easily deceived about Vietnam, because it was on television every night. Nevertheless, many Americans blamed our Vietnam soldiers for not perpetuating the glorious war myth.

The American government and society in general made the returning combat veterans feel like failures because America was not successful in Vietnam, and feel weak because they suffered from adjustment disorders. Our leaders ignored the situation because they did not want to be reminded of the strategic mistakes made in their management of the Vietnam War or admit to the American public a truth about war, which is that countless surviving combat soldiers engage in another mental war for survival when they return home, a war that some win and some lose.

Today this post Vietnam syndrome is called post-traumatic stress disorder (PTSD) and is recognized as a diagnosable medical condition that any human can expect to develop who has gone through significant trauma, such as an automobile accident, rape, or accidental shooting. In the case of a combat veteran who has lived through the extended terror and horror of war, post-mental complications of varying degrees are certain to develop. Many of these men came home with crippled souls from what they did and witnessed. America dumped the Vietnam soldier back into society with no adjustment preparation and in essence said, "Survive, buddy." Unfortunately, this is basically what they also did to this soldier when they dumped him in Vietnam.

Post-traumatic stress disorder is manifested in many forms and can lead to crime, illegal drug use, alcohol abuse, extreme and overreactive anger, depression, and even suicide. It is ironic that a soldier who fought so hard to survive in war would later take his own life. We now know that mental damage from war can be buried and unpredictably surface much later in life, manifesting itself in behavioral problems.

Combat veterans of all wars struggle with psychological conflict, moral revulsion, and even madness.

Although soldiers often asked God for help during combat, they are less likely to when they return home. The pre-eminence of death during war silently bonds many soldiers with God—a bond that is difficult to understand without the experience of continually facing death over a long period of time. A soldier's mantra becomes "Yea, though I walk through the valley of the shadow of death, I will fear no evil: for thou art with me." There are few atheists in the foxholes.

The religious concept of God and the afterlife is often all the soldier has to hold himself together in the darkest moments of combat. This initiates a tremendous intellectual battle within the combat soldier as he tries to rationalize the morality of war and his individual actions within the parameters of human goodness and love. He is faced with the dilemma of looking for the best of situations in the worst of circumstances. In his thoughts, the soldier looks for a god who offers forgiveness for his actions, protection, and the hope of a hereafter. The intensity of this introspective search accelerates with escalating combat action, deteriorating morality, and time.

Combat soldiers face decisions that require them to put their lives at extreme risk to improve their friends' and unit's chances for survival. Seldom if ever in normal life do we encounter even a momentary situation where we must make a conscious decision to give up our lives for our fellow man. Although ministers, doctors, social workers, teachers, and other goodwill servants talk about and try to improve the human condition and in their own way save lives, and perceive their occupations to be somewhat of a personal sacrifice for the betterment of humanity, these people usually risk little and never have to make the decision to give up their own lives by taking a bullet through the heart for another person.

But combat soldiers are put into situations where they are often confronted with such life-and-death decisions.

Some soldiers develop what I call a Jesus complex from continually risking their lives to save others or a guilt complex for not continuing to do so. They experience, at its extreme, the great dichotomy of humanity, the split soul inherent in our nature in which we willingly sacrifice our life for one worthy man yet slaughter another unknown but equally valuable person.

After the war, as the combat veteran moves farther away from death but continues to extend the intellectual analysis begun on the battlefield, he can become disenfranchised from the God he moved closer to during the war. This shift is not caused by the increased distance from death but by what the soldier sees in the world when he returns home. Sometimes little in the civilian world makes sense to these men. The wonderful anticipated postwar life is at best a distant vision.

Many combat veterans feel a horrible loss because the closely bonded, pure relationships developed in war are corrupted in a more complex civilian existence. The opportunities to create similar interdependent, respectful, caring friendships are much harder to find at home in a comparatively self-centered and superficial world. Here we are more inclined to compete with one another, whereas in war we tend to compete only against the enemy.

The war tragedies make it hard for combatants to communicate with people who have not had the same experiences. The risk, intensity, and commitment from living life at this extreme level further isolate the combat soldier from other people and institutions who might be able to help him. He becomes more introverted and distant. Life can never be the same again. He tries to ignore the fear, brutality, and sadness of combat violence and the suppressed anger that steams inside. Even with the great gift of survival, the soldier's frustration, cynical bitterness, and anger impede healing.

Without doubt, I have suffered from PTSD. My personal symptoms were a powerful need to control and a spontaneous anger that I suffered from for many years before I corrected the problem. I have had more depression than normal for an upper middle class American. My extreme competitiveness in business gives me adrenaline charges to drive off depression. Unfortunately, anger does also. Writing this story has been very therapeutic. As I once said to a friend, the process was like chemotherapy for cancer. I had to get sicker to get better.

This regression into the past took a severe toll on me mentally and physically. To go back in time to relive these horrible experiences and feelings was tough, but the relentless pacing into the wee hours of the morning are now over. The closer I get to the end of this project, the less I think about Vietnam and the more balanced my behavior is becoming. I can sleep again. Writing this story has been a healthy, healing catharsis for me and helped me find the path back to full humanity.

My Vietnam experiences were not bad considering the risks and dangers of each day. I was lucky. In Vietnam I tried to avoid looking at the horrors of war. My job was to control the future, and I could do nothing about what had already occurred, so I always focused on the next decision. Unless I was forced to look at an ugly scene to get information for the next decision, I tried never to stare at it. I tried to step over or around the bodies as though they were logs lying on the ground. I even left much of the gruesome and revolting description out of this story, for it served no purpose.

However, many Vietnam soldiers—officers and enlisted men—did not have the luck, foresight, or ability to control the game. For some, their lives now are a living hell as they engage in destructive escapes such as drugs and alcohol to help them cope with the horrible memories and mental disorders. My heart goes out to them. I do not consider them weak soldiers, only less fortunate people. But for a little change in luck here or there, I could just as easily be like them.

Jan Scruggs, God bless his soul, did a wonderful service for America when he initiated the actions that led to the Vietnam Veterans Memorial in Washington, D.C. His work benefited the Vietnam vet and the American public because it started the healing process that should have begun in the 1970s but was ignored. This memorial brought about the public and private healing needed by our country. The Wall is a monument to those noble men who gave their lives, but it also united the living veterans with the American public because it established a common bond and ground for grief.

The Vietnam veterans will live their lives to the best of their ability. Some will continue to struggle mightily with PTSD for the rest of their lives. In the future, as the Vietnam vets' physical and mental strength weakens in the normal process of aging, as the fragile self-confidence and self-esteem of many diminish and their vulnerability becomes more apparent, what is buried within the borderline PTSD veterans may surface, and we may see significantly greater behavioral issues with this population group, and more Vietnam casualties.

In the golden era of the "great American capitalistic democracy," Vietnam will always be recorded as a dark chapter. It will not be because we lost the war, but because of what we let our politicians and military leadership do to our own men—our sons, our brothers, our fathers, our friends, our own soldiers—in the execution and aftermath of this war. Our leaders knew better and did little because they did not care enough about their soldiers. They also showed a lack of respect for the American citizen and thought they could deceive the population without repudiation. We must be careful never to let this happen again. If we do, the shame is on America.

LETTER TO MY SONS

My employer, CYRO Industries, had a company function on April 14, 1997, and Carl Yastrzemski, Hall of Fame Boston Red Sox baseball player, was the guest speaker. I watched the events with an unusual philosophical perspective. The day Capt. Dan Monahan, Lt. Art Gray, and Pvt. Bruce McKee died, April 14, 1967, thirty years before, was the worst day of my life, and always will be unless I am predeceased by one of you. April 14, 1997, was also the day I decided to write you my Vietnam story.

The year 1967 was the best and worst year of my life. I can never be stronger than I was then. I can never do more to help others than I did then. I can never have more responsibility than I had then. I can never have more power than I had then. And I have never been more emotionally hurt than I was then.

As I watched CYRO's Carl Yastrzemski ceremonies, I thought back to 1967. I thought of what a glory year it must have been for Yastrzemski, and I thought of myself in the mud and the blood in the jungles and rice paddies of South Vietnam. I thought how, in 1967, I would so much have preferred to be Carl Yastrzemski rather than Lt. Joe Callaway.

But thirty years brings significant changes in perspective, and in 1997 I was very comfortable being Joe rather than Carl. In fact, as I look back on 1967, I am glad I went to Vietnam. I was the right guy for the job. I am now happier that I was Lieutenant Callaway in 1967 than if I had been Carl

Yastrzemski. I saved a lot of lives. He only won the American League Baseball Triple Crown and Most Valuable Player Award.

Never discount the probability of unforeseen changes and events in your life. In the spring of 1961, my International Relations high school teacher in New Canaan, Chris Collier, said, "You students better pay attention to what is going on in Southeast Asia because we are moving toward a war, and it is going to affect your lives." He was adamant in his position.

I was a terrible student during those years. In fact, Mr. Collier elected to teach me a lesson. He refused to round my 59.5 percent grade up to 60 and instead gave me a 58, which flunked me, causing me to miss my high school graduation and forcing me to attend summer school in order to graduate. For some reason, I always remembered Mr. Collier making that prophetic statement regarding potential war in Southeast Asia—especially as I trudged through the steaming, insect- and reptile-infested Vietnam jungles, rice paddies, and swamps fearfully hunting for the VC—yet at the time I did not have the slightest understanding of his ominous and foreboding warning. He was unknowingly talking directly to me, although you can be sure that his statement caught me between daydreams and was the only thing I heard all semester. I was just a weak, skinny underachiever with a two-second attention span who was trying to escape the responsibilities of life. No one, and I mean no one, in 1961 would have put me in the army much less as an infantry officer dead center on the battlefield at Macho Grande in 1967–68.

In June 1965 I had started basic combat training as an army private, and by June 1968 I was a captain in Special Forces with considerable combat experience. In life, with a little luck anything is possible, so play your options. But remember, it is always one step at a time, and all improvement comes from hard work. Also, never give up on any of your friends. You never know, when put in circumstances that require them to assume responsibility, who is going to step up when they are needed.

Life's greatest lesson is to learn never to give up. No matter how difficult the circumstances or how insurmountable the task or how bad your mistakes may appear to be, tomorrow is always a new day with new opportunities to recover. I am a profound example of why you should never give up. Life is about recovery. It is not who wins the most but who recovers the best.

Always keep life in perspective, understand that everything will not go your way no matter how hard you try, and enjoy the challenges presented by the complications of living. There is nothing better than turning a negative into something positive. Every day and every problem is an opportunity to improve. When you look at life from this perspective and see the challenges as opportunities, living can be a great joy.

One of the greatest memories of my Vietnam experience was being part of the camaraderie, friendship, concern, and caring that many Vietnam soldiers had for one another. In the middle of this environment of death and destruction, where we were forced by our government to kill our fellow man in the process of defending our own lives, the emotional bonds among many of the soldiers I fought with were extremely strong.

In this destructive environment of chaos, violence, fear, and remorse, there were times when I never felt closer to my fellow man. It was an emotional bond of friendship and respect built through companionship in great adversity.

These days, in summer when working in the yard, I hear the occasional Huey, probably a reserve helicopter pilot on two-week activation, fly up the San Ramon Valley. I hear the distinctive clatter of the chopper blades and I sometimes freeze, look down at my shadow on the ground, and reflect on a time of great strength, fear, and sadness. The chopper blades are the sound of terror and death.

When in San Francisco, I look at the Golden Gate Bridge and reflect back to that day in November 1966 when young men sailed out into the Pacific. It was long ago, and we were so young to get so old so fast. The vast majority of the American Vietnam soldiers were not killers. They never even thought about killing anyone. They were simple young men, souls with good hearts, trying to do what their country asked them to do. They were obedient, loyal, hardworking, and courageous. They were soldiers of America, and they had to do what they were ordered to do, unless it was illegal.

It is the American citizen's responsibility to control the politicians. The soldier has no choice by law. The system has to work that way. It is the only way you can run an effective, functional military organization. The American Vietnam soldiers had a difficult job in a complex situation. They were great Americans and good human beings.

The Vietnam Veterans Memorial is a fine tribute to the Vietnam soldier. There are now more than 58,000 names etched in the black marble of The Wall honoring these noble men who gave their lives. I visited the memorial for the first time in October 1984. My visit had to be done in a certain way. I arrived at 5 A.M., sat alone in the dark on the grassy knoll in front, tried to cry, talked a bit to my dead friends, thanked God for saving my life, and watched the sunrise, the dawn's first light, which was always the happiest moment of an infantry soldier's day in Vietnam. I have many friends whose names are on that wall. There are also many I just passed by on the battlefield without even knowing their names. I always visit the memorial when I have a trip to Washington and will continue to do so until I die.

I often think of the families of those who lost their lives in this tragedy. I think of McKee's parents, Billy Joe's mother, Florey's mother, Monahan's daughter, Payne's sons, even

Ray's son, and more. From 1985 to 1998, I stayed in contact with Dan Monahan's mother. Her husband, Francis, had died in the mid 1980s, and her relationship with most of her family, including her granddaughter, Maureen, was tenuous and strained for reasons I do not know. She was a lonely old lady. We often talked about her son Dan, and it made her feel better. Edith Monahan died in May 1998 at the age of eighty-six.

It brings me great personal pain to reflect this way and contemplate how this war affected all these unfortunate souls' lives. On the other hand, when I think of the guys, it makes me happy because I think of them only as they were. They always stay the same. I do not see them as decaying corpses or skeletons. But the pain and grief for the families never goes away. The older I get and the more my life grows with you, the more I understand and feel these poor souls' pain. I must live with it forever. Think of the years of anguish, the grieving pain these unfortunate people have endured, and for what reason? Because some manipulated, ignorant politicians embarked on an irresponsible course of action allegedly in the name of democracy and America.

Vietnam has left me with a great need to rebuild life. This, of course, has made a tremendous impact on your lives. I was perhaps harder and more demanding, restrictive, and protective than was normal, but my approach was all with good purpose and intention. Rebuilding life has helped me deal with the death and destruction in which I was, in essence, a conscript, but also a willing participant. Your lives have not been the same as your friends', but I would like to think I have made yours better.

It is important to understand that to develop the character and knowledge for a meaningful and successful life does not require you to experience the horrible extremes and tragedies of war. Every opportunity you would ever need to build your character and value structure is right before you every day of your life. It is right there with you in every decision and action you take each day. It is always your choice. You either build strength or drift into weakness. You have the opportunity to move forward or fall back every day.

All you have to do is open your eyes and make the effort to improve every day, and you will become a better, more capable, and more successful person than you could ever imagine. You have the opportunity every day, but you must be willing to recognize it and willing to try to give your best. Engage life and add direction and significance to it. Life is not just achievement and relationships; it is also a bonding with nature. Do not forget to appreciate the majesty of nature—the breathtaking marvels, the colors, the sounds, the scents that are often the overlooked beauty of each glorious and wonderful day of life. Listen carefully to the song of the meadowlark. Life is such a beautiful experience. Enjoy it.

I tried to raise each of you to be strong. In our world, it is much easier to be kind and caring if you are strong and happy. Strong does not necessarily mean high achievement, recognition, and physical development. Strong is strength of character, vision, and philosophy of life. Be strong enough to be kind.

I have a broad and complex vision of life, and it is not always easy to understand, even for me. I believe we are evolving into something better than the human race is now, and if we keep working hard at it through the generations, we will eventually get there. You need to be able to see into your soul. I know this is difficult for young men to understand, but you may when you get older.

I wrote my Vietnam story because I am tired of remembering the events, and these are significant things I wanted you to know. Vietnam was indeed the garden of good and evil. I have carried the grief, anger, and memories around with me far too long. I suppose I have used the experience over the years. Anytime I needed fire or will, I just tapped into that Vietnam anger. It was an instantaneous power resource.

Now I want to let it go. It is getting too heavy for me to carry, and I am not as strong as I used to be. I want to forget it forever and enjoy what is left of my life. To help in this process, I needed to record these troubling, sad, and wonderful events to the best of my ability. Hopefully, my story will be educational or meaningful to you at some point in your life, so I am just not howling at the Vietnam moon. I learned much in this experience, and I have always tried to pass my knowledge on to you young men.

The irony of all this is, the person you know and the life you enjoy were born in Vietnam. It was an experience that changed me forever. It forged in steel what I am today. One Joe Callaway died in Vietnam and another was born. My new life was born not out of destruction, although it was all around me, but out of love for my men and the knowledge that I had the skills to help them. The introspection, anger, and intellectual growth that followed all came from that love. But the greatest irony of all is that I miss the old Joe Callaway. He could not get anything done, and he screwed up most everything, but he was not a bad guy. Unfortunately, he never came home. He died in a Vietnam rice paddy in 1967.

I know that the past thirty plus years have been a special gift to me. I have tried to use the time well. Most of it has been devoted to our family, and I have enjoyed every minute. Death is something I know well, and when death comes my way again, I will fight for every breath just as in the old days. In some of the most frightening situations, near the end of my six months as a platoon leader, when I started to get bitter, I would snarl at death and challenge it. Someday I will lose, and I want you to know I have enjoyed every day. When my time comes, it should not significantly affect your lives. You should all be well prepared to handle the challenges ahead.

When you were all still in school, before you went off on your own paths, our family spent many Memorial Day weekends in Yosemite National Park. I was proud the year you three, in less than one day, climbed Half Dome and returned to the valley floor. My pride was not so much in the physical task but the fact that you did it together. As you know, to experience Yosemite's greatest beauty you must get beyond the valley into the High Sierra, away from all the people. If there is a God, he lives there. It is the most beautiful place on Earth. When I am there, I reflect back and remember my courageous Vietnam comrades and their sacrifices. My strength and soul grew from their light.

My Vietnam friends never grow old as we do. I remember them so vividly I could almost reach out and touch them. I want to forget the Vietnam events, but I never want to forget these soldiers. Their blood will never dry. Their courage and sacrifice represent the indomitable spirit of humanity, and its will to struggle against all odds in the worst of conditions. On Memorial Day weekend, I celebrate their spirit. They will always be part of me, and you will always be part of them. I have tried to build you that way. God bless you three young men. You are the first light of my soul and have made my life much more than Vietnam. Please enjoy your lives and be strong and kind. I am proud of you, and I love you. I hope we will all have many more years together.

The Greek philosopher Aristotle once said, "The search for truth is in one way hard, in another way easy. For it is evident that no one of us can ever master nor miss it wholly." In the last line of *The Great Gatsby*, F. Scott Fitzgerald says, "So we beat on, boats against the current, borne back ceaselessly into the past." We forever struggle into the future to discover the truth. God bless us all.

AFTERWORD:
POWER VERSUS PASSION

In Vietnam the American leadership experienced the humiliation that ultimately follows sheer and unbridled arrogance.
The Vietnam War was a human tragedy of enormous propor-
tions—a major political blunder.

The Vietnam War was lost not because American troops
failed in the field. In fact, we won every major battle and 85
percent of the small firefights. Although the VC and NVA
had unbelievable courage, determination, and perseverance,
were admirable soldiers in work ethic and in fighting skills,
and were probably the best light infantry the world had ever
seen, we had significantly stronger firepower, were airmobile, and were pretty tough soldiers.

We tactically destroyed the VC and NVA. Even though we
were caught by surprise in the 1968 Tet Offensive, we
slaughtered the VC and NVA. It turned out to be a suicide
mission. North Vietnam's General Giap and his commanding officers had lied to their own men. The Tet prisoners said
they expected this to be the final battle of the war. Their leaders told them the population would rise up against the South
Vietnamese regime and the Americans. North Vietnam sent
their men into destruction because they knew that this stage
of the war was not completely about body count but more
about passion—North Vietnam's passion to prevail, and
America's lack of passion for this war. The Vietnamese

knew we would lose interest in our body counts, ultimately lose patience, and eventually go home.

The war was lost not because it was immoral. A moral war is an oxymoron, because all wars are immoral. It was lost not because the Vietnamese valued life less than Americans did, which is the stereotype of Asians from the World War II mind-set. Vietnam is a family-oriented culture, and they loved their families, friends, and life as much as we did.

The war was lost not because of poor support back home. Sure the war lasted too long, few young people wanted to go, and the support base for the war was eroding. The American population became confused and intolerant because they saw nothing to gain. This was a contributing problem but not the determining factor.

The war definitely was not lost because Jane Fonda posed with North Vietnamese antiaircraft gunners, although she can never be completely forgiven for this act. One of the pilots the gunners were shooting at was my lifelong friend Jack Keegan in his navy A-6 Intruder, a small tactical, low-altitude contour bomber that worked off the USS *Midway* aircraft carrier.

If U.S. leaders had identified something in Vietnam of true value, something tangible, they would not have engaged in a limited war. The United States would have adopted a more aggressive strategy and pressed harder in the beginning. We perhaps would have established a second front in North Vietnam, but certainly would have sealed off their harbors and destroyed their transportation infrastructure, food supply, factories, and power resources to take pressure off the South.

We would have starved the North Vietnamese and bombed them back into the Dark Ages. The war would have been short and ended in a quick, negotiated compromise. We would have declared victory, then gone home. Eventually the Vietnamese would have started it all over again, but significantly fewer American lives would have been lost.

We engaged in the greatest strategic bombing campaign in world history to stop resupply and NVA troop movement into South Vietnam, but we never used this capability in the early critical stages of the war to cripple North Vietnam. We destroyed insignificant targets and jungle forests in most of our early bombing missions. We killed more trees than any nation in history. Through gradual escalation we tried to coerce the North Vietnamese into the behavior and decisions we wanted.

Our politicians said we were fighting a limited war because we were afraid a front in the North might bring China, communist since 1949, into the war to support North Vietnam. Perhaps, but the Vietnamese and the Chinese are traditional enemies who share a common border, and the Chinese had invaded and occupied Vietnam on numerous occasions throughout history. For centuries, Vietnam was the southernmost part of China's empire, but it never accepted Chinese rule. The Vietnamese discriminated against ethnic Chinese already living in Vietnam, and they had a deep-seated, historically based dislike for one another.

Vietnam was a comparatively small country of fifty million people, whereas China, the giant neighbor to its north, had a population of more than one billion people. Vietnam had been fighting foreign domination for more than a thousand years. The Vietnamese did not want a standing Chinese army in their country that might stay there forever because they wanted Vietnam's rice paddies to help feed China's huge population.

To invade Vietnam, China would have had to make its armies vulnerable to devastating American airpower, because they would have to move as conventional forces, not guerrilla soldiers, through restrictive mountain terrain and be easy to locate. United States airpower was now significantly more formidable than it had been in the Korean War, when the Chinese had invaded Korea to help the North Koreans.

Our tactical air would literally have destroyed the Chinese air force, and strategic air would have inflicted enormous casualties on their exposed conventional armies in static positions. It is highly unlikely that the Chinese would have been willing to endure the heavy losses incurred by rushing to Vietnam's defense, particularly because they knew that the Vietnamese were extraordinarily fierce and experienced guerrilla fighters, and the American ground troops would be tortured by the climate and terrain.

In the late 1970s, some years after our war was over, Vietnam invaded Cambodia to stop the human atrocities and instability occurring there. China, upset by Vietnam's aggression, tried to invade Vietnam and used its frontline combat troops. As the tactical ground units crossed the border, Vietnamese reserve infantry units, not the frontline combat troops already committed in Cambodia, engaged the Chinese army and quickly and soundly defeated them. In fact, they downright kicked the Chinese butts.

Vietnam could easily have become an ally of the United States after World War II, but our alliance with the French, who wanted to continue their colonial control over the country, actually forced the Vietnamese into their relationship with the communists at the end of that war. Before we abandoned the Viet Minh to the French, Ho Chi Minh was reading excerpts from our Declaration of Independence to the Vietnamese population and once even had an airplane fly over Hanoi displaying the American flag. The people of Hanoi cheered as the flag passed overhead.

In 1954 we could have just as easily adjusted to a more moderate position on North Vietnam after the Viet Minh defeated the French at Dien Bien Phu in the final battle of the French Indochina War, but we were locked into our longtime friendship with the French, and, because of our inflexible anticommunist mentality, pictured North Vietnam as another North Korea. With effective diplomacy, financial and industrial support, and simple salesmanship, we could have developed a relationship with a united Vietnam and probably steered it away from communism. In either diplomatic opportunity, at the end of World War II or after Dien Bien Phu, America could have adopted a position that would have avoided the Vietnam War.

The Vietnam War was lost because it was a nationalistic civil war of passion—a domestic dispute over control and assets—and North Vietnam had more to gain than we did. It was that simple.

We were a confused supporter of South Vietnam, hoping to find an easy victory without our intervention evolving into a full-blown war. For a while, the undeclared war was called a "police action," but this ended as the American body count and casualties increased to the point that the terminology became ridiculous.

American politicians made decisions based on a false sense of our own superiority and embraced the domino theory, the belief that all countries in Southeast Asia would systematically fall to communism if we lost South Vietnam. We had concrete tactical but somewhat limited strategic military objectives and could never define what we hoped to gain from victory, even to ourselves.

When asked why we were fighting in Vietnam, the American soldier gave only the ambiguous "we're fighting communism." Our troops had no clue why Vietnam was important to America and saw no reason for this useless war.

North Vietnam was stronger, better organized, and more dedicated than South Vietnam. Therefore, it won. In the more industrialized North, the French used Vietnamese as managers in their colonial operations; as a result, North Vietnam had a hundred-year head start in the development of their organizational and managerial skills.

In the South, the French were the direct managers of the

significantly more lucrative agricultural colonial operations. As a result, the South Vietnamese did not develop the managerial talent or experienced infrastructure to run their army or country effectively.

North Vietnam also boasted an army, the Viet Minh, which had already proven itself when it decisively defeated the French—almost 200,000 soldiers strong, stopped their colonial domination, and drove them out of the country. Positions in the South Vietnamese Army were based on family status; in the North, rank was based solely on ability and performance.

The charismatic and legendary Ho Chi Minh, meaning "He Who Enlightens," was the symbol of North Vietnam's passion and national identity. The people revered him as a great patriot, and his persona and godlike stature were the cohesive and driving force that gave energy to their relentless will to fight under conditions that required unbelievable determination and personal sacrifice. In later life he preferred to be called "Uncle Ho" to soften his political image and develop a closer, almost paternal link with his people.

Our politicians and military underestimated the Vietnamese resourcefulness, courage, and determination. Even in losing almost every battle, they wore us down with their perseverance. Their unrelenting will finally convinced U.S. politicians that North Vietnam would never give up, no matter how badly and how often we pulverized them.

The spiritual and philosophical leadership of Ho Chi Minh and the overall strategy and tactics of Gen. Vo Nguyen Giap's military leadership combined to create among the Vietnamese population a national purpose, confidence, and resolve to endure the suffering and self-sacrifice required to win this war. They were focused, driven, and willing to continue without regard for personal or national pain. They won by continuing to stand.

Many U.S. politicians decided after the 1968 Tet Offensive, in "the year of the monkey," to give up on the war, but it took years to end it because our administration did not want to admit we had made a mistake in thinking we could beat such a small, poor, third world country. How would it look to our powerful, formidable cold war enemy, the Soviet Union?

When President Nixon was in office, his administration coined the phrase "Peace with Honor," which meant, I do not know how to get out of this war. Unfortunately, about 20,000 of the 58,000 plus men killed in Vietnam were killed after Nixon took office in 1969 and tried to find a way to bow out gracefully.

I have great respect for General Giap and his staff, the North Vietnam Army, and the Viet Cong. They were phenomenal soldiers. They took one of the most brutal beatings in modern military history but still won the war. They would never give up, but they knew we would because we were driven only by ego. They had endless patience and unlimited time and knew politically we would eventually run out of both. It would have made no difference to them if the war had lasted another thirty years. The presence of our armies only fueled hatred that motivated their passion to fight.

America was and is an extremely aggressive, wealthy, and resourceful country, yet little North Vietnam stood up under its withering power, which was formidable even in the limited war America conducted. North Vietnam's determination is one of the great examples in world history of national character. The people won on sheer will, and they have to be admired. It was hard to believe that the VC and NVA shared the same heritage as the noncommunist South Vietnamese.

The United States could have worked its way through the limited war situation more effectively if we had left it to MACV advisers, Special Forces, and the CIA. The outcome would probably have been the same, but we would have negotiated a better deal for everyone because it would have been easier to find a face-saving way out. There would have been considerably less pain and suffering for everyone, Vietnamese and Americans alike.

Because America saw all communist countries as a cooperative, monolithic block and a common enemy, the fear of communist expansion around the globe caused the United States to support almost any anticommunist regime. In this strange symbiosis, regimes did not have to be democratic, only anticommunist. We would support any anticommunist thug. President Diem of the Republic of Vietnam exploited this American fear. He had no popular support in South Vietnam and had to use the United States to stay in power.

American diplomats had little training in the history and cultures of Asia and few available consulting experts. As a Eurocentric country, we could not understand that Vietnam would not fall under Soviet and certainly not Chinese control. By the time of the Vietnam War, China and the Soviet Union were already feuding over their common border, and cracks in the theory of a monolithic communist block were rapidly becoming apparent. Nationalism is a much more powerful force than communism, but we were in a paranoid anticommunist war mind-set.

We need always to demand adherence to the built-in checks and balances in our government's separation of powers. We need always to build a politically smarter, less trusting, better educated, and more active population. It is our task as a free society to ensure that our politicians take America in a responsible, constructive, and honorable direction.

If our free society does not exercise its power over the government, the government will usurp power, justify its actions as being in the best interest of the people, and systematically take away the freedoms we enjoy. It is the nature of organized power.

Our leaders will lie to the public if they feel comfortable

and will rationalize it as operating in the best interest of the people. We can never let them feel comfortable with lying. That is our responsibility and also that of the much maligned press, who can be leeches, but they also protect our rights. America's leaders must be constantly reminded for whom they work.

America's citizens must also be careful not to be manipulated by politicians. The politicians and military are particularly adept at using patriotism as a tool to serve their personal objectives, which may not necessarily be in the best interest of the United States. The Vietnam War taught the American public the fallibility of its most powerful leaders and their inclination to deceive the public if it suited their purposes. Our country was easily deceived in Vietnam. The politicians deceived even themselves.

We rode into the Vietnam War on World War II patriotism, cold war fear of communism, the power and influence of the so-called military-industrial complex, and our enormous ego. The war's direct and indirect cost reportedly approached $500 billion—an enormous expenditure in the 1960s and 1970s—and helped create the rampant, runaway inflation America experienced in the 1970s. The war was good for big business, but the American public paid the final bills with their children and their earnings. This war had no purpose and was not worth the pain or expense.

I harbor a deep-seated disregard for distrust of the federal government for how it managed the Vietnam War. I loathed President Lyndon Johnson for what he did to the Vietnam soldier. I cannot say this about any other human being, but I was a happy man the day President Johnson died. What happened in the political arena was the most disgusting aspect of the war. President Johnson was a weak, incompetent man. He made decisions based totally on politics rather than reason and human concern.

President Johnson served as a government employee for his entire working career. He started as a schoolteacher, then advanced through the political ranks all the way to president by virtue of President Kennedy's assassination. Yet when he died in the 1970s, Johnson had an estate valued at more than $9 million, an extraordinary amount of money at the time and impossible for a public servant with his earnings history to accumulate.

The CIA, on many occasions, warned Johnson against deploying conventional troops into the Vietnam guerrilla war environment. It was a simple, clear-cut request, but Johnson acquiesced to the military-industrial power base political pressure and placated conservative politicians, many with military bases in their states, by trading with them to gain their reciprocal support for his liberal "Great Society Programs."

President Johnson sent many thousands of American soldiers to a needless death and returned home hundreds of thousands of severely wounded and mentally disturbed and mentally impaired men. The war also took the lives of millions of Vietnamese soldiers and civilians. Johnson destroyed more lives and families than any other participant in the war and traded lives for his own personal political agenda. The Vietnam soldier was nothing but political cannon fodder to President Johnson. I can never forgive him for his failure as commander in chief.

President Nixon, an equally vile politician, campaigned for the American presidency in 1968 with an alleged "secret plan to end the war," which he never revealed even after being elected. It appeared to be Vietnamization of the war—he was giving their war back to them—but everyone knew that this would not work because North Vietnam was much stronger than the South.

Nixon used his whole first four-year term trying to end hostilities. Only when he was running for a second term did we have a Paris peace conference. Nixon sent almost as many men to their death in Vietnam trying to get out as the ill-advised and irresponsible Johnson sent in trying to stop alleged communist expansion.

Ironically, it was not only President Ronald Reagan's massive 1980s military buildup in high-technology weaponry that eventually brought about the demise of the Soviet communists. The totalitarian nature of communism failed to accommodate basic human needs for freedom and creativity. The incredible advances in American industrial productivity emerging from expanded use of computer automation technology created an accelerating high-tech industrial revolution. American free enterprise and our passion to achieve, not just Ronald Reagan, brought down the Soviet Union.

Vietnam will always be regarded as a conflicted war for America. After World War II, we renounced colonialism yet supported French recolonization of Vietnam. We openly supported South Vietnamese dictators, engineered the assassination of Diem, would not allow free elections to be conducted in Vietnam, and at the same time represented ourselves to be the champions of democracy.

Vietnam's twentieth-century history was not unlike American history. America carved out its democracy by revolting against a colonial master. We fought a vicious Civil War to maintain the integrity of our country just as Vietnam did, yet America wanted to deny Vietnam's nationalistic unification.

Communism was our bitter cold war enemy, but in Vietnam, America read the geopolitics incorrectly. Because of our alliance with the French and our failure to adopt a functional diplomatic position that recognized Vietnam's nationalistic spirit, we implemented a strategy that served only to push Vietnam more and more into the communist camp. This will some day be corrected and capitalism and democracy will come to this country.

The Vietnamese have a driven enduring spirit and are extremely hard-working people. They are a resourceful people of strong character. They will not forever be shackled with the limitations of communism. Capitalism and democracy are powerful forces, and the Vietnamese people will prosper in this environment. It is inevitable that the Vietnamese society will grow into these political and economic systems. The inherent values of the Vietnamese are much more consistent with capitalism and democracy. It may be an evolutionary process, but when these changes eventually come about, that will be the end of Vietnam's internal war, and these industrious people will finally have their freedom.

"No one has ever treated the
infantryman's role in Vietnam with more
sympathy or thoroughness."
—*Booklist*

A LIFE IN A YEAR

The American Infantryman in Vietnam,
1965-1972

by James R. Ebert

Finally, here's a book that focuses exclusively on
the life of the "grunt" in Vietnam. The voices of
more than sixty Army and Marine Corps infantrymen speak of their experiences, from induction to
the jungles and rice paddies of "Indian country"
to their return to "the World."

From I Corps in the north to IV Corps in the
south, and from the early days of 1965 to the
American withdrawal in 1972, *A Life in a Year*
offers a unique look at the grunt's war in
Vietnam—war as experienced from the edge of a
foxhole, as seen through the eyes of the combat
riflemen themselves. The experiences are woven
together, giving the reader a true understanding
of what it was like to serve in an infantry unit
fighting Viet Cong guerillas and North Vietnamese
regulars.

Published by Presidio Press
Available wherever books are sold

For firefights in the swamps, ambushes in the jungle, or just facing the enemy dead-on, Recondo trained LRRPs to win.

RECONDO

LRRPs in the 101st Airborne

by Larry Chambers

They will never be able to duplicate the 5th Special Forces Recondo School and the training that gave its grads something they desperately needed—the skills to survive Long Range Patrol missions in jungles that the NVA considered its own. Vietnam veteran Larry Chambers vividly describes the grit and courage it took to pass the tough volunteer-only training program in Nha Trang and the harrowing graduation mission to scout out, locate, and out-guerrilla the NVA.

Here is an unforgettable account that follows Chambers and the Rangers every step of the way—from joining, going through Recondo, and finally leading his own team on white-knuckle missions through the deadly jungle of Vietnam.

Published by Presidio Press
Available wherever books are sold

*On the front lines with the
bravest men in the bloodiest
year of the war*

WARRIORS

An Infantryman's Memoir of Vietnam

by Robert Tonsetic

It was the tumultuous year 1968, and Robert
Tonsetic was Rifle Company commander of
the 4th Battalion, 12th Infantry in Vietnam. He
took over a group of grunts demoralized by
defeat but determined to get even. Through
the legendary Tet and May Offensives, he led,
trained, and risked his life with these brave
men, and this is the thrilling, brutal, and honest story of his tour of duty. Tonsetic tells of
leading a seriously undermanned ready-reac-
tion force into a fierce, three-day battle with a
ruthless enemy battalion; conducting surreal
night airmobile assaults and treks through
fetid, pitch-black jungles; and relieving combat stress by fishing with hand grenades and
joyriding in Hueys.

Published by Presidio Press
Available wherever books are sold

*Seventy-seven deadly days
in combat*

WEST DICKENS AVENUE

A Marine at Khe Sanh

by John Corbett

In January 1968, John Corbett and his fellow leathernecks of the 26th Marine Regiment fortified a remote outpost at a place in South Vietnam called Khe Sanh. Within days of their arrival, twenty thousand North Vietnamese soldiers surrounded the base. What followed over the next seventy-seven days became one of the deadliest fights of the Vietnam War—and one of the greatest battles in military history.

"In this short, readable account, Corbett describes his days at Khe Sanh in almost dispassionate prose and in great detail. . . . effectively convey[ing] the siege from a Marine grunt's point of view."
—*Publishers Weekly*

Published by Presidio Press
Available wherever books are sold